C. S. Lewis
and
Christian Postmodernism

C. S. Lewis
and
Christian Postmodernism

Word, Image, and Beyond

KYOKO YUASA

Foreword by Bruce L. Edwards

☙PICKWICK *Publications* · Eugene, Oregon

C. S. LEWIS AND CHRISTIAN POSTMODERNISM
Word, Image, and Beyond

Copyright © 2016 Kyoko Yuasa All rights reserved. Except for brief quotations in critical publications or reviews, no part of this book may be reproduced in any manner without prior written permission from the publisher. Write: Permissions, Wipf and Stock, 199 W. 8th Ave., Eugene, OR 97401.

Pickwick Publications
An Imprint of Wipf and Stock Publishers
199 W. 8th Ave., Suite 3
Eugene, OR 97401

www.wipfandstock.com

PAPERBACK ISBN 13: 978-1-4982-1938-9
HARDCOVER ISBN 13: 978-1-4982-1940-2

Cataloguing-in-Publication data:

Yuasa, Kyoko.

C. S. Lewis and Christian postmodernism : word, image, and beyond / Kyoko Yuasa ; foreword by Bruce L. Edwards.

xii + 198 pp. ; 23 cm. Includes bibliographical references and index.

ISBN: 978-1-4982-1938-9 (paperback) | ISBN: 978-1-4982-1940-2 (hardback)

1. Lewis, C. S. (Clive Staples), 1898–1963—Criticism and interpretation. 2. Postmodernism. I. Edwards, Bruce. II. Title.

PR6023 E926 Y83 2016

Manufactured in the U.S.A.   04/18/2016

Contents

Foreword by Bruce L. Edwards | vii
Acknowledgments | ix

    Introduction: Harbinger of Christian Postmodernism | 1
1 Philosopher of Christian Postmodernism | 10
2 Novelist of Christian Postmodernism | 36
3 Pre-Historic Magician Awakens in the Modernist Age | 66
4 Medieval Paradise: East, West, and Beyond | 102
5 Re-Writing Mythology: Greco-Roman and Norse | 139
    Conclusion | 174

Bibliography | 181
Index | 193

Foreword

Born in 1898 in Belfast, Northern Ireland, C.S. Lewis, was educated in Oxford, England, served in the British army during World War I, and completed a long and fruitful teaching career in Oxford and Cambridge that lasted from the mid-1920s until his death in 1963. Lewis thought much of his published work would be forgotten, but has long been an influential figure in the English-speaking world and continues to have a sustained impact on three continents, particularly in the British Isles, in Australia and New Zealand, and in North America. He is regarded with high esteem well into the twenty-first century in his multiple vocations as a literary historian, cultural critic, fantasist, Christian apologist, poet, and memoirist, and, one can say usefully, as an astute eulogist of the presumed values inherent in Western civilization. What has gone relatively unremarked is the rise of Lewis's popularity and reputation in world letters—seen in the growing scholarly attention and translation he has received in the last two decades in Germany, the Netherlands, France, Spain, Russia, China, South Korea, Brazil, and, now, as evident in Dr. Kyoko Yuasa's innovative new publication, in Japan.

It is important as Lewis's readership continues to expand that there arise gifted, informed, and diverse critics who come along to meet the challenge of translating and interpreting—as well as extending—the impact of Lewis's oeuvre in languages and traditions different from his own. It is thus a truly happy occasion to welcome Dr. Yuasa's adventurous new voice to Lewis Studies. I was first privileged to meet Professor Yuasa in a seminar I was teaching on Lewis in the Kilns, his Oxford home, under the auspices of the C.S. Lewis Foundation in the Summer of 2004. It was here shared with me as well as seminar participants insights from her growing inquiry into the efficacy of Lewis's fantasy as well as the effectiveness of his rhetorical

Foreword

criticism. Her scholarship has since flourished to include many insightful articles published in both Japanese and English, translations of previous English monographs into Japanese (including a work of my own, *A Rhetoric of Reading: C.S. Lewis's Defense of Western Literacy*), and, presently, this unique volume that reintroduces and reimagines C.S. Lewis for a worldwide audience under the rubric of "Christian postmodernism."

Dr. Yuasa offers a unique take on the meaning of the pregnant but problematic term, "postmodernism," and the reader of this volume would do well to follow her development and deployment of this term. *Christian postmodernism*, in particular, is the platform she endeavors to establish and recalibrate—to "baptize," if you will, the term, "postmodernism," in the manner Lewis asserts Scottish author, George Macdonald, "baptized his imagination"—all in the service of explaining Lewis to an emerging world audience. She undertakes this challenging task because she wishes to equip Lewis to speak eloquently out of his own time and cultural context. To do so, Dr. Yuasa, argues, Lewis must be artfully migrated from his original milieu and inserted into the critical consciousness of a post-Western, post-Enlightenment era. Through an elucidation of Lewis's Christian postmodernism, she hopes to enable a truly world audience to bypass the inhibitions of an errant modernist typology, who can then directly encounter Lewis's ideas and his fiction through the lens of his mythopoeic imagination.

Since we live in an era of instant punditry, of conclusion-drawing from the thinnest of reconnaissance, out of a reductionist default mode based upon the whimsy of an idea, Dr. Yuasa's work is particularly valorous. She helps to address this malady with a carefully argued exposition that provides welcome new insight into Lewis's achievements and ongoing relevance for readers everywhere, of all times. Put simply, it is C.S. Lewis's uncanny "anachronicity," recognizing his pivot that situates between time and eternity, that Dr. Yuasa uncovers: his audacious ability to be "neither/and" within fiction and nonfiction texts that serves us as a tool for recovery of perspective and true insight. For this accomplishment alone, we must be thankful—and thereby properly chastened.

Dr. Bruce L. Edwards
Emeritus Professor of English and Africana Studies
Bowling Green State University
Willow, Alaska, March, 2015

Acknowledgments

This book is a modified version of my PhD thesis, defended at Hokkaido University (Japan) in September 2014. During the writing of this book, I have inevitably accumulated many debts. I must first mention in particular my PhD supervisor, Dr. Eijun Senaha of Hokkaido University, for his time, expertise and constructive criticism on all of the most crucial parts of this manuscript. I am also indebted to my committee members, Professors Hidemitsu Takahashi and Yasuhiro Takeuchi, also of Hokkaido University, for allowing my defense to be an enjoyable moment, and for their brilliant comments and helpful suggestions. Additionally I acknowledge Professor Yukihiro Takemoto for his valuable feedback on my research and Dr. Kei Chiba for always being so spiritually supportive of my work.

I am especially thankful that Dr. Bruce L. Edwards, Professor Emeritus of English and Africana Studies, Bowling Green State University, consented to write the Foreword to this text. I was deeply saddened when Dr. Edwards passed away on 17th November 2015, during the final stages of preparation for publication. Dr. Edwards gave me opportunity in 2007 to translate and publish in Japanese his book, *A Rhetoric of Reading: C.S. Lewis's Defense of Western Literacy*, which served to get my PhD career started on the right track. I first met Dr. Edwards and his wife Joan at the C.S. Lewis Summer Seminar at The Kilns, Oxford, in 2004. I remain sincerely grateful for the encouragement of Dr. and Mrs. Edwards, and the other participants ("The Twinklings") at that seminar for sharing their views on Lewis, and inspiring me to undertake a further academic study on his works.

I am also indebted to Dr. Gayne J. Anacker (California Baptist University), Vice President for Academic Affairs of the C.S. Lewis Foundation (US), who was the first person to motivate me to pursue doctoral studies on C.S. Lewis. I am also grateful to Dr. Sanford Schwartz (Pennsylvania

Acknowledgments

State University), and Dr. Charles Huttar (Hope College) for their guidance and feedback on my prospectus, to Dr. Joy Alexander (Queens University, Belfast) and Dr. John Gillespie (University of Ulster, Coleraine) for their insightful discussion on my thesis in progress, and to Dr. Kazuo Takeno (Nihon University) for his valuable advice and constructive criticism on my work. I pay homage to the late Dr. Christopher Mitchell, the then Director of the Marion E. Wade Center at Wheaton College, for guidance given for my PhD prospectus in 2009. I can only show appropriate thanks to him through my future work.

This book has greatly benefited from numerous comments and critiques made by the participants at several international conferences: C.S. Lewis Oxbridge Conference in July 2005; the Oxford University C.S. Lewis Society in June 2009; Conference of Christianity Literature at Wheaton College, Chicago, in September 2009, and at Houston Baptist University in October 2009; The C.S. Lewis Conference at Lille Catholic University, France in June 2011; The Conference of English Literature Society of Japan between 2011 and 2013; and The Conference of Christianity and Literature Society of Japan in 2012.

I would also like to extend my appreciation for the unending encouragement and personal attention of the Meas family, Ho, Laura-Jane, Joseph and Yoshiya, for providing me so much needed support in what could have otherwise been a somewhat stressful environment. Laura-Jane willingly spent so much time proofreading my thesis and giving me excellent suggestions, which always enabled me to gain so much drive to tackle challenges head on. I am also deeply thankful for the friendship of Keiko Suzuki, Toshiko Ogiwara, Michie Kuroda, Dieter and Shelley Schmidt, and the Sapporo International Church members. Thanks to their prayers, I endured and survived the experience of doctoral work.

I also thank my editor, Dr. K. C. Hanson, and Assistant Managing Editor, Matthew Wimer, and Administrative Assistant Brian Palmer for all their help, and also my publishers, Pickwick Publications, a division of Wipf and Stock Publishers. I cannot attempt to mention by name everyone who helped me during the writing of this book. Nevertheless, I would like to honor each and every one. It goes without saying that whatever faults remain are entirely my own responsibility.

Finally I wish to express my deep appreciation of my mother, who passed away during the writing of the thesis in 2009, and also my gratitude to my father who went to heaven during the writing of this book in 2015; I

Acknowledgments

treasure their love and support. I give all glory to God, and thank the Lord Jesus Christ, who provided me with the blessing of completing this project.

Introduction
Harbinger of Christian Postmodernism

C.S. Lewis (Clive Staples Lewis) (1898–1963) is best known as a writer of children's literature, but he writes not simply "for juveniles."[1] He writes to overcome the inhibitions not only in children's minds, but in the minds of readers of all ages. He insists that the taste of children should be considered "human taste"[2] and not of less value simply because the literary establishment does not appraise juvenile taste highly. By inhibitions, he means the imperfection of humanity and the limited construction of language. He writes to question the modern critics who confine the boundaries of literary genres by age, the marginalization of the perspectives of mythology and Christianity, and the sidelining of "science fiction" and "fantasy literature."[3] He is, however, a pioneering writer of "Christian postmodernism" who rehabilitates the values discarded by modernist thought.

Lewis critically discusses the spiritual crisis of the modern world in fantasy and science fiction through philosophically accepting both multiple views and ultimately what transcends the limitation of humanity, as well as through rhetorically expressing the clash and integration of both "word" (rational explanation) and "image" (imaginative expression).

The definition of word and image in this paper includes what Stanley J. Grenz expresses with the same terms, but is not limited to his definition.[4] He means the different communicative styles between modernism and postmodernism, while this paper covers not only communicative styles, but also divided world views including literary genres, literary approaches

1. Lewis, *On Stories and Other Essays on Literature*, 48.
2. Ibid., 51.
3. Ibid., 55–56.
4. Grenz, *A Primer on Postmodernism*, 2.

(fact and fiction), academic disciplines, gender, and philosophy (naturalism and supernaturalism, history and myth, observation and faith).

Christian postmodernism is a new term not yet used in other publications, but a seemingly unconventional rhetoric that Lewis must have employed to reach the mindset of the postmodern world. The terms "word" and "image" are used to mean language available not only rhetorically but also theologically.[5] Although the meaning of the term "postmodern" or "postmodernism" differs according to author, "postmodern world" is more often observed, while Carl Rascheke uses "theological postmodernism" and "religious postmodernism."[6] The term "postmodernism" is generally used to mean the anti-modernist movement in and after the 1960s that advocates a multiplicity of philosophical and cultural notions, focusing on the peripheral values undermined by modernist thinkers. Crystal L. Downing associates postmodernism with the cultural trends between the 1960s and 1980s.[7] Grenz explains the developing attention on postmodernism in the 1970s.[8]

As postmodernism does, Lewis deconstructs the modernist's single interpretation of the truth—elevating reason (word) over faith (image)—and instead advocates the multiple perspectives of the world as well as what they transcend. He deconstructs the interpretation commonly accepted by the previous generation, stating that human interpretation is influenced by our cultural models in each time period, which Lewis calls "the accepted Model of the universe."[9]

Lewis's concept of Christian postmodernism is based on his understanding of the Gospel as a story of reconciliation between two incompatible worldviews: Christianity and mythology. By the term "Gospel," he means a true story which really happened in "actual human history."[10] He claims that the mythological stories of gods dead and risen are historically incarnated in the life of Jesus of Nazareth.[11] He affirms that what is vaguely

---

5. In an interview conducted by the author with Dr. Eijun Senaha, Professor at Hokkaido University (Nov. 2008), he suggested the term "Christian postmodernism."

6. Rascheke, *The Next Reformation*, 69.

7. C. Downing, *How Postmodernism Serves (My) Faith*, 86–87.

8. Grenz, *A Primer on Postmodernism*, 22.

9. Lewis, *The Discarded Image*, 222.

10. Lewis, *The Collected Letters of C.S. Lewis Volume I*, 18.

11. "Jesus of Nazareth" is a term used to mean the historical figure Jesus; "Nazareth" in Galilee was Jesus's childhood hometown.

Introduction

seen through mythologies comes into focus in the Gospel. By the term "myth," he means not a fake story fabricated by human beings, but a tool for communicating truth. He distinguishes between a fake story and fiction: the former is fabricated to deceive others, but the latter (as well as story and myth) is a medium for conveying truth.

This concept of mythology may sound contradictory to modern theologians, but its uniqueness is based on Lewis's personal experience when he converted to Christianity in 1931. He explains this conversion as being the result of history and mythology in a letter to his friend Arthur Greeves (Oct 18, 1931): God reveals Himself "through the mind of poets."[12] As a natural consequence, Lewis doubts modernist thoughts which separate mythology from Christianity. He rejects the modernist theologian Rudolf Bultmann (1886–1978) who demythologizes Christianity by excluding the supernatural from the Bible. Lewis refers to modernized Christianity as "watered down" Christianity.[13] He similarly rejects the modernist critics who separate the poiema (external frame) and logos (myth or meaning), affirming that poetry (language) exists but has no meaning. He, however, claims that a poem is both Logos (something said) and Poiema (something made).[14] As Lewis scholar Bruce Edwards states, a poem is both *Logos* and *Poiema*: "Lewis would respond that such theorists forget or ignore."[15]

Lewis deconstructs the previous interpretations of the text influenced by the cultures of the time in order to invite the reader's participation in interpreting the meaning of the text. He does not emphasize the reader's single interpretation, but rather their collaboration with the author to reach an understanding beyond human interpretation. He asserts that the single viewpoint of a reader is not perfect for reading literature because humanity is not perfect. In his last work, *An Experiment in Criticism* (1961), written two years before his death, He compares the modernist way of reading to being imprisoned—as if the reader is in a prison of his/her own value.[16] However, he proposes the transcendence of limited human construction in order to rehabilitate the joy of reading damaged by modernist thought: "I transcend myself; and am never more myself than when I do."[17] As Bruce

12. Lewis, *The Collected Letters I*, 977.
13. Lewis, *God in the Dock*, 24.
14. Lewis, *An Experiment in Criticism*, 132.
15. Edwards, *A Rhetoric of Reading*, 61.
16. Lewis, *An Experiment in Criticism*, 36.
17. Ibid., 141.

Edwards states, Lewis's reading lies in seeking "an enlargement of our being."[18]

Other Lewis scholars also contribute to the dialogue. David Downing discusses an echo between Lewis and Jacques Derrida: they both deconstruct modernist interpretation which is embedded by culturally generated languages.[19] James K.A. Smith similarly re-interprets the slogans of Jacques Derrida, Jean-François Lyotard, and Michel Foucault in the context of Christianity.[20] Crystal Downing also opposes the general interpretation of taking the French philosopher's famous slogan, "nothing outside the text" as the abolition of meaning, and instead claims that Derrida resisted the modernist values along with other post-structural thinkers.[21]

Lewis's understanding of Christianity through the Gospel is creatively reflected in his approach to writing novels. This is especially true in descriptions of the identities of his characters moving between the ambiguous borders of fact (history) and fiction (mythology). This analysis of his works which challenge modern thought will reveal that he is a novelist of Christian postmodernism who advocates literary techniques not only of word and image but also beyond: supernatural understanding beyond human interpretation.

The first two chapters deal with his non-fiction, mainly selected to highlight his conviction of anti-modernism and his postmodern sensibilities. The other chapters deal with a discussion of three of his fictional works: *That Hideous Strength* (*THS*) (1945), *The Voyage of the Dawn Treader* (*VDT*) (1952), and *Till We Have Faces* (*TWHF*) (1956), demonstrating his philosophical strategy as a novelist of Christian postmodernism. The selected works cover roughly his entire writing career as a novelist, and each work commonly features a female protagonist who is in a search of self-recognition. His Christian postmodernism is most vividly reflected in his female characters' activities of writing, reading, and speaking.

In chapter 1, a comparison of Lewis's thoughts with the generally reviewed opinions of modernism and postmodernism will reveal that he is an anti-modernist philosopher who welcomes postmodern sensibility as a contributor to multiple interpretations of the text among readers, and that he is a promoter of peripheral cultures. He respects the postmodernist

---

18. Edwards, *A Rhetoric of Reading*, 64.
19. D. C. Downing, "C.S. Lewis Among the Postmodernists," n.p.
20. Smith, *Who's Afraid of Postmodernism?*, 23.
21. C. Downing, *How Postmodernism Serves (My) Faith*, 135.

Introduction

process of exchanging arguments within the community in order to reach an understanding of meaning. He enjoys story-telling and discussions with his friends: when meeting regularly with his scholar-friends in the Inklings at Oxford; all through his life with close friend Arthur Greeves in Ireland; and in his later life with American poet Joy Davidman as his shadow-editor.

Lewis revived the forgotten genre of fantasy literature within the literary group named "the Inklings" who held an informal gathering twice a week (at Lewis's office in Magdalen College, Oxford, and the local pub, "Bird and Baby"). Colin Durietz evaluates the literary contribution of the Inklings' friendship, especially that of Lewis and Tolkien, to the birth of two works: *The Lord of the Rings* and *The Chronicles of Narnia*.[22]

A discussion of modernism and postmodernism reveals that each thinker presents an individual definition. The difficulties of defining both thoughts are expressed by a number of critics, including Matei Calinescu, Brian McHale, Michael Bell, and Louis Markos, but modernism is commonly assumed by them as a background against which to define postmodernism, even though each specifies a different emphasis. Philosophers of Christian postmodernism, such as A.E. McGrath and Crystal Downing, similarly express the complexities of Christian postmodernism, but within the chosen terms, commonly express the value of multiple ideas situated in the context of community.

A discussion of Lewis in the context of postmodernism is not necessarily welcomed by many Lewis scholars. Some conclude that he is neither modernist nor postmodernist. The reason for their antipathy is a fear of both thoughts, based on their conclusion that both modernism and postmodernism are the dethroning of God. They negatively interpret these ideas, especially "postmodernism," according to two proposals by French philosopher Jean-Francois Lyotard, as: "incredulity towards meta-narratives"[23] and "micro-narratives."[24] Louis Markos is one who interprets both as the abolishers of meaning in language, who alienate logos from poiema, word from image, and the natural from the supernatural.[25] Teruo Kuribayashi analyzes how modernist philosophy de-Christianized Western

---

22. Durietz, *Tolkien and C.S. Lewis*, 141.
23. Lyotard, *The Postmodern Condition*, xxiii.
24. Ibid., xxiv.
25. Markos, *From Achilles to Christ*, 112.

society and was adopted for Christian ministry and mission around the turn of the twentieth century.[26]

The positive voices for Christian postmodernism do not deny the complicated nature of Lewis's writings. In his *A Rhetoric of Reading* (1986), Bruce L. Edwards discusses Lewis's rhetoric of reading as the "antidote" to help the modern reader resist imposing their own consciousness upon the text. In his essay "The Lion Still Roars" (2010), he observes two different counter-reactions to Lewis and postmodernism in academic circles, stating that he is both a rationalist and a romantic. More sharply than Edwards, David Downing views Lewis as a postmodernist, discussing him in the context of postmodern philosopher Jacques Derrida: "Like Derrida, Lewis emphasizes that all analysis is situated, that there is no position of utter objectivity from which one may think about thinking itself."[27]

Crystal Downing positively categorizes Lewis within Christian postmodernism, as she welcomes the ethos as a possibility to have her rejected story accepted. She states that postmodernism allows her to more often present her Christian views in an academic platform.[28] Harry Lee Poe also favorably estimates postmodernity as a good opportunity for Christians to define the new culture.[29]

In chapter 2, the discussion firstly analyzes Christian postmodernism in comparison with modernist and postmodernist novels, and secondly, explores the reason behind Lewis as a traditional thinker choosing the seemingly unconventional rhetoric of Christian postmodernism. The novels of Christian postmodernism will be defined through two comparisons: firstly, between his anti-modernist notion and his first novel *The Pilgrim's Regress* (1935), and secondly, between the postmodern literary techniques of four selected British postmodern works and the source material for his literary approaches.

The study of sources for Lewis's literary approaches will reveal that his reading experience, especially medieval literature, produces his literary approaches which happen to fit the mind in a postmodern world. The medieval writers use word and image in order to seek not only spiritual discovery but also self-recognition—the approaches echoing contemporary style.

---

26. Kuribayashi, "Kindai-go O Saguru Posutomodan Shingaku: Gendai Amerika No Shingaku Jijou," 11–55.

27. D. C. Downing, "C.S. Lewis among the Postmodernists," n.p.

28. C. Downing, *How Postmodernism Serves (My) Faith*, 104.

29. Poe, *Christian Witness in a Postmodern World*, 21.

Introduction

Through reading classical literature, including the Bible, Lewis is possibly inspired by such postmodern approaches as: the Apostle Paul's method of speaking within the discourse of the reader, the dialogic potential of language, the joy of reading in any genre, and the reader's participation. Many of the characters of his novels are described as moving between the borders of genres, fact and fiction, and the time-zones between the contemporary and the mythological (Greco-Roman, Irish, and Nordic). Further, the ambiguous identity of a persona can change between narrator, writer, and reader.

Reviving the joy of reading fiction is what Lewis wishes to rehabilitate in every genre, including those of science fiction and fantasy. He denounces the modern critics' dogmatic attitudes that exclude the works of William Morris and George MacDonald simply because they are "popular works"[30] and that ignore fantasy literature as the anti-canon in the history of literature.[31] As Bruce Edwards states, the joy of reading beyond genre is Lewis's strategy for "revitalizing and reintroducing forgotten works and authors."[32]

Lewis speaks within the discourse of the reader, in a similar way to the Apostle Paul—the writer of the epistles in the New Testament. When Paul talks to the Athenians, the Hebrew speaker not only switches languages (between Hebrew and Greek) according to the audience, but also recites a Greek poem familiar to the Greeks in order to make his message more accessible to the local citizen (Acts 17:29). He re-interprets Greek poems within the context of his worldview—the Gospel—and recounts a retold story of the poems to the Greeks. Lewis adapts this strategy of story-telling into his novels: the author enters Greek, Irish, and Icelandic mythologies, reinterpreting the old stories within the context of the Gospel and regenerating a retold myth for his contemporary reader in the form of word, image, and beyond.

As a writer, Lewis sought to restore the reader's participation in the process of interpreting, rehabilitating, and harmonizing the roles of both the author and reader as interpreters. Through his war experience on French battlefields during World War I, he finds modern minds numbed because of an inability to interpret meaning. His autobiographical book, *Surprised by Joy* (1955), recounts his memory of an increasing fright at the impending experience of the fight, rather than the experience of the fight

---

30. Lewis, *On Stories*, 90.
31. Ibid., 51.
32. Edwards, *A Rhetoric of Reading*, 84.

itself. Young Lewis arrives at the front line trenches on his nineteenth birthday in November 1917.[33] On the actual battlefield, he is devoid of emotion due to the deprivation of his interpretive power. Through his war experience, he comes to realize that his contemporary readers are troubled by the changing values of language.[34]

For an analysis of postmodern literature, four British novels will be under discussion, in the chronological order of their publications: Iris Murdoch's *Under the Net* (1954), Muriel Spark's *The Prime of Miss Jean Brodie* (1961), Doris Lessing's *The Golden Notebook* (1962), and John Fowles's *The French Lieutenant's Woman* (1969). These British novelists, selected from Patricia Waugh's *Metafiction*, started writing around the 1960s—a time approximately corresponding to Lewis's death—and composed metafictional works to reflect language in the dialogic process, as insisted by Mikhail Bakhtin. Waugh introduces the novels which Bakhtin refers to as dialogue-oriented and which opposes the determination.[35] Although the conflict of voices is rectified in realistic fiction through their subjection to the supreme voice, she affirms that meta-fiction reveals the impossibility of such a resolution.[36]

Lewis enjoys literary encounters with female writers, both real and imaginary, including two contemporary writers, Dorothy L. Sayers and Joy Davidman, as well as one medieval philosopher, Julian of Norwich (Julian). In addition to Sayers and Davidman, Lewis exchanges ideas with a number of female pen pals, including an American woman (name unspecified, but later revealed as Mary Willis Shelburne)[37] and Sister Penelope.[38]

Very little has been critically discussed concerning Lewis and women writers, but Sayers, Davidman, and Julian all affect his literary styles. Although the male-oriented world of Oxford was strictly cautious about female writers in the mid-twentieth century, Sayers encourages Lewis to think of a new image for a novel featuring a female character, while Davidman inspires Lewis with the complete image of Psyche for his last novel *TWHF* (1956). Julian's mystic words lead him to approaches echoing contemporary

---

33. Lewis, *Surprised by Joy*, 217–19.
34. Edwards, *An Examined Life*, 79–101.
35. Waugh, *Metafiction*, 6.
36. Ibid., 6.
37. Lewis, *Letters to an American Lady*.
38. Lewis, *The Collected Letters of C.S. Lewis Volume II*, 264, 452, and 495. Lewis, Walter Hooper's *C.S. Lewis: A Complete Guide to His Life & Works*, 719.

Introduction

style. She writes of her mystic experience with both word and image, and beyond, in order to seek spiritual pursuit as well as self-recognition. The contemporary reader will be impressed by an echo between Christian postmodernism and the medieval female writer.

Chapters 3 through 5 chronologically review Lewis's selected novels and cover his entire writing career. An analysis of his concept of language, philosophy, and literature in chapters 3, 4, and 5, illuminates him as a novelist of Christian postmodernism who writes not only to access postmodernist readers through the clash and harmony of word and image, but also to claim supernatural understanding beyond human interpretation.

Also in chapter 3, the last book of his space trilogy, *THS*, invites readers to respond to the interpretation of the sleeping magician, Merlin, and to rehabilitate language beyond the limited image of self-identity. In chapter 4, the multiple directions of the major characters in *VDT* demonstrate Lewis's notions of directions, not only of the ship, but also the other main characters, which are a reflection of the postmodernist sensibility in *VDT*. Just like the medieval Irish imram—a literature genre about adventurous voyages—the modern imram *VDT* sails eastward to find paradise not just in and beyond the east, but also to the west and beyond. In chapter 5, the tremors, or radiating influences, of four characters (three women and one man) in Lewis's last novel, *TWHF*, reveal that he presents a drama of death and resurrection through his retelling of both Greco-Roman and Norse myths.

The new century saw a rise in academic discussions of Lewis's writings. The year 2005, in particular, saw an increased number of academic publications on Lewis, in the run up to the release of a cinematic production of part of the Narnia series.[39] Lewis scholars have been editing more books and papers, which is adding significantly to the total number of academic papers about him. This discussion of Lewis as a harbinger of Christian postmodernism will contribute to illuminating him as a novelist still relevant in the twenty-first century.

---

39. The academic responses to Lewis literature in and around 2005 are analyzed in the introduction of my annotated bibliography written in 2007, "An Annotated Bibliography 1989–2007: C.S. Lewis's Thoughts on Mythology, Paganism and Christianity in *The Horse and His Boy* and *Till We Have Faces*," *Eijun Senaha's Torch*. http://rose.hucc.hokudai.ac.jp/~p16571/libraries/bibliographies/pdf/yuasa.pdf.

1

Philosopher of Christian Postmodernism

C.S. Lewis accepts the conflicting values of realism and supernaturalism, but ultimately reaches an understanding which exceeds both views. The philosophical stance of accepting this dichotomy is in direct opposition to the spirit of his modernistic age, which prefers to divide realism and supernaturalism, highlighting either thought or a singular point of view. He advocates not the conflicts but the harmony of the contrasting values of the natural and the supernatural. He claims that we have no reason to vie for superiority by regarding "the one or the other as inferior."[1] He finds it illogical for the modernist to insist on looking inside the mathematician's brain to find "timeless and spaceless truths about quantity."[2] An analysis of Lewis's concept of modernism will conversely reveal that he shares a postmodernist sensibility, in the sense that he is suspicious of the modern theorists who claim a superiority of realism to supernaturalism or insist on either aspect of worldviews, realism and supernaturalism, and that Lewis contributes to the reconciliation of worldviews divided by modernistic beliefs. As to Lewis's trust in the ability of language, Bruce Edwards states that a growing number of scholars (including philosopher John Beversluis) try to rehabilitate Lewis above contemporary charge.[3] He thinks that although Lewis is an insightful guide for literary criticism, "his name will not be listed among the first rank of critics contemporary with him—men like T.S. Eliot

---

1. Lewis, *God in the Dock*, 212.
2. Ibid., 213.
3. Edwards, *A Rhetoric of Reading*, 9.

or F.R. Leavis."[4] But Lewis's anti-modernistic argument has spurred and inspired discussion amongst scholars of interdisciplinary fields, not only in literature but also in theology and science, in the twentieth and twenty-first centuries. The negative response from the modernist critic and the positive feedback from the different disciplines, theological and scientific, regard him as an anti-modernist. The discussion of him as an anti-modernist will reversely reveal that he is a writer of Christian postmodernism, contributing to a reconciliation of conflicts between realism and supernaturalism.

MODERNISM AND POSTMODERNISM

The difficulties of defining modernism and postmodernism have been indicated by a number of critics, including Matei Calinescu, Brian McHale, Michael Bell, Stanley J. Grenz, Louis Markos, and Crystal Downing. All of these critics assume modernism as the background against which to define postmodernism, even though each has a different emphasis. Calinescu emphasizes the continuity between modernism and postmodernism[5]; McHale claims that the two concepts begin with clash but finish in a circle[6]; Bell reviews the two notions as different stages of the same metaphysic[7]; Grenz observes a shift from the modern era of manufacturing "goods" to the postmodern period of manufacturing "information"[8]; Markos views modernism as "the bottom to top paradigm,"[9] counter to the traditional paradigm in which human thought is a divine gift (top to bottom); and Crystal Downing welcomes postmodernism which works to undermine modernist foundations.

Matei Calinescu historically clarifies the changing relation between modernism and Christianity. In *Five Faces of Modernity: Modernism, Avant-Garde, Decadence, Kitsch, Postmodernism* (1987), he analyzes the historical shift of ideas of modernity, changing from non-religious notions (the Renaissance period) to religious conflicts against Christianity (modern time), in four phases: the Middle Ages, the Renaissance, the Romantic period, and the modern times.

4. Ibid.
5. Calinescu, *Five Faces of Modernity*, 265.
6. McHale, *Postmodernist Fiction*, 4–5.
7. Bell, "The Metaphysics of Modernism," 46.
8. Grenz, *A Primer on Postmodernism*, 17–18.
9. Markos, *Lewis Agonistes*, 36.

C.S. Lewis and Christian Postmodernism

Calinescu points to the difficulty of defining modernism, as its thought appears to be paradoxical: it advocates the death of God, while preserving its positive imagination of Christianity. The term becomes associated with both "unbeliever"[10] and "a free-thinker."[11] He also finds a paradox between modernism and romanticism. The Romantic period shares a modern feeling of a dying God, as well as the anti-modern sensibility that integrates mythology and Christianity. He concludes that modernity is a concept that changed from non-religious to religious at the beginning of the twentieth century.

Michael Bell also finds it hard to date the emergence of modernity, but broadly outlines modernism as having peaked between 1910 and 1925, and argues that its intellectual formation is associated with lines of thought that include Marx, Freud, and Nietzsche. In "The Metaphysics of Modernism" (2011), Bell defines modernism as the age of "relativistic consciousness,"[12] describing the ethos of relativism with the term "the world picture," borrowed from Martin Heidegger. The twentieth century philosopher Heidegger characterizes the relativistic consciousness of modernity with the well-known phrase "the world becomes picture."[13]

Brian McHale concludes that the dominant of postmodernism is not singular, but plural. He bases his conclusion of dominant on Roman Jakobson's definition of dominant.[14] Jakobson views the dominants as the components of a work of art which rule the remaining components. McHale proposes that the dominant of modernist fiction is epistemological, which deploys strategies on how to know the world,[15] while the dominant of postmodernist fiction is ontological, which deploys strategies based on which world you are in.[16] He asserts that text depends on different dominants, historical and cultural.[17]

Stanley J. Grenz observes the postmodern ethos expanding as a cultural phenomenon between 1960 and 1990. He states that the term "postmodernism" was first used in the 1930s by Spanish writer Federico de Onis

---

10. Calinescu, *Five Faces of Modernity*, 58.
11. Ibid., 59.
12. Bell, "The Metaphysics of Modernism," 13.
13. Heidegger, "The Age of the World Picture," 131.
14. McHale, *Postmodernist Fiction*, 6.
15. Ibid., 9.
16. Ibid., 10.
17. Ibid., 6.

and historian Arnold Toynbee. Although Toynbee analyzes the postmodern era as the decline of Western civilization and a shift from the West to a new pluralist world culture, Grenz finds the postmodern spirit emerging in various fields of the humanities, such as architecture, art, theology, philosophy, and literature. In *A Primer on Postmodernism* (1996), he also writes that in the postmodern age of cultural diversity, the information society reflects "differing tastes and styles."[18]

Louis Markos claims the four founders of modernism to be Marx, Darwin, Freud, and Nietzsche. In *Lewis Agonistes: How C.S. Lewis Can Train Us to Wrestle with the Modern and Postmodern World* (2003), he affirms that these four are responsible for the materialistic trends of modernism changing the focus of humanity from the spiritual to the physical. He explains that Darwin changed the notion of modernism from "the physical" to "the spiritual," from "the less complex" to "the more complex," and from "the material" to "the immaterial"[19]; Freud examines the effect of natural process upon the human psyche, believing in the existence of the physical origin; Marx posits that human beings are products of material structures; and by declaring that God is dead, Nietzsche means to deny the existence not only of God but also of all absolutes. Crystal Downing similarly views modernism as the period when Marx, Freud, and Nietzsche hypothesize about human nature replacing ecclesiastical Christianity."[20]

Crystal Downing interprets the story of "the Tower of Babel" (Gen 11:4–7) as that of modernized Christianity: the Tower of Babel is an account about people who are scattered by God from one to many places, and who communicate with from one to multiple languages at the result of their desire to construct a tower in order to reach Heaven. She finds a similar interpretation of the Tower of Babel in K. A. Smith, J. Richard Middleton and Brian J. Walsh, and Reinhold Niebuhr. The modernist Christian world similarly sets up one discourse as an absolute truth for reaching Heaven, so that they get confused with multiple interpretations in the postmodern world.

Through arguing modernism and postmodernism, these theorists present a discussion of a relationship with God, of a relative consciousness, and of a diversity of values. McHale and Bell focus on the relative consciousness of human-centered modernism rather than the absolute

---

18. Grenz, *A Primer on Postmodernism*, 19.
19. Markos, *Lewis Agonistes*, 34.
20. C. Downing, *How Postmodernism Serves (My) Faith*, 186

value. Calinescu, Grenz, Marcos, and Downing discuss the sensibilities of modernism and postmodernism in relation to God. Scientific modernists and fundamentalist Christians seem to be on opposite sides, but they actually shared the same worldview of logical positivism in the first half of the twentieth century. Crystal Downing attributes the cause to their emphasis on reason.[21]

PHILOSOPHICAL CONCEPTS OF CHRISTIAN POSTMODERNISM

Lewis as a protector of old Western tradition cannot be related in the postmodern movement if it means simply the dethroning of meaning in language. Such a postmodern proposition is the antithesis of Lewis, but if it means re-evaluating cultures ignored by modernism, the Christian fantasy writer is worthy of attention, because both Christianity and fantasy literature are marginalized by modernist thought. Although postmodernism and Christianity seem contradictory at first glance, both are compatible from Lewis's point of view.

The term "postmodernism" was first used in the 1930s and culturally expanded in the 1960s. Born in the twentieth century, the term meaningfully serves in the twenty-first century in the field of Christianity. The Christian world, such as churches, seminaries, and field missions, have not yet sufficiently discussed the thought.[22] The modern patterns of thought are introduced not only into Western Christian societies but all over the world by twentieth century Christian missions. Commonly cited phrases, such as postmodern Christians or Christians living in the postmodern world, are used to mean the cultural impact of post-modernity on Christianity, but not on the reading experience of literature.

Among Lewis scholars, there is a negative response to discussing his literature in the context of postmodernism. The reason is their fear of the term "postmodernism." Those scholars negatively interpret the notion of "postmodern" as the dethroning of God based on two propositions by French philosopher Jean-Francois Lyotard (1924–1998): one is incredulity towards "meta-narratives"[23] and the other is "micro-narratives."[24] By the

21. Ibid., 105.
22. Kuribayashi, "Kindai-go O Saguru Posutomodan Shingaku," 11.
23. Lyotard, *The Postmodern Condition*, xxiii.
24. Ibid., xxiv.

former phrase, they understand Lyotard to mean the rejection of the traditional values in Europe: values that include dualism, either by science or absolute belief. By the latter phrase, they understand the French thinker to mean language in the context of authority and power.

Unlike modernist Christians' interpretation of postmodernism, the postmodernist scholars of Lewis re-evaluate the positive effect of postmodernist thought. They consider postmodernism not as a challenge against a Christian society per se, but as an opportunity to use the postmodern ethos for the deconstruction of the previous modernist mindset of excessive emphasis on individual autonomous faith. These theorists re-evaluate, from a Christian perspective, the significance of individual varieties based on the postmodern philosophers' phrases that respect multiple opinions: not only Lyotard's micro-narratives but also Wittgenstin's "language game."[25]

Lyotard develops the idea of micro-narratives from Wittgenstein's notion of language game. The term language game is Wittgenstein's concept of system of language based on his *Philosophical Investigations* in which he introduces the use of language as "the process of naming the stones and of repeating words after someone might also be called language-games."[26] Such a positive approach to postmodernism encourages the embodiment of the Gospel situated within the contours of postmodern society.[27]

Christian scholars in favor of postmodernism include James K. A. Smith, A. E. McGrath, Stanley J. Grenz, John Caputo, and Crystal Downing. They individually use their chosen terms to express the multiple ideas situated in the context of community: Smith's "a living community on interpretive pluralism,"[28] Grenz's "the individual-within-community,"[29] and Caputo's "hyper-realism."[30]

In *Who's Afraid of Postmodernism* (2004), J.K. Smith introduces postmodernist thinking reflected in multiple interpretations of the text. He embraces "interpretive pluralism" as a countermeasure against the modernist's elevation of enlightenment: "On the one hand, . . . On the other hand, . . .

---

25. Wittgenstein, *Philosophical Investigations*, 7.

26. Ibid.

27. Concerning a "postmodern paradigm shift" in the Christian churches, refer to John Milbank's *Radical Orthodoxy* (1999).

28. Smith, *Who's Afraid of Postmodernism?*, 50.

29. Grenz, *A Primer on Postmodernism*, 168.

30. Caputo, *What Would Jesus Deconstruct?*, 44.

pluralism is endemic to our postlapsarian (post-fall) conditions."[31] Smith sees the first interpretive pluralism within the church, based on his hermeneutic perception that one (single) world is composed of multiple (plural) factors, as may be seen in the Trinity, in the events of the Pentecost, and in the Creation.[32] The One God consists of a Trinity of three persons: Father, Son, and Holy Spirit; in one event of the descent of the Holy Spirit, the message of the Gospel is understandable to various native language groups. During Creation, one human is created as a synthesis of soul, spirit, and body. The second post-lapsarian pluralism he regards as "the given situation"[33] for different interpretations of the nature of reality: "both are interpretations; neither is objectively true."[34]

Smith affirms that the Christian church is the storyteller of the contemporary world. He emphasizes the community's commitment as "a community of love and justice,"[35] the stage where God's drama is played out, claiming that "Our storytelling should be supported by our story living."[36]

As Smith echoes Lewis in accepting multiple interpretations of the text, Alister E. McGrath reflects Lewis in regarding literary criticism as the way to read. Lewis asserts that "the literary reader(s)"[37] should be re-reading attentively, reflecting repeatedly on their favorite lines, and exchanging views about books with each other. He disagrees with what he calls "Vigilants"[38]: modern critics who categorize books as superior or not. Among them, he includes I.A. Richards who emphasizes close reading of poetry. Bruce Edwards explains Richards's modernist reading as a kind of "religious faith."[39]

McGrath is aware of a similar approach through his own reading of two fourteenth century medieval writers: Geert Zerbolt van Zutphen and

---

31. Smith, *Who's Afraid of Postmodernism?*, 50.

32. "The Trinity" is, according to the Oxford English Dictionary, the three persons of the Christian Godhead: Father, Son, and Holy Spirit; "Pentecost" is the Christian festival celebrating the descent of the Holy Spirit on the followers of Jesus after his Ascension, held on the seventh Sunday after Easter; and Creation is the beginning of the universe, regarded as act of God (Acts 1:8).

33. Smith, *Who's Afraid of Postmodernism?*, 50.

34. Ibid.

35. Ibid., 79.

36. Ibid.

37. Lewis, *An Experiment in Criticism*, 2–3.

38. Lewis, *Christian Reflections*, 12.

39. Edwards, *A Reading of Rhetoric*, 81.

Ludolf of Saxony. He details this reading experience as if he were projected into the story.[40] He emphasizes Zerbolt's claim on the importance of meditating on the same lines in the text, using both reason and imagination, until he experiences a paradigm shift of understanding.[41]

Through the study of medieval works, McGrath, in conclusion, highlights the image of adopted family in the postmodern reading approach. He presents a parallel between Christianity and adopted children: both are invited to share individual stories and images and to restore the social bonds of a small community.[42] He affirms that the use of "word" and "image" empowers readers to understand the true essence of adopted family. He proposes that the reader use their imagination to mediate on the form and content of truth and to picture the world.[43] He considers postmodernity as an opportunity to release readers from the conventional methods of elevating reason at the expense of imaginations and emotions.[44]

Stanley J. Grenz also explains his stance with the two basic concepts "word" and "image." He contrasts the different communicative styles between modernism and postmodernism and explains each style with word-based communication (rational explanation) in contrast to image-centered participation (individually told stories). In *A Primer on Postmodernism* (1996), he does not use the term "Christian postmodernism," but he is conscious of it because he speaks to the Christian community on the approach of sharing the Gospel with a postmodern world. He defines postmodernism as "the individual-in-relationship" in the community of faith.[45]

John D. Caputo similarly focuses on the relationship with other people. He regards the hyper-real relationship with "the other person" as if readers make a journey that is incomplete, but he affirms that incompleteness means "not an imperfection but testimony to the perfect excess of the other."[46] He defines postmodernism with the same "hyper-realism"—a

40. McGrath, *The Journey*, 18.

41. Ibid., 15.

42. McGrath, *Postmodern Sekai No Kirisutokyo: 21 Seiki Niokeru Fukuin No Yakuwari*, 111–15. As the original text of *Christianity in a Postmodern World* is written in Japanese, the cited parts, including the title, are translated for this paper into English by the author. *Christianity in a Postmodern World* is a collection of McGrath's lectures originally presented in Japan in 2003, and published in Japan in 2004.

43. Ibid., 104.

44. Ibid., 100.

45. Grenz, *A Primer on Postmodernism*, 168–69.

46. Caputo, 45.

search for reality that transcends the present horizons—and an ability to admit an unexpected future event and to imagine that there are different thoughts according to different periods. He explains "the other person" as not "one of our possibilities" but "one of our impossibilities."[47]

Crystal Downing likewise emphasizes postmodernism as the relation to others in the recognition of conflicting truths through re-evaluating the context of others. Although some fear postmodernism on the assumption that taking all truths equally leads to relativism, she asserts that this conclusion is wrong, and she concludes that it is not God but human language that is situated. She concludes with a quoted statement from Lewis: God is un-describable by "being too definite"[48] for the indefiniteness of human beings.

All of these Lewis scholars refer to a relationship with others in some way: McGrath and Grentz emphasize the reading experience; Caputo focuses on the speaking effect; while Downing stresses the incompleteness of human language. This paper suggests labeling this new genre "Christian postmodernism," in which Lewis introduces the reader to a new literary world beyond the boundaries of genres, enabling them to accept the plural perspectives of both "word" (rational explanation) and "image" (imaginative expression), as well as an understanding that transcends human language. He discusses with the contemporary reader a spiritual crisis in the modern world, and ultimately aims at a transcendent understanding which is created when "word" and "image" meet. Word and image are intended to mean not only the theological clash between the human and the divine, but also the rhetorical confrontation between rational explanation and imaginative story-telling.

Lewis questions the literary boundaries between "popular" and "serious" borders,[49] and he chooses to write in literary genres that modern critics do not consider to be "serious." In his essay "On Science Fiction," he disagrees with modern critics who label science fiction as either popular or serious.[50] Lewis adds to his argument on the "serious" modernist novelists in his letter (26 Jan. 1954) to a writer of science fiction, Arthur C. Clarke: "What is called 'serious' literature now. . ."[51]

47. Ibid., 44.
48. Lewis, *Miracles*, 160.
49. Lewis, *On Stories*, 55–56.
50. Lewis, "On Science Fiction," 55–56.
51. Lewis, *The Collected Letters of C.S. Lewis Volume III*, 52.

Philosopher of Christian Postmodernism

Lewis scholars such as Louis Markos, Bruce Edwards, David Downing, and Crystal Downing share the opinion of C.S. Lewis as an anti-modernist writer. Markos, however, regards Lewis as a challenger of the twentieth century mainstream of modernism. He presents examples of Lewis's opposite side of modern criticism in the *Chronicles of Narnia*. Markos defines modernism as "the bottom to top paradigm," in which human thought is a divine gift (top to bottom). He discovers a parallel between anthropocentrism and the developing impact of modernist paradigm.

Contrary to the other Christian postmodernist scholars mentioned, Markos disagrees on the point of discussing Lewis as a Christian postmodernist. He dismisses both modernism and postmodernism as anti-Christianity and rejects both Ferdinand de Saussure and Jacques Derrida as "dethroning" critics.[52] He affirms that Saussure (modernist) and Derrida (postmodernist) are products of the spiritual and linguistic world espoused in Nietzsche's proposition that "God is dead."[53] Markos further writes that Saussure is far from God, and that Derrida abolishes "the relationship between signifier and signified."[54] He asserts that as Christianity has nothing to share with modernism and postmodernism, so Lewis should be categorized as neither: the deconstructionists would be "the greatest threat to the status and meaning of poetry."[55] He sharply identifies Lewis as an anti-modernist and anti-postmodernist writer.

Unlike Markos, Bruce L. Edwards claims that it is difficult to place C.S. Lewis's rhetoric of reading in clearly defined categories as it is hard to identify words such as modern, postmodern, and romantic. Although in his *A Rhetoric of Reading* (1986) he does not directly discuss Lewis's rhetoric of reading in terms of the postmodernist approach, he identifies Lewis as the antidote in helping the modern reader to resist the imposition of their consciousness upon the text. He affirms that the purpose of Lewis's reading is not to be in the main stream of modern critical trends, but on the periphery for the purpose of rehabilitating the text and the reader: "unfolding the text before the reader, to help him resist rather than embrace the imposition of his consciousness upon it."[56]

---

52. Ibid.
53. Nietzsche, *The Gay Science*, 120.
54. Markos, *Lewis Agonistes*, 141.
55. Ibid., 117–22.
56. Edwards, *A Rhetoric of Reading*, 108.

Fifteen years after *A Rhetoric of Reading*, Edwards refers more emphatically to Lewis's use of postmodern rhetoric. In an essay (2010), he declares that Lewis is both a rationalist and a romantic, even if he sees two different counter-reactions to Lewis and postmodernism in academic circles: one opinion is that Lewis is "too much a 'Modernist' to help postmoderns cope with the Enlightenment's fall from grace"; the other is that Lewis is "too much a 'Romantic' to escape the self-centeredness that postmodernism corrects."[57]

More sharply than Edwards, David C. Downing views Lewis as a postmodernist in relation to postmodern philosopher Derrida. He compares the two emphasizing that all analysis is situated, "there is no position of utter objectivity from which one may think about thinking itself."[58]

Crystal Downing most assuredly classifies Lewis among the postmodernists—Lewis deconstructs past models in the same way that Thomas S. Kuhn argues in *The Structure of Scientific Revolutions* (1962). Kuhn defines scientific paradigm shifts as "beliefs."[59] Downing claims that postmodernism is unexpectedly connected with Christianity as both are undermined by the modernists who depend on a dualistic elevation of reason over multiple values.[60] She insists that Lewis is a postmodernist, in the sense that he deconstructs the modernist concept of scientific objectivity. He exposes the modernist's construction of another model, which he indicates in *The Discarded Image*: "No model is a catalogue of ultimate realities."[61]

Lewis scholars such as Bruce Edwards, David Downing, and Crystal Downing discuss Lewis's philosophy in the context of Christian postmodernism in different terms: Crystal Downing highlights the conceptualization of the Other[62]; Edwards's "limited human construction"[63] suggests that Lewis uses deconstructive expressions to seek the finiteness of human knowledge rather than for "the easy equations with things-in-themselves"[64]; and David Downing's "multiple interpretations"[65] suggests that Lewis views two kinds

57. Edwards, "The Lion Still Roars," n. pag.
58. D. C. Downing, "C.S. Lewis Among the Postmodernists," n. pag.
59. Kuhn, *The Structure of Scientific Revolutions*, 175.
60. C. Downing, *How Postmodernism Serves (My) Faith*, 21.
61. Lewis, *The Discarded Image*, 222.
62. C. Downing, *How Postmodernism Serves (My) Faith*, 3.
63. Edwards, *The Taste of the Pineapple* 29.
64. Ibid.
65. D. C. Downing, "C.S. Lewis Among the Postmodernists" n. pag.

of reality in the same way as T.S. Eliot does in his poem "Burnt Norton" of *Quartet*.[66] These scholars discuss the philosophical and theological sides of Lewis's thoughts, but pay little attention to his imaginative approach as a writer of fiction. Lewis as a novelist of Christian postmodernism will be discussed in chapter 2.

LEWIS AS AN ANTI-MODERNIST

Throughout his writing career, Lewis feels a sense of crisis against modernistic sensibility and expresses the unpleasantness he attributes to the trends of the twentieth century. In his theological book *Mere Christianity* (1952), he indicates his concern over the modernized interpretation of miracles: "reality is very odd."[67] A discussion of a selection of his non-fictional works, including articles and books, will reveal the philosophical foundation for his anti-modernist thought, preparing the reader to appreciate his fictional world in both word and image. From his non-fiction works written in the 1940s and 1950s, a chronological selection will reveal his anti-modernistic notions: "Bulverism" (1941), "The Poison of Subjectivism" (1943), *The Abolition of Man* (1941), "Meditation in a Toolshed" (1943), *Miracles: A Preliminary Study* (1947), the "Introduction" to *Letters to Young Churches* (1947), *Surprised by Joy* (1955), "De Descriptione Temporum" (1955),[68] and *Mere Christianity* (1952).

With the term "Bulverism," in his 1941 essay of the same name, Lewis challenges twentieth century mainstream thought in modernism, characterizing the origin of modern mind-sets. By "Bulverism," he means a mistaken method of discourse which explains the reason for the argument before providing the argument itself. He creates this fictional character, "Ezekiel Bulver," to represent people with a preference for logical fallacy. Through Mr. Bulver, Lewis explains the modern practice of psychologizing those whom we disagree with, instead of arguing the cause of their different opinions. Bruce L. Edwards compares Mr. Bulver to the modernist critics:

---

66. Eliot, *Four Quartet*, 15 and 18.

67. Lewis, *Mere Christianity*, 23. *Mere Christianity* was originally presented as a radio series for the BBC between 1942 and 1944, and later published in 1952.

68. "De Descriptione Temporum" was delivered in Cambridge, on 29 November, 1954, published in 1955, reprinted in 1962 (*They Asked for a Paper*) and in 1969 (*Selected Literary Essays*).

arguing (as does Derrida) that language is only about itself and cannot refer to a 'transcendental signified' or contending . . . that the text is not an objective entity but rests in the eye of the beholder and thus prevents the 'only real issue' from ever being raised.[69]

With the term "the poison of subjectivism" in his 1943 essay of the same name,[70] Lewis criticizes the modernist tendency that arose during the age of Enlightenment which based knowledge and morality on subjective experience and feeling, claiming that "The very idea of freedom presupposes some objective moral law."[71]

With the phrase "the head with no chest," Lewis returns to the same subject in his 1943 philosophical work on modern education, *The Abolition of Man*. This term means rational thought and the raised objection to modern attempts to debunk objective values. He describes the dehumanizing tendencies in modernism that depend on pure reason (the head) leading to a lack of objective value to judge what behavior is right and wrong. The modern mind-set separates mind from body, causing the loss of normal human feelings (the chest), thus creating "men without chests." Lewis develops the same theme of "the head with no chest" in his scientific fiction *That Hideous Strength* (1945). He creates main characters devoid of emotional sensibilities as well as moral abilities so that they fail to judge their behaviors. This novel will be analyzed in chapter 3.

In the essay "Meditation in a Toolshed" (1945), Lewis voices his resistance against modernist epistemology—the dualistic notion which endorses either hyper-realism (science) or supernaturalism (religion).[72] He describes his experience of viewing light in two ways: "look at" (which indicates the law of nature) and "look along" (representing the law of super-naturalism).[73] He recounts the experience of viewing light in a dark toolshed: he looks at the beam and sees spots of dust floating in it; but he is struck by a different sight when he looks along the beam and traces it to its source. He realizes that the beam actually originates from "90 odd million

---

69. Edwards, *A Rhetoric of Reading*, 40.

70. "The Poison of Subjectivism" originally appeared in the periodical *Religion in Life*, vol. XII (Summer 1943), was posthumously reprinted in *Christian Reflections* (1998), and in *C.S. Lewis: Essays Collection and Other Short Pieces* (2000).

71. Lewis, "The Poison of Subjectivism," 665.

72. Originally published in *The Coventry Evening Telegraph* (July 17, 1945) and reprinted in *God in the Dock* (1970).

73. Lewis, *God in the Dock*, 212.

miles away, the sun."[74] His glance chases the beam through the crack and sees a different view—the leaves of a tree beyond its crack in the door—and continues to trace the beam through the leaves of the tree and beyond. He concludes that we must "look both along and look at" everything,[75] because these two human values are completely conflicting and incompatible.

In *Miracles: A Preliminary Study* (1947), Lewis similarly presents his antithesis to modernist persistence of naturalism and its danger of excessive dependence on empiricism: "It is useless to appeal to experience before . . .the philosophical question."[76] Lewis's ethics of miracles is in opposition to modernist thought, emphasizing cause and effect while rejecting purpose. He affirms that it is not logical to deny that something or someone can enter into a dimension or realm beyond the laws of nature if one believes in a supernatural being.

Lewis's argument with the King James Version of the Bible, translated into English by order of King James I in the seventeenth century, similarly reflects his notion against modernism. He asserts that the *KJV* is subject to the erosion of time and that its interpretation is changeable over time,[77] His concept of language is in counterpoint with the scientific interpretation of the Bible which led to "the *KJV*-only movement" in the twentieth century. The movement started as an anti-modernist response to the scientific critical analysis of the Bible in the nineteenth century, but the modernist *KJV*-supporters became like the seventeenth century dualist Christians who adhered to a single interpretation of the seventeenth century English Bible. John Ankerberg and John Weldon affirm that the seventeenth century obsession with the Latin version was similarly repeated in the twentieth century: both generations were absorbed with the older translation of the Bible, revealing their dualistic nature of adhering to a single interpretation.[78]

Although Lewis understands the laborious human efforts to improve Bible translation, he affirms that a newer translation provides better access to the modern reader.[79] Even though he appreciates the beautiful rhythm of *KJV*, he believes that the ultimate beauty of Scripture is not in the liter-

---

74. Ibid., 213.

75. Ibid., 215.

76. Lewis, *Miracles*, 1.

77. Lewis, "Modern Translations of the Bible," 229. This essay was originally published as an Introduction to J.B. Phillips' *Letters to Young Churches* (1947).

78. Ankerberg and Weldon, *The Facts on the King James Only Debate*, 11.

79. Lewis, *God in the Dock*, 229.

ary rhetoric but in the holiness and humility of the Incarnation embodied when the divine became human.

As Lewis affirms that language is a reflection of imperfect human beings, translation is no exception. The dualist influence of the Enlightenment expanded into Western society through modern readings of the Bible. Biblical criticism was a critical approach to the biblical text in which the scientific thinking of the eighteenth century was applied to the study of the Bible, promoting a dualistic interpretation in which only one translation of the Greek and Hebrew original text was preferred. The scientific approach to biblical criticism led to the nineteenth century discovery of the translation errors in *KJV*, which invited an excessive protection of the version. The increasing concern over the seventeenth century version caused excessive promotion of the twentieth century *KJV*-only movement. Lewis recommends Phillips's post-war translation (portions of the New Testament). Philips' version is of Christian postmodernism as he translates not only the words but also the images behind them through paraphrasing the words of Jesus: he communicates with the contemporary readers while valuing the emotions of the authors.

Lewis discusses the concept of chronological snobbery in his 1953 inaugural speech at Cambridge and again in his autobiography *Surprised by Joy* (1954). He and his friend-critic Owen Barfield coin the term "chronological snobbery" when they argue about outdated religion. Chronological snobbery refers to the erroneous argument that the thinking of an earlier time is innately inferior when compared to that of the present. Lewis realizes that he also holds to the modernist notion with regard to chronological snobbery. He feels a shock when he shouts "medieval" to Barfield, an anthropologist, to mean "as terms of abuse."[80]

In the essay "De Descriptione Temporum," Lewis again reveals his anxiety about the spirit of modernism with a particular term: "the post-Christian."[81] He warns to the reader that the modernist's small action results in a severe consequence. Through the dividing of all history into three periods: "the pre-Christian," "the Christian," and "the post-Christian,"[82]

80. Lewis, *Surprised by Joy*, 206.

81. Ibid., 5. The speech "De Descriptione Temporum" was presented in his inaugural lecture at Cambridge in 1954 and published in *They Asked for a Paper* in 1962 and in *Selected Literary Essays* in 1969. In 1954, Lewis accepted the newly founded chair of Mediaeval and Renaissance Literature at Magdalene College, Cambridge University, where he continued his career until death in 1963.

82. Ibid.

he assumes a story of post-Christianity. Post-Christianity originated in the period of the Renaissance, which promoted a belief in rational theory. Lewis's concept of the history of modernism is that modernists accept the Renaissance, as if they've opened Pandora's Box, and invite the far-reaching consequences: the atheistic modernist thought of the twentieth century, including Sigmund Freud's psycho-analysis and Darwin's natural selection.

To illustrate the developing picture of modernism, Lewis employs an interesting parallel between a lion cub and the thoughts of modernists, including Darwin (empiricist), Freud (reductionist), and Marx (rationalist). The modernists were responsible for causing three results: a lion cub, a lion inside the cage, and a lion outside the cage. Darwin plays with a lion cub (the ancestry of Man); Freud plays with a lion inside the cage (his ancestry and his soul), even though he is shocked by the cub growing up to be a savage lion; but the worst result comes when Marx mechanically uses everything so that the lion gets out of the cage. Lewis anxiously predicts that the rational use of humanity will produce the abolition of humanity.[83]

Modernized Christianity is what Lewis calls "watered down"[84] or diluted by modernist thought. Using the term "Christianity-and-water," he criticizes the German theologian Rudolf Karl Bultmann (1886–1978) for leaving the supernatural out of the Bible to de-mythologize Christianity. Bultmann regards demythologizing the New Testament as an evangelical task so that he concludes that the biblical image alienates modern people from the Christian faith.[85]

In his theological publication *Mere Christianity* (1955), Lewis expresses a sense of unease over the modernized interpretation of miracles. He argues that by "diluting Christianity,"[86] Bultmann removes the miraculous stories of Jesus Christ from the Bible, hoping that Christianity will survive even under the modern threat of enlightenment. Lewis asserts that Bultmann's compromise with dualism excludes the essential twin pillars of the Gospel—the Incarnation of the Divine born into humanity and the Resurrection of the dead. Counter to Bultmann, Lewis presents Christianity as the historical fulfillment of pagan mythologies, writing as a novelist to dramatize the reconciliation of two incompatible worldviews: Christianity and mythology, as well as naturalism and supernaturalism.

83. Lewis, *Selected Literary Essays*, 7.
84. Lewis, *God in the Dock*, 24.
85. Bultmann, *Kerygma and Myth*, 3.
86. Lewis, *Mere Christianity*, 23.

CHRISTIAN POSTMODERNISM
BEYOND ACADEMIC DISCIPLINES

Lewis is a writer who deserves feedback from scholars beyond the boundaries of academic disciplines. His concept of miracles has invited contrasting reactions: a negative one from modernist critic Kathleen Nott (1905–1999), as well as positive responses from scholars of interdisciplinary fields, such as theologian Lesslie Newbigin (1909–1998) and scientist Francis S. Collins (1950-). An analysis of these three scholars' arguments on Lewis's proposition for miracles, reveals that the writer of Christian postmodernism contributes to a reconciliation of modernist conflicts between science (naturalism) and religion (supernaturalism) and promotes the postmodernist coexistence of both views in the twenty-first century.

Nott is a firm believer in rationalism, while Newbigin and Collins oppose modernist thought that separates dual worldviews: naturalism and supernaturalism; history and myth; as well as observation and faith. As a writer of Christian postmodernism, Lewis functions to reconcile these divided worlds. He accepts two different views and expects complete understanding that transcends human abilities. In the 1940s and 1950s, he had already established a frontier project for restoring the philosophical cracks. His efforts, championed by theologian Newbigin in the twentieth century, continue with scientist-thinker Collins in the twenty-first century.

Lewis is widely discussed as a Christian apologetics writer, but is not popularly known among his contemporary modern critics. Modernist critic Kathleen Nott has rebutted the writers of the 1950s at Oxford. Although Lewis as a critical philosopher is not largely discussed by his contemporary theorists her denial conversely illuminates Lewis as a critic. She is ironically the only modern critic among his contemporaries who has focused on him as a critic.

Nott criticizes not only Lewis but also other leading writers at Oxford, including T.S. Eliot, Graham Greene, and Dorothy L. Sayers. This is made clear by the title of her book: *The Emperor's Clothes: an Attack on the Dogmatic Orthodoxy of T.S. Eliot, Graham Greene, Dorothy Sayers, C.S. Lewis, and Others* (1953). She refutes their theological ethos, rejecting their works as detestable: "their stance is dogmatic Christian orthodoxy."[87] She disagrees with Lewis who set forth his theological argument for miracles in his book *Miracles: A Preliminary Study* (1947). Surprisingly, Nott makes an

---

87. Nott, *The Emperor's Clothes*, 68.

excellent summary of his book, stating that "these are the central dogmas of the Christian faith, the sine qua non of orthodoxy."[88]

Nott is a rational thinker who defends the scientific approach to logical reasoning, demanding a separation of the inner world (faith) from the public life (knowledge based on the scientific approach). She is convinced that knowledge based on observation and that logical thinking should be limited within the public field. She, therefore, charges Lewis with being a transgressor, as he adopts a theological approach to literature and literary critics. She concludes that his description of miracles is not logical knowledge.

One example of the sort of argument that makes Nott feel uncomfortable is Lewis's re-evaluation of Milton's *Paradise Lost*. In 1941, Lewis presented a lecture, "*A Preface to Paradise Lost*," for the Ballard Matthews Lectures at the University College of North Wales. Nott dismisses Milton simply because the author writes about God's Creation. Nott not only debunks Lewis's notion of writing as creative activity, but she also laments his lack of logical reasoning or syllogism.

For Nott, Satan is a wish fulfillment, but for Milton and Lewis, Satan is a reality. The two writers describe Satan differently: Milton's Satan in *Paradise Lost* is of grand appearance, while Lewis, in his novel *The Screwtape Letters*, strips Satan of thrilling glamor with his depiction of a farcical, delirious, and guileful figure. Although Milton's vision of Satan is considered to be a hero, Lewis denies the proposition, situating Satan not as tragic but as laughable. He assumes that if sin is insanity, vice would be ridiculous. He thus describes a young demon of *The Screwtape Letters* as comical and less experienced, and the White Witch of *The Chronicles of Narnia*, as risible and eccentric, intentionally depriving her of any mysterious aura.

Nott proposes that knowledge should be obtained based on rational inference as a result of experiment and observation. She cannot understand Lewis's postmodernist concept of accepting knowledge through both rational and imaginative inferences. It seems to her that Lewis is too confused to distinguish between the two words "thought" (knowledge) and "reasoning" (rational inference). She uses these words interchangeably: reasoning or thought: "All possible knowledge depends on the validity of reasoning or thought."[89] She concludes that he lacks logical reasoning or syllogism because his knowledge is based on irrational meditation, not on logically as-

---

88. Ibid.
89. Ibid., 259.

sumed premises, so she claims that he does not give any insightful thought to the realistic premises. For Nott, theological dogma for reaching truth is the scientific and deductive method of thinking, but for Lewis it is to advocate the unity of two ways: realism and supernaturalism.

Counter to Nott's demand for a single interpretation of rationalism, Lesslie Newbigin appeals for the unification of both the public experience (science) and the private one (religion) in the 1980s. His voice is an echo of Lewis in the 1940s. Lewis's Christian postmodernism is endorsed by this modern scholar. Although Lewis is popularly known as a theological and philosophical writer among his contemporary modernist critics, his epistemological notion of the two worlds is re-confirmed by Newbigin's theological study based on his missionary experience in India.

Newbigin agrees with Lewis's analysis of a modern world in which mutual understanding is completely abolished and humanity has fallen. In *Foolishness to the Greeks: The Gospel and Western Culture* (1986), he echoes Lewis's anxiety over the possible danger that a social scientist might degrade humanity, like a biologist regarding humans as earthworms.[90] He finds a similar theme in Lewis's scientific novel *That Hideous Strength* (*THS*) (1945). To his contemporary world, Newbigin introduces Lewis as a prophetical voice.

Newbigin's demand for the unification of the discrepancy between profession and practice is the echo of Lewis's desire to embrace the inconsistency within Christian life. Lewis reveals his fear of the dichotomy of modern thought throughout his writing life, in both his fiction and his non-fiction. As he indicates in "Meditation in a Toolshed," Lewis observes a modernist demand for more empirical data against inner experience.[91] He believes in an understanding reached through both realism and supernatural experience, but due to the limitations of the human construction of language, he feels that the two experiences can never happen at the same time. However, he claims significance in sharing both viewpoints.

For theologian Newbigin, embracing both worldviews is the key to true understanding. He regards the syllogism as an imaginative way of thinking that unexpectedly requires a technique proposed by Thomas S. Kuhn. In *The Structure of Scientific Revolutions* (1962), Kuhn presents a paradigm shift in which thinking is based on "that body of belief" or the premises beyond and outside logical reasoning.

90. Newbigin, *Foolishness to the Greeks*, 84.
91. Lewis, "Meditation in a Toolshed," 212–15.

Emphasizing a discontinuity between the old theory of physics (Newtonian physics) and the new theory of physics (Einsteinium physics), Kuhn reveals that the new theory is not the result of reasoning based on previous premises, but that of a visionary conversion. Natural history cannot be interpreted in the absence of at least some implicit body of intertwined theoretical and methodological belief that permits selection, evaluation, and criticism. According to Kuhn, there is a need for "a current metaphysic," or "another science," unless the knowledge is tacit.[92]

Newbigin finds a similarity between Kuhn's notion of the paradigm shift and the Bible. His ethos is that we face a discontinuity when we try to understand biblical conversion (repentance to a godly life) as the theological action is unexplainable according to the model of interpretive cycle.[93] By discontinuity, he means a new awareness that is not reached by logical reasoning, but is rather a type of knowledge of which we are not aware. In Scripture, he discovers a number of biblical examples that emphasize the impossibility of understanding the Gospel with human wisdom. One example is Jesus speaking to his disciples: "they may indeed look, but not perceive, and may indeed listen, but not understand; so that they may not turn again and be forgiven" (Mark 4: 12, NRSV).[94]

Newbigin merges the two separated worldviews—fact and value. After returning from forty years of missionary work in India, he witnesses the separated identity within the same believers in his home country: an observation of post-Christianity in England. He realizes that his second mission is to restore the split worlds between naturalism and supernaturalism and the dichotomy between the public world (facts) and private world (values): "the central clue to the ideology that governs our culture."[95]

As a proponent of merging the separated worlds, Newbigin disagrees with theologian and sociologist Peter Berger (1929-) who endorses

---

92. Kuhn, *The Structure of Scientific Revolutions*, 16–17.

93. Newbigin, *Foolishness to the Greeks*, 74.

94. There is a consensus of scholars that the New Revised Standard Version (NRSV) of the Bible is the best and most reliable version despite the King James Version (KJV) being more familiar. This thesis uses the NRSV, except for the obvious adaptations of the KJV by Lewis and other authors. Theologian Bruce M. Metzger regards the NRSV as an authorized revision of the Revised Standard Version: "officially authorized for use by all major Christian churches: Protestant, Anglican, Roman Catholic, and Eastern Orthodox" (*The C.S. Lewis Bible*, xxvii). In an interview conducted by the author, one of the committee members for *The C.S. Lewis Bible*, Bruce L. Edwards suggests that "An American PhD committee would likely recommend the NRSV..." (June, 2014).

95. Newbigin, *Foolishness to the Greeks*, 132.

the division in Christian belief, the deductive standard for escaping into a private region out of the public world (modern society). In *The Heretical Imperative* (1979), Berger writes extensively about the possibility that Christianity can be affirmed as a major voice in the context of modern Western culture. He argues that this culture has no generally acknowledged "plausibility structure."[96] The term "plausibility structure" means a social structure of ideas and practices that creates conditions determining what beliefs are plausible within the society in question.

Lewis would call Mr. Berger "Mr. Bulver," an individual who assumes that someone is wrong without discussing the reason why. Lewis creates this fictional person "Mr. Bulver" to criticize this modern method, and then endlessly explains their stupidity. Like Lewis, Newbigin argues that principle is "the tacit component in knowing."[97] He affirms that mutual understanding is the key to restoring the discontinuity of two worlds. The tacit component of knowledge is what Thomas Kuhn calls in his scientific work: "paradigm shifts."[98] With paradigm shift or Christian postmodernism, Lewis writes as if he is a heretic, speaking to the modern reader from an alien culture. Although Lewis advocates the notion of miracles embodied in the Gospel, he is a trans-cultural communicator, similar to missionaries such as the Apostle Paul and Newbigin. As a novelist, Lewis purposely speaks to the reader with a different cultural background as if he is a missionary transplanting the Gospel into an unfamiliar land.

Newbigin witnesses the negative result of the dualistic thinking which is demanded by Kathleen Nott. Regarding the Incarnation (the Divine identified in humanity) as the embodiment of the Gospel born into human cultures, he supports rehabilitating the dualistic separation of the two cultures, private space from the public in one's religious behavior to the world. From his perspective, Kathleen Nott limits knowledge within one culture, which is understanding reached by reasoning based on scientific observation.

In conclusion, Newbigin insists that mutual understanding between the two thoughts should be promoted, not only the dualistic thoughts of public and private, but also an understanding of the Gospel as a merger of two cultures, both countries of the sender and the receiver of the Gospel:

96. Ibid., 10.
97. Ibid., 80.
98. Ibid., 52.

"To accept it is to make the surrender the early church refused to make—at the cost of the blood of countless martyrs."[99]

Newbigin metaphysically explains the merging of discontinuity, while Lewis illustrates the unity of the two worlds (tacit knowledge or paradigm shift) through the imaginative character in Arthurian legend, Merlin. In *THS*, Merlin is portrayed as an intermediator who connects two worlds in a variety of dimensions: a sleeper (alive and dead), reviver (past and present), and interpreter (ancient and modern worlds).[100]

Just as Newbigin speaks to the theological field of the twentieth century, Francis Collins (1950-), a geneticist, appeals to the world of the twenty-first century scientists for a coexistence of the two philosophies of science and religion. Inspired by Lewis's discussion on science (naturalism) and religion (supernaturalism), Collins affirms, in his *The Language of God* (2006), that the two perspectives should be mutually complementary tools in the search for truth. Although he does not gain a unanimously positive reaction from either side, as a scientist (the director of the Human Genome Project) and as a believer in God, he asserts that both values are God's creation, as he can see God's hand in the magnificent coding of the DNA double helix. He affirms that our hope, joy, and future lie not in the binary option but in the reconciliation of both science and religion.

Lewis, through his writings, contributes to Collins's understanding that another option exists beyond the binary selection of naturalism or supernaturalism. An analysis of Lewis's influence on him will reveal that Lewis denies a dualistic choice of either the spiritual (divine guidance) or the scientific (human interpretation), but he is a Christian postmodernist who longs for truth reached by an understanding that transcends the limits of human language. The novelist Lewis discusses the topic with the rhetoric of reading, while the scientist Collins explains the same subject with the laws of nature, the origin of the universe, and evolution and creation.

Collins is in search of the reason for his longing for something sacred and righteous beyond human understanding. He realizes, through reading Lewis's book on the law of nature, *Mere Christianity* (1952), that this experience is "the God-shaped vacuum,"[101] a well-known phrase coined by the French philosopher and scientist Blaise Pascal in *Pensées*. In the first five chapters of *Mere Christianity*, Lewis argues that the law of nature (the

---

99. Ibid., 132.
100. Lewis, *That Hideous Strength*, 34.
101. Collins, *The Language of God*, 38.

moral law) is an inclination among human beings pleading for a principle of absolute truth.

Collins's experience of the "God-shaped vacuum" was to be dismissed as "wishful thinking" by modernist thinker Sigmund Freud. In *Totem and Taboo* (1913), the Austrian psychologist states that such longings for the supernatural are not an indication of sensations of awe toward a belief in God, but nothing more than wishful thinking, phrasing it as ". . .at bottom God is nothing other than an exalted father."[102] In *The Question of God* (2002), however, Armand M. Nicholi, opposes Freud's proposition. The Harvard scholar, who studies and teaches on the subjects of Freud and Lewis, and has done so for more than thirty-five years, concludes that: Freud's wish would be "a very different kind of God . . . in the Bible."[103] The crucified deity would not be what people would wish for.

Collins realizes, through reading Lewis, that this longing is equivalent to the desire of scientists to know the great truth. He emphasizes the moment when science transcends an action of discovery: the scientist is involved in rejecting "a completely naturalistic explanation."[104] Lewis calls this sense of longing for another world "the Joy."[105] By "Joy" he means "an unsatisfied desire which is itself more desirable than any other satisfaction."[106] With this technical term, he distinguishes the desire for another world from the one in this world.[107] He concludes that if no experience in this world can satisfy the longing, it is "made for another world."[108]

A clash of interpretations of the biblical account of Creation exists not only between scientists and believers in God, but also among believers—between modernist, literalist, and non-literalist. Their opinions differ according to the interpretations of chapters 1 and 2 of the Book of Genesis. The modernist ignores the account; the literalist interprets it as a literal history; and the non-literalist interprets it as an allegory. Collins echoes Lewis who interprets the account as a moral lesson rather than a history: "we

---

102. Ibid., 37.
103. Ibid.
104. Ibid., 36.
105. Ibid., 18.
106. Ibid.
107. Ibid.
108. Lewis, *Mere Christianity*, 115.

have no idea in what particular act, or series of acts, the self-contradictory impossible wish found expression."[109]

Lewis's understanding of Genesis looks, at first glance, contradictory to modernist Christianity, but he stands by the same stance as the traditional notion. He concludes not only that Genesis is myth, but that in being myth, it is perfectly acceptable. Although he interprets the Creation as "myth," that does not automatically mean *false* for him. He evaluates myth as a highly imaginative way of explaining the truth in a way similar to history and science. Lewis alludes to the paradigm for his approach in the tradition of Christianity that includes a Roman Catholic theologian Saint Jerome and a principal figure of Calvinism during the Protestant Reformation, John Calvin.[110]

Collins stands by "theistic evolution" even though the term is still a stumbling block for most believers—the concept that evolution appears to be accidentally operated from a human perspective, but the outcome would be identified from God's point of view. He distinguishes between evolution as a biological process and the same term used as the world's concept.[111] To more commonly communicate this stance on society, Collins proposes a new term: "BioLogos"—the belief that God is the source of all life and that life represents the intention of God.

In recent discoveries on the theory of universe, Collins finds positive evidence for a harmony of both positions, as he states that "Only a supernatural force that is outside of space and time could have done that."[112] The Big Bang is one example indicative of a divine explanation for the beginning of the universe. The study of genomes is another example. He finds a close connection among all living things as the master plan of God who created the universe "to allow the creation."[113]

Faced with increasingly antagonistic voices between proponents of creation and proponents of evolution, Collins requests that readers on either side continue exploring the interpretation of Genesis 1 and 2, because, despite twenty-five centuries of debate over the story of Creation, no human understanding has ever reached what the passages were precisely intended to be. Collins upholds the lesson learned from Galileo that God

109. Lewis, *The Problem of Pain*, 71.
110. Lewis, *Reflections on the Psalms*, 94.
111. Collins, *The Language of God*, 55.
112. Ibid., 67.
113. Ibid., 199.

who created the universe and bestowed on human beings the intellectual abilities to discern its workings would not want us to ignore his gifts.[114] He again turns to Lewis when he is faced with a choice of multiple interpretations of miracles between eccentric supernaturalism (literalist) and complete ignorance (modernist). Lewis emphasizes the rarity of miracles and the purpose behind miraculous events: "they are found at the great ganglions of history."[115]

Collins denies interpreting miracles as the purposeless acts of a whimsical trickster, and also doubts the interpretations of potentially miraculous events presented both by committed materialism (rejection of miracles) and religious conservatism (rejection of science).[116] He observe the opposite opinions of miracles between the materialist and the conservative spiritualist: the former ignores miracles, while the latter seeks miracle status for things that can be explained by the laws of nature. He does not deny the possibility that there might be, on rare occasions, an invasion from something or someone outside nature, possibility not an invasion of political or social history, but that of spiritual history which cannot be fully known by men. He echoes theoretical physicist and Anglican priest John Polkinghorne who also asserts that the laws of nature are the expressions of God's will.

Collins realizes, through reading Lewis, the significance of individual assumed perception; what the novelist Lewis calls "a philosophy"[117] and what the scientist Collins calls "presumption."[118] This occurs when he is challenged by the compatibility of embracing two worldviews—scientific explanation and spiritual understanding of miracles in Christianity, e.g. the Incarnation or Christ's birth in the flesh and the Resurrection or his rising from the dead.[119] Lewis affirms that: "If we hold a philosophy which excludes the supernatural, this is what we always shall say."[120]

---

114. Ibid., 56.
115. Lewis, *Miracles*, 167.
116. Collins, *The Language of God*, 93.
117. Lewis, *Miracles*, 3.
118. Collins, *The Language of God*, 51.

119. To calculate the probability of miracles, Collins uses the mathematical method of Bayes' Theorem—a simple mathematical formula used for calculating conditional probabilities ("Bayes' Theorem," Stanford University, Sep. 30, 2003).

120. Lewis, *Miracles*, 3.

Philosopher of Christian Postmodernism

Collins concludes that no miracles can be allowed if the presumption is that supernatural events are impossible: "a natural explanation."[121] Although science is a method of studying nature and is governed by the laws of nature, it is a constantly self-modifying approach, not a perfect way to seek the truth. In the same way, although the Bible is God's Word, human interpretations of biblical accounts are not perfect, as revealed by the millennial debate on the meaning of chapters 1 and 2 of the book of Genesis.

For Collins, the wisdom of Lewis serves as a signpost for accepting the two worldviews. He envisions that the greatest miracle is revealed through understanding beyond the binary selection of naturalism or supernaturalism: what he calls *agape*. He affirms that it is impossible for the Darwinist to explain *agape* or people who sacrificially give themselves. This is because, for the modernist, altruism is always supported by evolution as it helps the group survive. The modernist, especially Darwinists' challenge against Collins, reveals that Lewis, as a writer of Christian postmodernism, contributes to a reconciliation of conflicts between science (naturalism) and religion (supernaturalism) and promotes understanding that transcends the coexistence of both views. Collins concludes by stating that God "can be worshiped in the cathedral or in the laboratory."[122]

---

121. Collins, *The Language of God*, 51.

122. Ibid., 39. Collins quotes the last phrase (modified) from Pulitzer Prize-winning author Annie Dillard's *Teaching a Stone to Talk: Expeditions and Encounters* (1982): "What is the difference between a cathedral and a physics lab?"

— 2 —

Novelist of Christian Postmodernism

C.S. Lewis's literary approach is the result of both his philosophical antipathy toward modernist thought and his literary passion for premodern classics, but he resolutely introduces himself as a writer with two cultural roots: Christian classics and pagan myths. His preference for old writings covers a variety of types of myths: Greek, Latin, Northern, and medieval. He is aware that his taste for the medieval world is negatively labeled as "old" by the modernist critics as he states in "De Descriptione Temporum."[1] However, he declares, in the same year, that he represents not only "the old Western culture"[2] but also "the mist . . . pagan, romantic and polytheistic in grain."[3]

Against the modernist age that elevates reason above faith, Lewis does not dilute reason and faith, but evaluates both the Gospel (Christianity) and pagan myths (pre-Christian stories). He speaks in a way that mixes both word (the human explanation) and image (the supernatural guidance). By employing the harmony of both styles, he questions not only the boundaries between popular and serious genres, but also the limitations of human language.

Lewis creates a harmony of contradictory worldviews—Christianity and pagan mythology. This euphonious tendacy is not only the reason

---

1. Lewis, "De Descriptione Temporum," 12.
2. Ibid.
3. Lewis, foreword to *Smoke on the Mountain*, 1. *Smoke on the Mountain* was published almost in the same year as "De Descriptione Temporum" was presented in 1954.

for his conversion from atheism to deism, but also his motivation to write novels through the contradictory perspectives and literary genres. As a critic, he expresses his comprehension of a modernist novel characterized by author-controlled autonomy. As a reader, even though he wishes to read fantasy works similar to medieval romances, he can find only a few among contemporary publications. J.R.R. Tolkien, Charles Williams, Dorothy L. Sayers, and Joy Davidman are the exceptional cases among the twentieth century writers.

As a writer, therefore, Lewis chooses fantasy as the literary form which is best for him to communicate to the contemporary reader—the reconciliation of Christianity and mythology. Although he has his first collection of poetry published before 1930, he keeps writing novels from the 1930s nearly until his death. Based on his own World War I experiences at the front, he finds his generation numb to the meaning of language because he was devoid of fear (human emotions) during the actual fighting.[4] As a novelist, he writes for the readers who have experienced wars, but after his death, his works come to speak to postmodernist minds.

To a post-war audience entangled in multiple values, Lewis speaks even after his death to his reader in the postmodern world. More of his books are posthumously published. The scholar of medieval literature appeals to postmodern readers as he writes his novels with literary techniques similar to those commonly used in the Middle Ages, including meta-fiction (a story within a story) and an ambiguous boundary not only between fact and fiction, but also between author, narrator, and character. The comparison of his works and postmodernist writings will reveal that his choice of speech is appropriate to appeal to the reader of a postmodern world.

Four postmodern British novelists have been selected for comparison with the postmodern approaches of Lewis from among the authors mentioned in Patricia Waugh's *Metafiction* (1996): Iris Murdoch, Muriel Spark, Doris Lessing, and John Fowles. All four started writing in Britain around the 1960s, about the time of Lewis's death. Their novels are characterized by their inclusion of a metafictional world that reflects language within the dialogic process. Waugh affirms that meta-fiction reveals the impossibility of such a resolution, counter to realistic fiction in which the conflict of voices is rectified through their subjection to the supreme voice.

The contrasting ground of two voices is a concept introduced by Russian philosopher Mikhail Bakhtin. He regards language as voices

---

4. Lewis, *Surprised by Joy*, 227.

"diametrically opposed to its original direction" as the word for "the arena of conflict between two voices."[5] As such, Bakhtin's semantic direction is a reflection of his assertion of human language being in a constant process.[6] He accepts two communicative styles—absolute truth and context-based perception. Crystal Downing affirms that Bakhtin's sign is related to a dialogue, context-situated.[7]

Lewis's approach is inspired mainly by reading both medieval romances and nineteenth century novels. An analysis of the main source material will clarify the rhetorical stance of his writing technique. The selection of materials is based on the book reviews recounted in Lewis's autobiography *Surprised by Joy* (1955), and also in his letters, mainly to his brother Warnie and his best friend Arthur Greeves in Ireland. The correspondence between Lewis and Arthur Greeves proceeded between the 1930s to his death in 1963.

LEWIS'S NOTION OF MODERNIST LITERATURE

Lewis could be categorized in the same religious paradigm as modernists until his conversion to Christianity in 1931. He became a theist in 1929, but became a Christian in 1931. Although nowadays he is well-known as a Christian author, he was an atheist until the 1920s. He can be categorized on the same philosophical platform as James George Frazer, who regards religion as the human effort to make sense of the incomprehensible. At the age of sixteen, as an ardent reader of Frazer's famous book, *The Golden Bough* (1890), Lewis became unexpectedly fascinated by Frazer's modernist concept of mythology: "dying gods" and "fertility rites."[8] He, however, loses his passion for modernistic concept of gods.

Lewis's first novel, *The Pilgrim's Regress* (1933), displays his change of notions about God. This novel, written two years after his conversion to Christianity, is an allegorical depiction of his anti-modernism. Late in his life, he orally describes himself as an anti-modernist when he accepts his Cambridge professorship in 1954. The analysis of both the Cambridge address "De Descriptione Temporum" and his first novel, *The Pilgrim's Regress*, will clarify the reasons for Lewis's shift away from his zeal for modernism.

5. Bakhtin, *Problems of Dostoevsky's Poetics*, 106.
6. C. Downing, *Changing Signs of Truth*, 300.
7. Ibid., 306.
8. Frazer, *The Golden Bough*, 386.

Novelist of Christian Postmodernism

Lewis presents modernist thought as the destroyer of the philosophical heritage of Western culture. He turns away from the visions of other contemporary poets. In his Cambridge professor acceptance speech in 1954, "De Descriptione Temporum," he highlights a separation between the Waverly works and the modern time. To the audience, he introduces himself as "a dinosaur of the old Western Culture, almost extinct."[9] He expresses astonishment at the impossibility of agreement of opinions in the modern age, referring to an academic conference where there was no agreement reached among attending scholars as to the meaning of modernist poet T.S. Eliot's poem "A Cooking Egg."[10] Although the two scholars of Oxford had no contact when "A Cooking Egg" was presented in 1920, they shared an interest in the medieval tradition, and gradually developed a friendship "on a personal level."[11] As discussed in chapter 1, their Christian thought was attacked by the modernist critic Kathleen Nott in 1953.

Lewis expresses his dismay at the modernist world in his poem "A Confession" which was published in the same year as "De Descriptione Temporum" (1954): "For twenty years I've stared my level best / . . . / In vain. I simply wasn't able."[12] He reveals his anxiety about the modernists' destruction of the historical association between the classical world and the modern society, by ridiculing Eliot's famous lines about a sunset in "The Love Song of J. Alfred" (1928).

Although Eliot seeks no meaning in this poem, Lewis expresses his doubts about Eliot and also counterattacks in his poem "A Confession": "To see if evening—any evening—would suggest / A patient etherized upon a table; / In vain I simply wasn't able."[13] Instead of "A patient" in the evening, Lewis re-evaluates the beautiful evening on the shore and the graceful departure of a ship.[14] Through his rejection of Eliot's work, Lewis uncovers the gap between stock responses (solid forms and shapes, conventional symbols) and new, subjective associations (modernist technique).

In his pre-Christian period, until the 1920s, the young Lewis shared the same concept of pagan gods as James George Frazer. By observing the visible rituals in every culture, the Scottish writer affirms that all the

---

9. Lewis, "De Descriptione Temporum," 13.
10. Ibid., 9.
11. Vaus, "Lewis in Cambridge: Professional Years (1954–1963)," 205.
12. Lewis, *Poems*, 34.
13. Ibid.
14. Ibid.

gods have no narrative with a particular place and time. Anthropologist Frazer highlights the universality of the gods to reject the historical reality of Christ. The modernist Frazer proposes that all pagan gods are of relative value. His rational proposition comes to the conclusion that the universal pattern of the gods, dying and resurrecting, is common to all cultures. Therefore, Christ is not unique, but of equal value to many other pagan gods, including the Egyptian mythological god Osiris and the Greek mythological youth Adonis.

For the teenage Lewis, Christianity is a supreme fiction. From the perspective of relativism, he describes the belief as "one mythology among many."[15] In a letter to his friend Arthur Greeves in 1916, he states that mythologies are "merely man's own invention—Christ as much as Loki."[16] In the poem "Couplets," (1917) written before his conversion, Lewis admonishes gods for their haughty attitude toward human beings: "the proud gods."[17] He clearly expresses his agnostic stance in this poem.[18]

Modernist philosophers fail to contain their confusion at the demise of the old values. Modernist novelists, in the same way, excessively react to the desolate state of their minds by writing fictitiously ordered reality in the form of novels. In "De Descriptione Temporum," Lewis selects two works to epitomize the modernist literature: Virginia Woolf's *To the Lighthouse* (1927) and James Joyce's *Ulysses* (1922). These two modernist novelists highlight desolation by proclaiming no reality within the fictional worlds of their creation.

To both writers, Lewis displays negative reactions, referring to their incompatibility of spelling and sound. He affirms that in his notion of language, spelling and sound are counter to Joyce's mutinous selection of words in *Finnegans Wake* (1939). Four months before his death, Lewis wrote that Joyce's *silvamoonlake* is "spoiled for me by the spelling which links it up with an advertisement slogan that we're all sick of here 'Drinkapintamilkaday.'"[19] For Lewis, the form and sound matter as much as the spelling and sound.

Virginia Woolf regards her literature as a tool of her aesthetics, and James Joyce describes his literature as an inescapable sign confined in a

---

15. Lewis, *They Stand Together*, 135.
16. Lewis, *The Collected Letters I*, 230–31.
17. Lewis, *The Collected Poems of C.S. Lewis*, 140–41.
18. Green, and Hooper, *C.S. Lewis: The Authorized and Revised Biography*, 31–32.
19. Lewis, *The Collected Letters III*, 1440.

linguistic prison. Patricia Waugh states that Woolf and Joyce mark the emergence in a new sense of being fictional,[20] while Ludwig Pfeifer asserts that Woolf and James do not represent reality in a literary sense but focus on perspectives of how to know.[21]

In "De Descriptione Temporum," Lewis contrasts his respect of history and Woolf's rejection of the past. He prefers "periods" in history, while Woolf rejects the tradition—she writes her novels in stream of consciousness to deny the past. Lewis states that: "We cannot use for literary history the technique of Mrs. Woolf's *The Waves*."[22]

Woolf and Joyce share a concept of language with the modern linguist, Ferdinand de Saussure. Just as the two modernist writers have no faith in meaning and purpose in language, so Saussure believes that the words people use are not a reflection of real ideas but sound images (signifiers) that point to some shady concept (signified). As Louis Markos states, Saussure's language lacks a link between image and concept.[23]

Modernist literature is characteristic of realism, a notion of illusion under which the language of a text can be interpreted as a reflection of facts in a real world. Patricia Waugh explains the notion through the listing of five features of modernist literature: 1. the appropriate organization of plot 2. the chronological proceeding 3. the omniscient author 4. the logical link between characters' action and each personality, and 5. the causal connection between apparent details and the philosophy of existence.[24]

She proposes that modernist literature is posited on the realist worldview of the materialist, positivist, and empiricist.[25] The fictional world is a hypothetically organized reality in plot, sequence, author, character, and law. Realism is a fictional illusion in which authors invoke belief in a common phenomenological world, directing the reader to daily reality. The reader of a modernist text is led into an illusion of self-reflexive reading in which an interpretation can be constructed by directly connecting the words of the text with objects in the real world.

Lewis presents his notion of anti-modernism in his first novel, *The Pilgrim's Regress* (1933), which was written two years after his conversion

20. Waugh, *Metafiction*, 6.
21. Pfeifer, "The Novel and Society," 61.
22. Lewis, "De Descriptione Temporum," 2.
23. Markos, *Lewis Agonistes*, 141.
24. Waugh, *Metafiction*, 7.
25. Ibid., 23.

to Christianity. The story begins with the escape of the atheist protagonist John from the castle of the landlord in the East Mountain to the sea of the West: the landlord is suggestive of the Creator and the sea reflects earthly paradise. During his journey, however, the young man is in distress due to his encounters with numerous modernist philosophies of the early twentieth century world, including atheism, Freudianism, nihilism, and fascism. In a dungeon, John feels like a miserable failure after facing phoniness, treachery, and hypocrisy through his meetings with modernists, including "Mr. Halways," "Gas Halfway," "Time Spirit," and "Neo Classic," who respectively represent decadence, Epicureanism, skeptic materialism, and plutolatry.

With the help of his companion, Virtue, who represents reason, John unexpectedly arrives at the back side of the East Mountain, opposite the Sea of the West which he desires to reach. Virtue, with his name suggesting a high moral standard, serves to help John, by providing moral support, restart his journey from the back side to the front side of the East Mountain. John makes a "regress" to the East, returning to re-start his journey, as the title indicates.

John's return to his home country is described with two literary forms: prose and verse. The integration of the two different forms is both a reflection of the restoration of his divided self and the suggestion of another world beyond the human construction of language. In this mixture of literary forms, seventeen poems (verse) are inserted into the allegorical work (prose). The two literary forms are exposed, tested, and rehabilitated through John's adventure. Both forms represent his divided mind between his desire to reach the Island in the West, and his desire for the Landlord in the East. In the last poem included in *The Pilgrim's Regress*, Lewis recounts the shift of John's communication from monophony to polyphony, from monologue to dialogue, until he sees joy over death: "Cannot understand / Love that mortal bears / For native, native land / All lands are theirs."[26] Lewis finally expresses the changing process of John's values as well as the true goal beyond the visible process.

At the end of *The Pilgrim's Regress*, Lewis uses a double construction similar to meta-fiction: one is the story of the protagonist John, the other is the vision of a dreamer who sees John traveling two courses. In the first journey, John makes progress, but in the return course, he makes "a regress." It is not clearly mentioned whether the dreamer will be awoken or

---

26. Lewis, *The Pilgrim's Regress*, 199.

not, but it is vaguely suggested that the dreamer can be united with the story of John and Virtue. This novel reveals a vision of unification of the divided selves of all people, including John, Virtue, the dreamer, and the reader. Even though the story is written in an allegorical form, the whole construction of the story is indicative of a forerunner of the postmodernist approach, as a story (John's regress) within a story (the dreamer's sleep).

APPROACHES OF POSTMODERN LITERATURE

Postmodernists react with suspicion not only toward the organized reality of modernist literature, but also to the modernist literary forms, especially their singular way of looking at reality in contrast with the postmodernist's multiple perspectives of the world. Stanley J. Grenz clarifies the different goals for the modern and postmodern writer: the former strives to seek for the fixed explanation for "a complex but ... singular reality," while the latter strives to question the coexistence of "different realities."[27] The postmodernist novels subvert the modernist trust in autonomous objectivity.

Postmodern novels depict the narrator not as a single trustful person, but one with limited ability and with multiple perspectives. The narrator of the postmodern novel, thus, misinterprets the things he/she describes. Further, multiple narrators report the same events in different ways. Postmodern literature invites the reader to join the interpretation of the text reading and to consider which side to believe. Crystal Downing affirms that the role of the reader is the key to postmodern novels. After she contrasts the role of the reader in modern novels and postmodern works, she concludes that the reader of postmodern novels is challenged to discern the distinction between fiction and history.[28]

An analysis of the distinction between fiction and history in postmodern literature is illustrated in this paper by the use of four British novels, discussed in chronological order of publication: Irish Murdoch's *Under the Net* (1954), Muriel Spark's *The Prime of Miss Jean Brodie* (1961), Doris Lessing's *The Golden Notebook* (1962), and John Fowls's *The French Lieutenant's Woman* (1960).

Iris Murdoch's first novel, *Under the Net* (1954), is a meta-fiction in which the author alludes to artificiality by parodying the first fictional world. In her story, language is not a perfect tool but a limited human

27. Grenz, *A Primer on Postmodernism*, 29.
28. C. Downing, *How Postmodernism Serves (My) Faith*, 88–89.

construction. The "net" in question is the net of language and the fiction within the fiction. The drama of protagonist Jake's chase and escape makes the reader see a double vision, both tragic and comic, serious and absurd. Patricia Waugh explains that the ability of the reader is limited in this novel.[29]

Muriel Spark (1918–2006) ultimately suggests to the reader another world beyond human imperfections in *The Prime of Miss Jean Brodie*. This novel of meta-fiction integrates two interpretations of what happens (a single choice by Miss Brodie and multiple preferences by her students), two periods (the 1930s and 1960s), two human relationships (the exclusive teacher–student group and the expansive author–reader communication), and the two identities of Sandy (a betrayer and a savior).

The leading protagonist, Miss Brodie, lacks an omnipotent viewpoint, but acts on the assumption that she is a perfect teacher. She mixes the assumed self-image with the reality, but the teacher emotionally acts in disguise, as if she is in her prime. She lives on a vague border between the assumption and the reality. All of her students realize the contradictions presented by Miss Brodie.

Doris Lessing's *The Golden Notebook* (1962) is a story within a story, in which the writing continues as if the author avoided stopping. The protagonist, Anna Wulf, is separately described in a story within a story, firstly in a realistic novel "*Free Woman,*" and next in four separate "Notebooks," colored black, yellow, blue, and golden. In the Golden Notebook, Anna writes the first sentence, passing it to another character, Saul Green. He continues to write a new story so that it is difficult to distinguish who the real author is.

Lessing tries to deconstruct the traditional discourse and construct a new reality, but she aims to not finish the plan. Although her attempt seems to be non-successful, the author purposely intends not to stop. As she inspires the reader to interpret the story in an endless process, she is as least successful in exposing the inadequacies of the modernist novels. Therefore as Waugh claims, Lessing wins a sense of discharge.[30]

John Fowles (1926–2005) similarly inspires the reader to participate by reading. In *The French Lieutenant's Woman* (1969), he presents to the reader the obscure self-identity of a nineteenth century woman named Sarah. He gives the reader three different endings to her affair with Charles.

29. Waugh, *Metafiction*, 119.
30. Ibid., 77.

His novel, in conclusion, suggests that we can win freedom if we accept the provinciality of history.[31]

All of these four writers express the author as a speaker to the reader, so that the reader is asked to respond to the author's call and cooperate with them in forming an understanding of the story. The reader is expected to enter into the narrative story and become involved in the inner world of the fiction, just like a character in the story. That is a reversal of the modernist way of author-controlled autonomous values.

LEWIS'S POSTMODERNIST APPROACH

In a similar way to these four novels, Lewis takes the approach of "the fugue," repeating the story through meta-fiction. "Fugue" is a musical term meaning a piece of composition in which a short phrase is introduced and then repeated in an interwoven pattern. He applies the repetition to represent his theological affirmation of divine reality "like a fugue."[32] He regards the fugue as the complicating harmonies of God through using the similar postmodern approach "like a fugue,"[33] not to avoid death but to expect another world beyond death: "All his acts are different, but they all rhyme or echo to one another."[34]

The same term, "fugue," is used by postmodernist philosopher J. Hills Miller who describes Jacques Derrida's way of reading as "fugue."[35] He claims that, as a postmodernist, Derrida never stops writing like "the fugue" in order to avoid death. With the repetitive expressions, "fugue," Derrida wishes to avoid facing the last goal—death—so that he can prevent the beginning and the ending of the story. Miller compares Derrida's rhetoric to Bach's aria in which the same melody is repeated, "as if it could never end, until, finally, it leads to the chorale,"[36]

By repetition, Miller means to state that postmodernists resist the chronological sequence of the story and continue to ask themselves where they are. As they fear a stranger inside the self, they emphasize the difference

31. Ibid.,125.
32. Lewis, "Miracles," 37.
33. Ibid.
34. Ibid.
35. Miller, "The Late Derrida," 146.
36. Ibid.

of gender and the strangeness of others, in order to erase this stranger in the self.

The postmodernists' nightmare of death makes a digression in writing, as Miller illustrates in Derrida's postmodernist reading of Daniel Defoe and John Donne. With the repetition of a story within a story, the author avoids the grand story of death and the self who is possessed by death: the protagonist of *Robinson Crusoe* repeatedly asks the question of who the footprints belong to, but avoids making a decision; and John Donne's *Holy Sonnet* is a poem obsessed with death.[37]

Unlike Derrida, who associates the flight from death with postmodernist repetition, Lewis compares the intertwined harmony of "the fugue" to the reality of God. As the postmodernist novelists do, Lewis purposely makes ambiguous boundaries between fact and fiction, presenting a blurring identity of narrator and character, but he writes to reveal not the terror of death as Miller proposes. He ends stories with death to uncover the ambiguity of life. For him, death is not the end. He describes the end of his stories with a protagonist's vague disappearance, as we can see in the ambiguous ending of some characters: Ransom in *That Hideous Strength* (*THS*), Reepicheep in *The Voyage of the Dawn Treader*, and Queen Orual in *Till We Have Faces)*. These characters disappear from the story with ambiguous ends, which suggests that each character is transported into an unknown dimension.

Lewis and postmodernist writers similarly employ the vague borders of fact and fiction to de-center traditional values, but he uses the same technique to doubt the modernist's dualistic dominance of reason over faith, naturalism over supernaturalism. When the narrator of *THS* enters into the fiction as a character, the persona "I" appears.[38] Although his identity and his relation with the other characters are unknown, he may be considered to be the same person as the narrator of the other books of the Space Trilogy. The persona "I" of *THS* is in a position to move freely between the borders of fact and fiction, between dream and reality.

Lewis's postmodern literary approaches are rooted in his reading experiences. His source materials widely cover Hebrew-Greco-Roman classics; Greek, Roman, and Nordic pagan mythologies; fantasy literature; and

---

37. Ibid., 157.

38. The persona I in this section is based on my oral presentation for *Perelandra Project* "*Perelandra*: the Postmodern Concept of the Persona *I*" at Oxford University on June 27, 2009.

the work of his contemporary female writers. Through reading these works, Lewis regards the act of reading as a collaborative effort of both reader and author: through the text, the author interacts with the reader. Bruce L. Edwards regards Lewis's meaning of a text as a blend of not only the reader's willing participation in the literary process, but also the author's intention to interact with the reader. Lewis makes detailed accounts of his reading experiences in his autobiography *Surprised by Joy* (1955), and in letters written between the 1930s and the 1960s. An analysis of Lewis's reading experience will clarify his roots in Christian postmodernist approaches to the Bible, mythology (Greco-Roman and Nordic), Western classics, and sexuality in another world.

The Bible

Lewis's literary approach is biblically influenced in two ways: the concept of limited human language and the Apostle Paul-type communication approach.[39] Lewis expresses his view of human language when he proclaims his belief in the Gospel, the basic story of Christianity in which the eternal divine and the limited flesh are integrated. In *English Literature in the Sixteenth Century* (1954), he compares this acknowledgment of language to the translation of the Bible, writing that "all translations of scripture are tendentious."[40] As to the biblical translation, he claims that the divine Word is incarnated within imperfect human language, so that [Tyndale's and More's Bible translations] are influenced by human interpretation: "translation by its very nature, is a continuous implicit commentary."[41]

In the Incarnation of Christ, Lewis sees the harmony of the divine Word (perfect) and human language (imperfect), affirming that language is a reflection of imperfect human beings: translation is no exception. As translation is subject to the erosion of time, he ultimately argues that the King James Version is changeable in time. He insists on a newer translation to provide better access for the modern reader.[42]

---

39. In this paper, I regard the Bible (including both the Old Testament and New Testament) as a comprehensive entity made of the original texts, Hebrew and Greek, and their translated versions by scripture scholars according to their vernacular languages and times.

40. Martindale and Root, eds, *The Quotable Lewis*, 75.

41. Lewis, *English Literature in the Sixteenth Century Excluding Drama*, 75.

42. The discussion of Lewis's concept of limited human language, is based on my

From his reading of the Bible, Lewis deepens his understanding of the Christian postmodernist approach of speaking differently to reach the contemporary reader. The Apostle Paul employs different approaches according to different cultures. He preaches in Hebrew directly out of the Scripture at the Synagogue (Jewish church) (Acts 17:2 NRSV), and he speaks to the Greeks through Greek poems while in Athens (Acts 17:28–29). Similarly, Lewis enters into the discourse of his target reader, telling his story with their discourse and finally subverting the retold story as a Gospel meta-narrative. When Lewis retells his story with the target discourse, he uses the same approach as postmodernist novelists.

Paul the Apostle, formerly called Saul of Tarsus (AD 5–67), is the first Hebrew missionary of Christianity in Europe. Standing on the Areopagus, he pays respect to his Greek audience by reciting a quotation from Greek poets, so that he prepares their minds before they listen to him:

> For 'In him we live and move and have our being'; as even some of your own poets have said, 'For we too are his offspring.' Since we are God's offspring, we ought not to think that the deity is like gold, or silver, or stone, an image formed by the art and imagination of mortals. (Acts 17:28–29, NRSV)

The first part of Paul's quotation "For in him we live and move and have our being" (Acts 17:28) is from the Cretan philosopher Epimenides (between the seventh and the sixth centuries BC). The second quotation "we are God's offspring" is from the poetry *Phaenomena* by Stoic philosopher Aratus. Aratus speaks of Zeus as being the supreme God: "Let us begin from Jove. Let every mortal raise."[43] By "his offspring," Paul originally means "Zeus's offspring" but he converts the story into a biblical context: "we are the offspring of God" (Acts 17:29).[44]

Paul first captures the minds of the Greek audience (Acts 17) by behaving according to the target community and ultimately retelling the Greek discourse according to his meta-narrative, the Gospel. The Areopagus, situated on the Hill of Ares, is a center of politics, culture, and religion in ancient Greece: Ares is the god of war in Greek mythology. The Areopagus

---

article "C.S. Lewis's *The Great Divorce*: Christian Postmodernism and 'The Inverted Telescope'" orally presented for the First C.S. Lewis Conference in France at Lille Catholic University (June 3, 2011) and later published in *Persona and Paradox: Issues of Identity for C.S. Lewis, His Friends and Associates* (July 2012).

43. Henry, "Matthew Henry Commentary on the Whole Bible (Complete)," n.p.
44. Ibid.

functions as a city–state institution where all Athenians and those from other countries come to hear new stories.

The Apostle Paul's strategy has not often been discussed until the twenty-first century. The strategy as the approach of Christian postmodernism is credited by four critics: D.A. Carson, Curtis Chang, Louis Markos, and Brian Godawa. Although the four writers do not use the term "postmodernism," it is certain that they regard Paul's approach to mean Christian postmodernism in the sense that he retells the target story and subverts the narrative according to his own story, the Gospel.

Just like the Apostle Paul, Lewis is vigilant regarding the best communicative way to reach the contemporary reader in "the post-Christian world."[45] Both Louis Markos and Brian Godawa evaluate Lewis's imaginative novels as equivalent to Paul's strategy, revised for the twentieth century. The four, in their publications in the twenty-first century, highlight Paul's approach though using different phrasing of the method, as D.A. Carson calls it "the priority" for example.[46]

Curtis Chang affirms that the subversion is a strategy found among three historical Christian writers, not only Paul but also St. Augustine and St. Thomas Aquinas. He explains the three-fold subversion as Paul's faith in taking "every thought captive to obey Christ" (2 Cor. 10:5 NRSV).[47] In his essay "Athens Revisited" (2000), D.A. Carson observes "the priority" that Paul adopts in his arguments (Acts 17:22–31) and establishes the biblical "metanarrative" before the Gospel. In *From Achilles to Christ* (2007), Louis Markos affirms that Paul uses the pagan verses in parallel with the Old Testament to draw the Greeks' attention from an unknown God to a God known as Christ. In *Word Pictures: Knowing God through Story & Imagination* (2009), Brian Godawa agrees with Chang about Paul's subversive way of uniting Christianity and the local culture, finally subverting the Greek concept of God.

---

45. Lewis, "De Descriptione Temporum," 5.

46. Carson, "Athens Revisited," 391. Confer to the other cases in Chang's *Engaging Unbelief* (136), Markos's *From Achilles to Christ* (16), Godawa's *Word Pictures* (136).

47. Chang, *Engaging Unbelief*, 136.

Mythology

Lewis applies the term "myth" to Christianity, regarding the Gospels as God's myth, stating that "stories happen in actual human history."[48] Colin Duriez, and David Porter affirm that Lewis believes that the Incarnation is the Myth (capitalized) which becomes "the Fact."[49] When people read and "taste" the story of myth, he affirms that we come closest to having an imaginative experience which "incarnates" the abstraction "God is love."[50]

Mythology influences Lewis in two ways: his concept of human language as imperfect construction and his view of an unsettled world with multiple values. Mythology represents a world of characters whose identities are ambiguous or indefinable: satyrs of Greek mythology are half-man and half-goat; Loki of Northern myth is depicted as a trickster who causes troubles for the gods but uses his cunning to help them; and Tuan mac Cairill of Irish myth survives through a series of animal transformations from the Antediluvian age to Christian times.

As a reader of mythology, Greco-Roman, Irish, and Nordic, Lewis is impressed by the sense of longing for another world. In his autobiography *Surprised by Joy* (1955), he connects his understanding of pagan myths with the Christian story in the Gospel and concludes that the Gospel (the story of death and resurrection of Jesus Christ) historically fulfills pagan myths (stories of death and resurrection of gods and goddesses). This acknowledgment of Christianity and mythology is united in his comprehensive understanding of language and literary approach.

Lewis's literary adaptation of ancient northern folklores can be traced back to his absorption in Irish myths beginning from listening to the stories of his Irish nanny Lizzie Endicott during childhood.[51] At public school, young Lewis starts reading Celtic mythology[52] and W.B. Yeats' poems of Irish myths.[53] More than forty years later, he recounts the memory of his childhood, describing his school days as colored with mythopoeic characters: Greek (satyrs, Maenads, and Helen), Irish (Deirdre, Maeve, Cuchulain,

---

48. Lewis, *The Collected Letters I*, 977.
49. Duriez, and Porter, *The Inklings Handbook*, 160.
50. Lewis, *God in the Dock*, 66.
51. Lewis, *Surprised by Joy*, 4.
52. Ibid., 132–33.
53. Ibid., 201–2.

and Conachar MacNessa), and Northern (Brynhild and Sieglinde).[54] Colin Duriez highlights Lewis's deep interest in Irish folklore by quoting Rev. Cosslet Quinn, a former rector of St. Mark's (Ireland) where Lewis was baptized.[55]

Lewis also gained a longing for another world through Nordic mythology by listening to Richard Wagner's opera "Ring of the Nibelung" and reading books of Nordic myths. He remembers his passion for Nordic mythology: "I passed on from Wagner to everything else I could get hold of about Norse Mythology. . ."[56] In particular, H. A. Guerber's *Myths of the Norsemen* (1908) serves to develop Lewis's literary world because he comes to know his "first friend,"[57] Arthur Greeves, through their common interest in Guerber's *Myths of the Norsemen*.

Lewis's friendship with Arthur is influential to his literature. His lifelong correspondence with this Irish friend provides a primary insight into understanding his notion of literature. He expresses "Joy" (capitalized) when he finds *Myths of the Norsemen* in Arthur's room: "both knew the stab of Joy and that, for both, the arrow was shot from the North."[58]

Among Irish folklore books, Lewis is attracted, in particular, to *The Crock of God* (1912) by Irish writer James Stephens. Included in the book is a story about the metamorphosis of an Irish hero, Tuan mac Cairill, who endlessly transforms himself and continues to live an everlasting life. In his letter to his Irish friend Arthur Greeves (July 24, 1917), he expresses his love for the Ireland of "Patsy Macan" (sic) and stated that if he ever were to become interested in politics, he would be a nationalist.[59] Patsy MacCann is a character in a novel *The Demi-Gods* (1914) by James Stephens. Around 1917, Lewis was attracted to the ideas of the Romantic Nationalist movement associated with W. B. Yeats and his circle. As such, as with Lewis's love for the Ireland of Patsy MacCann, Ronald Bresland affirms that Lewis's literature has a combination of both fantasy and realism.[60]

---

54. Ibid., 137–38.
55. Schultz and West, eds., *The C.S. Lewis Readers' Encyclopedia*, 141.
56. Lewis, *Surprised by Joy*, 89.
57. Ibid., 151.
58. Ibid.
59. Lewis, *The Collected Letters I*, 330.
60. Bresland, *The Backward Glance*, 58.

Fantasy Literature

Lewis regards fantasy literature as the ideal form to convey what he wants to say. He simply declares that "I fell in love with the Form."[61] He is critical of disparaging comments about fantasy literature made by other writers in many of his writings, including *Surprised by Joy*, several of his essays, and his letters to Arthur Greeves. An analysis of his literary comments on fantasy stories, including Arthurian literature, will reveal their impacts on his writing. The other selected works for comparison in this paper include Dante's *Divine Comedy*, Laurence Sterne's *Tristram Shandy*, Edmund Spenser's *The Faerie Queene*, George MacDonald's *Phantastes* and *Princess and the Goblin* and William Morris's *The Well at the World's End*.

Arthurian literature is a paradox of multiple representations. In *That Hideous Strength*, Lewis uses the indefinable images of Merlin by drawing on several sources, including Robert de Boron's Grail books, *Joseph d'Arimathie* and *Merlin*, in addition to Geoffrey of Monmouth's *Vita Merlini* (1150), Chretian de Troyers' *Perceval* (1170–1190), and Thomas Malory's *Morte D'Arthur* (1485). Unlike the magician of the pre-modern time, Lewis re-interprets Merlin as a wizard re-awoken into the modernist community, and throws a question to the contemporary reader as to whether the unidentified ancient man, Merlin, is a friend or a foe.

Through Dante's *The Divine Comedy*, Lewis learns the simultaneous performance of multiple roles by one persona as author, character, and narrator. In his essay "The Seeing Eye,"[62] he discusses Dante as a persona with two separate entities: an author "outside the poem"[63] and a character "inside the poem."[64] However, he sees Dante as the integrated being.

In his novels, Lewis expresses the complexity of a persona with both author and character. He finds the similar complexity in the structure of the work in Edmund Spenser's *The Faerie Queene*. He affirms that Spenser's allegorical world is characterized by "labyrinthine complexity,"[65] by which

---

61. Lewis, "Sometimes Fairy Stories May Say Best What's to Be Said," 46.

62. "The Seeing Eye" was first published as "Onward, Christian Spacemen" in the American periodical *Show*, 3 (Feb. 1963), and later renamed for publication in *Christian Reflections* (1998), and published again for *C.S. Lewis: Essays Collection and Other Short Pieces* (2000).

63. Ibid., 62.

64. Ibid.

65. Lewis, *The Collected Letters I*, 170.

he means that the structure of the work is "pluralistic,"[66] while the centers of it are unresolved.

Lewis marks *The Faerie Queene* with two words: complication and novelty. In *Spenser's Image of Life* (1967), he characterizes *The Faerie Queene* with "special complications."[67] By complications, he means that Spenser uses a polyphonic technique of combining different elements "in an intricate way"[68] as well as the simple system of iconography of "verbalizing now one from now another,"[69] even though there is a variety of imaginative resources. In *The Allegory of Love*, he constitutes a feature of *The Faerie Queene* by its "novelty"[70] in two senses: firstly Spenser borrows the form of the Italian epic, modifies it, and turns it into conceit; secondly the poems result in the final form of courtly love as reflection of "the romantic conception of marriage."[71]

Lewis compares the complexity of Spenser's literary composition to the landscape of Surrey, England, where he was educated in his teens. He read *The Faerie Queene* for the first time when he was at a private school in Great Bookham, Surrey. In his letter to his friend Arthur Greeve in Ireland, he states that he's finished reading *The Faerie Queene*.[72] Even after over forty years of reading the allegory as a scholar of medieval and Renaissance literature, he again expresses the intricate composition of *The Faerie Queene* in a comparison of the geographical features in Surrey and in Ireland: walking in Surrey is "in the labyrinthine complexity."[73] Elizabeth Baird Hardy focuses *The Faerie Queene* as Lewis's literary source of the Narnian series, comparing Lewis's motif of the sea to the first two books of *The Faerie Queene*.[74]

Lewis, however, finds the "Shandeyian" world more complicated than "the labyrinthine complexity"[75] of *The Faerie Queene*. He describes the contradictory natures of *Tristram Shandy* (1759–1767) by Laurence Sterne as

66. Ibid.
67. Lewis, *Spenser's Image of Life*, 1.
68. Ibid., 4.
69. Ibid.
70. Lewis, *The Allegory of Love*, 297.
71. Ibid., 298.
72. Lewis, *The Collected Letters I*, 170.
73. Lewis, *Surprised by Joy*, 169.
74. Hardy, *Milton, Spenser and The Chronicles of Narnia*, 121–22.
75. Lewis, *Surprised by Joy*, 169.

"humanity of a pleasant Shandeyian,"[76] by which he means the unexpected combination of confusion and bliss. Through reading this work, Lewis discovers unexpected twists and turns against the rigid styles of novels. He repeatedly discusses *Tristram Shandy*, not only only in his letters, but also in his autobiography *Surprised by Joy*[77] and his essays.[78] He refers to the word "Shandeyian"[79] in a letter to his brother Warnie in 1929, and in a letter to Arthur Greeves in 1917.[80] In order to express his various literary tastes, he contrasts Sterne's vulgarity with Jane Austen's delicateness.[81]

George MacDonald's *Phantastes* is instructive for Lewis to learn the "postmodern" sense in a double way: the multiple roles of the author/character and the meta-fiction. Just as Lewis depicts the Italian writer Dante as a persona with complex roles, author and character, he also regards the nineteenth century writer MacDonald as an indefinable identity in history and fiction. This Scottish man is, in history, the author of *Phantastes* (1858), but is, in fiction, a character. Lewis paints MacDonald as if the man represents both identities: in his novel *The Great Divorce* (1945), an old man named MacDonald is the Master for a nameless young man called "I." The persona "I" may be considered as MacDonald himself. Readers of *The Great Divorce* will find a similarity suggesting that the nameless man might be the author Lewis, especially when the protagonist confesses his reading experience. That said, there is not a perfect correlation between the historical figure Lewis and the man in the fiction. The nameless man is not able to recognize his master when he encounters the character MacDonald.

With reference to *Phantastes,* which Lewis discovers in 1916, he is absorbed in reading a story within a story: the protagonist Anodos re-reads the story of another character, Cosmo, and recounts the second story of Cosmo to the reader. Anodos experiences both life and death through a life of being buried and risen in books. In reading *Phantastes*, Lewis is impressed by the celestial reality—sensations—which he would not be aware of in the earthly life: "Holiness."[82] He sees a majestic vision of the bright shadow entering his common world.

76. Lewis, *The Collected Letters I*, 810.
77. Lewis, *Surprised by Joy*, 139–40.
78. Lewis, *On Stories*, 16.
79. Lewis, *The Collected Letters I*, 810.
80. Ibid., 332.
81. Ibid., 810.
82. Lewis, *Surprised by Joy*, 207.

Novelist of Christian Postmodernism

Lewis expresses the spiritual impact of Holiness with these three words in the Vulgate version: "Unde hoc mihi."[83] The phrase is originally based on the biblical account of Elizabeth who makes joyful exclamation when she welcomes the visit of Mary who is pregnant with Jesus Christ: "And why has this happened to me" (Luke 1:43 NRSV). Just like Elizabeth, Lewis sees the Holiness coming into his life, describing the spiritual effect of reading *Phantastes* on him as being "baptized by imagination" in several books including the preface to *The Anthology of George MacDonald* (1946), the fiction *The Great Divorce* (1945), and the non-fiction *Surprised by Joy* (1955).

Lewis also explains the impact of *Phantastes* on his imagination in a different way. In non-fiction, he expresses the spiritual effect on his soul more sensibly. He hears the mysterious sound surrounding him: "with me in the room, or in my own body, or behind me . . . with me."[84] His exclamation rhymes with part of an anonymous prayer popularly known as "St. Patrick's Breastplate." The prayer includes phrases such as: "Christ within me, / Christ beneath me, / Christ above me, / . . . , / Christ in the heart of all who thinks of me."[85] Unlike the imaginative descriptions in his non-fiction, his fiction expresses the impact with a more descriptive tone, simply summarizing his reading impression with one word: "holiness."[86] He seems to express the truth in the indistinct border of genres between fiction and non-fiction.

Through reading another of George MacDonald's books, Lewis is again inspired by the Scottish author's twilight world between wake and sleep. The male protagonist Curdie of *The Princess and the Goblin* (1872) keeps dreaming a dream. In his letter (15 June, 1931) to Arthur Greeves, Lewis explains the ambiguous boundary as both the endless repeat of a dream and people's fear of this rational world: "It is so fatally easy to confuse an aesthetic appreciation of the spiritual life with life itself."[87]

Just as Lewis is fascinated by both of MacDonald's novels and his intriguing personality, so is he enamored of William Morris's fictional world (but not his lifestyle). He read Morris's *The Well at the World's End* for the first time in 1915. In his letter to Arthur Greeves, he expresses his

---

83. Ibid., 209.
84. Ibid., 208.
85. Kinsella, ed., *The New Oxford Book of Irish Verse*, 14.
86. Lewis, *The Great Divorce*, 66.
87. Lewis, *The Collected Letters I*, 906.

excitement at the reading of the novel as a happy experience, "another Adventure."[88] He discusses Morris's fictional world even when he simply uses the term "Morris": "Morris himself escapes definition."[89] He describes Morris's literary world as "a dance."[90] He means that Morris's writing shifts, restarts, and moves in a vague border between sleep and awake: "Everything is always beginning over again."[91]

Lewis affirms that *The Well at the End of the World* nearly succeeds in "catching the bird."[92] By the bird, Lewis means an indescribable feeling that may remain in the reader's mind after reading the stories: "entangled in the net for several chapters."[93] The male protagonist of *The Well at the End of the World*, Ralph, passes away like a bird flying off, moving from this world to another. Morris thus ends his story in an ambiguous style. The author remains silent as to where Ralph goes after his death. His reader is left between the sharp contrast of his silence on death and his verbosity on an earthly paradise.

Lewis asserts that Morris has no spiritual word to indicate eternal life after death except revealing "the tension" of life and death.[94] He concludes that in Morris there is "no conclusion,"[95] because Morris escapes definition of life after death, and that Morris is neither a Christian nor a materialist. As David Downing states, Lewis discovered the polyphonic narrative revealed in the quality of perpetual irresolution he found in the works of William Morris.[96]

---

88. Ibid., 153.

89. Lewis, "William Morris," 229. The essay "William Morris" was originally read to the Martlets Society on November 5, 1937 and published in *Rehabilitations* and *Selected Literary Essays* in 1969. (The Martlets was an undergraduate Oxford literary society to which Lewis belonged).

90. Lewis, *The Collected Letters I*, 153.

91. Ibid.

92. Lewis, *On Stories*, 28.

93. Ibid., 19.

94. Ibid., 45.

95. Ibid., 65.

96. D. C. Downing, "C.S. Lewis among the Postmodernists," n.p.

Sexuality in Another World

Christian postmodernism is most reflected in Lewis's description of his female characters who are involved in writing and reading. His literary style regarding these protagonists reveals a significant change from the 1930s to the 1950s, as his concept of sexuality undergoes a transformation from the male-oriented world to sexuality in Heaven. His approaches are influenced by his varied encounters with female writers, real and imaginary. The former includes Dorothy L. Sayers (1893–1957) and Joy Davidman (1916–1960), and the latter is the medieval author Julian of Norwich (ca. 1342–ca. 1416).

Although the bachelor scholar Lewis enjoys a sheltered male-oriented academic community at Oxford, discussion by correspondence and in person with Sayers and Davidman serves to encourage him to find a new image for the female character of his last novel *Till We Have Faces* (*TWHF*), and Julian's mystic world inspires him to express with word and image the heroine who is in search of both a spiritual breakthrough as well as self-recognition.

Lewis presents the ideal image of humanity in the illustration of Orual, the protagonist of *TWHF*, as both man and woman and beyond. He envisions humanity beyond opposite sexes in another world, reflecting the reality of humanity in Heaven upon the sexuality of man and woman in this world. This world for Lewis is a shadow-land of the true homeland, another world, in gender.

Lewis begins arguing that gender matters in the 1940s, when the discipline was not as much a major concern for the literary community as it is today. He, however, displays contradictory views toward gender in these early works. He is negative about presenting women as public speakers in his essay "Priestesses in the Church?" (1948), while positively expressing his interest in gender in his fiction, including *Perelandra* (1943) and *That Hideous Strength* (1945). The three female writers' influence on Lewis's concept of sexuality will, however, reveal his choice of a changing literary style.

In Lewis's novels of the 1930s and 1940s, the protagonists, their companions, and the narrators are all male. These works include *The Pilgrim's Regress* (1933), *Out of the Silent Planet* (1938), *Perelandra* (1943), *The Screwtape Letters* (1942), and *The Great Divorce* (1945). The readers of Lewis of the 1930s and 1940s are mainly considered to be the male members of "The Inklings," even though he received passionate feedback from numerous female readers.

C.S. Lewis and Christian Postmodernism

The Inklings was a literary group at Oxford University, a private circle of male friends including J.R.R. Tolkien and Charles Williams. This group of people gathered twice a week, reading academic papers and literary drafts to each other and exchanging critical comments on the papers. They met at a pub, "The Bird and Baby," every Tuesday morning and at Lewis's room of Magdalen College every Thursday night.

Lewis socialized primarily with the dominantly male bachelor scholars of Oxford University, where celibacy was obligatory until the nineteenth century. Most of the scholars had a living space on campus, like a monastery even in the middle of the twentieth century, where marriage was considered a sign of degraded scholarship. There were religious restrictions on scholars in Oxford of the nineteenth century.[97]

Very little has been written about Lewis's gender theory and next to none of this has been written by male scholars of literature. As Candice Fredrick and Sam McBride write in *Women among the Inklings: Gender, C.S. Lewis, J.R.R. Tolkien and Charles Williams* (2001), there is a missing zone in the gender study of the Inklings.[98] One reason for this, Fredrick and McBride explain, is probably because of the presumption on both sides of the feminist and Christian communities that feminism is incompatible with Christianity. After Fredrick, a female scholar, and McBride, a male scholar, declare that they are feminists and Christian, they claim that both perspectives are compatible.

Fredrick and McBride categorize feminism into three perspectives: liberal (seeking equality with men), radical-separatist (seeking to overturn all male-defined culture), and materialist-feminist (presuming gender as a social contract).[99] They believe that the third perspective is opposed to The Inklings' assumption that gender precedes embodied sexuality. Judging from the significant change in Lewis's depictions of female protagonists, Fredrick and McBride conclude that he sees a more real image of women in the world in his later works.

There has not been much discussion about Lewis and gender, but two opposing views are presented by a female and a male scholar in the open journal debate "C.S. Lewis and Gender" in the *Christian Scholar's Review* (*CSR*) (2007). Mary Stewart Van Leeuwen, a psychologist, argues that across his lifetime, Lewis's views on gender relations shift from traditional

---

97. Dougill, *Oxford: A Literary Guide*, 1.
98. Fredrick and McBride, *Women among the Inklings*, xi.
99. Ibid., xii.

views about male authority to a more egalitarian view of gender relations through his positive relationships with women, especially his intellectual peers including Joy Davidman.[100] Philosopher Adam Barkman, however, comments on Lewis's faithful attitude to the hierarchical conception of gender as taught by "Scripture, nature and our forbearers."[101]

In that journal debate, four leading Lewis scholars, Joe R. Christopher, Harry Lee Poe, Doris T. Myers, and Diana Pavlac Glyer, two male and two female, respond to arguments concerning Lewis and women, exchanging lively opinions. The editor of *Christian Scholar's Review*, Don King, comments that the discussion of Lewis and gender is lively and heated: "far from settled."[102]

Mary Stewart Van Leeuwen continuously claims that Lewis accepts multiple gender stereotypes. In her book, *A Sword between the Sexes?: C.S. Lewis and the Gender Debate* (2010), she affirms that Lewis supports both an essentialist and a hierarchical view of gender because he does not allow any monopolistic appeal to empirical social science. Even though Van Leeuwen is a psychologist, she warns of the danger of appealing simply to the findings of social science, which may result in abolishing "Lewis's dualistic notion"[103] that human bodies should be studied by natural science but minds should be by the humanities.

Van Leeuwen implies that Lewis is a writer of Christian postmodernism, although she does not use the phrase. She affirms that he supported both views of gender, essential and hierarchical.[104] From the perspective of Christian postmodernism, she agrees that he accepts multiple interpretations of gender or "stereotypes" (the term used by Van Leeuwen),[105] reaching an understanding that transcends binary selections of the interpretation—essential or hierarchical. These arguments regarding Lewis and gender, however, focus on seeking his philosophical and theological views of women, not necessarily on his writing struggles to communicate his concept of heavenly sexuality to modern readers.

Both Dorothy L. Sayers and Lewis are writers of Christian postmodernism as they accept multiple interpretations under God's guidance. As

---

100. Van Leeuwen, "C.S. Lewis and Gender," 391.
101. Ibid., 415.
102. King, "Introduction to the Colloquium Issue," 388.
103. Van Leeuwen, *A Sword between the Sexes?*, 167.
104. Ibid.
105. Ibid., 54.

scholars and alumni of Oxford in 1915, they exchange critical views on each other's works through their correspondence and in person. She is a writer of theological books and a scholar-as-translator of *The Divine Comedy*. Her beliefs contribute to Lewis's understanding of language and sexuality that transcends the human limitation.

It may sound contradictory to modernist writers that these two writers, Lewis and Sayers, have faith in the Divinity, while respecting the variety of human perspectives. Sayers's postmodern concept of multiple worldviews is, however, the reflection of her theological understanding of the Trinity. The creativity of writing and reading is her testimony of God. In her theological essay *The Mind of the Maker* (1941), Sayers affirms that the Trinity of God is comparable to a writer whose creativity is involved in three aspects of writing: idea, energy, and power. The activity of reading makes the reader interact with the mind of the maker through these three characteristics of the author.

In the 1930s, Sayers was far ahead of Lewis in her notion of gender. She spoke live to audiences, conveying that the primary task for any human being is to do the work which he or she was created for, as "both men and women are fundamentally human."[106] Sayers re-defined the mystery novel ten years before Lewis wrote his *Space Trilogy*. Instead of the general assumption that humanity should be eliminated from the detective story, Sayers integrated both plot and theme in the mystery novel, directing her literary style to the popular manners of the nineteenth century writers.

Unlike the classic hero, such as the adventurer and the knight, the modern heroes (heroines) no longer hunt mythical animals; instead, they hunt murderers and analyze prisoners in order to protect the weak. Sayers evaluates the detective as "the true successor of Roland and Lancelot."[107] The editor of *The Art of the Mystery Story*, Howard Haycraft asserts that Sayers advocates the amateurism and the democracy embodied in a detective— the spirit of thinking freely, acting alone, and democratically criticizing.[108] Barbara Reynolds lays out four themes in Sayers's fiction and non-fiction writing: 1.the need for redemptive human activity; 2.the image of the True

---

106. Sayers, *Are Women Human?*, 49. Sayers made this statement originally as an address to a women's society in 1938, but it was later published as *Are Women Human?* (1971).

107. Sayers, "Gaudy Night," 76.

108. Haycraft, *Murder for Pleasure*, 317.

God; 3. the grief over a mechanistic capitalist society; and 4. the capitalist society that degenerates education for commercial ends.[109]

Reynolds's classification can be applied to Harriet Vane, the female protagonist, and writer by occupation, of Sayers's mystery novel *Gaudy Night* (1935). Harriet recovers her identity through writing a sonnet—a process in which she has to attach her life to the supreme good of "detecting" the most appropriate words for a poem of fourteen lines as the infinite transcendent good. The detection in poetry leads her to detecting a scandal at Oxford University.

Harriet Vane is a reflection of Lewis's concept of creativity. In his scholarly work *A Preface to Paradise Lost* (1942), he distinguishes two parents for every poem: its mother is "the matter" (thought inside the poet) and its father is the pre-existing "Form" (the epic, the tragic, and the novel). He rephrases the two parents as Logos (the poet's opinion and emotions) and Poiema (an organization of words which the poet chooses): "The matter inside the poet wants the Form."[110]

Harriet is disappointed by the world which looks like it is sleeping, like "a great top on its everlasting spindle."[111] Through this imaginative process of composing a poem, Harriet undergoes a hands-on, creative experience of Sayers's theology, "a diversity within its unity."[112] While combining what she means and what she receives in the form, Harriet discovers the synthesis of meaning and form. She *intends* as an author but *receives* the revealed spirit in the form. As an author, she has to accept herself as a human construction—imperfect and limited. The process not only allows her to comprehend the true meaning of vocation, but also to overcome her inferiority complex toward her suitor, Peter. Her recovery of self-confidence, conversely, leads to an evil attack on her from the "poison pen" of another character who was the cause of the scandal in Shrewsbury, a fictional college of Oxford.

In *Gaudy Night*, Sayers presents a world that contains both a mystery fiction and a novel of manners by demonstrating how Harriet seriously handles life as a human, the term including both woman and man. Mary McDermott Shideler claims that Sayers prophetically declares to modern

---

109. Reynolds makes this comment in Chris Armstrong's article, "Dorothy Sayers: 'Dogma is the Drama" written based on his interview with her in 2005.

110. Lewis, *A Preface to Paradise Lost*, 3.

111. Sayers, *Gaudy Night*, 220.

112. Sayers, *The Mind of the Maker*, 4.

society as a whole that the category of "personhood" is adequate for meeting the needs of women: "we cannot afford to discard any human resources . . . , even though it is women who possess them."[113]

Harriet's act of composing a sonnet is an ideal combination of Lewis's proclaimed duality of creativity, but it is not until his last novel, *Till We Have Faces* (*TWHF*) (1956), that he reveals to the reader his ideal integration of the metamorphosis of humanity embodied in the life of a woman who assumes multiple roles as narrator, author, character, and reader.

As opposed to Sayers's obvious influence on Lewis's literature, Joy Davidman makes, as the shadow editor, an almost unknown contribution to the completion of Lewis's last novel *TWHF*. In the early stages of this novel, he talks with this American woman writer, who helps him to re-organize his premature ideas of the literary form. He receives sharp comments as well as warm motivation from her, as she inspires him to establish a literary structure for the story, the pinnacle of which is the protagonist Queen Orual, who is depicted between beauty and ugliness, man and woman, narrator and character.

The boundaries of Orual's identity, physical and spiritual, become blurred to the reader, especially after her last word, "might." With this indefinite way of ending the story, Lewis suggests that humanity in another world transcends our inherent human nature, including languages and sexes. Through Davidman, who has a contradictory background of non-orthodox Jewish then Communist atheist turned to theist, Lewis can see an ideal image of sexuality in another world that is beyond the limitation of languages, personalities, and sexes.

As Don King notes, Davidman increasingly serves "as a collaborator and shadow editor" for Lewis.[114] Although Lewis was stagnant in writing *TWHF*, he was inspired to advance just by talking with her one night. In her letter to William Gresham (March, 1955), she describes her involvement as an editor of *TWHF*: "We kicked a few ideas around till one came to life. The next day, without further planning, he wrote the first chapter!"[115] After only one and half months, Lewis is able to finish writing three-quarters of the work. His discussions with Davidman contribute to the swift progress of the work. *TWHF*, published in 1956, is dedicated to her.

---

113. Sayers, *Are Women Human?*, 12.
114. King, ed., *Out of My Bone*, 242.
115. Ibid., 242.

Novelist of Christian Postmodernism

Through Davidman's personality, Lewis sees a variety of lights simultaneously reflected in different colors, which he states as "my trusty comrade, friend, shipmate, and fellow-soldier. My mistress; at the same time all that any man friend."[116] In the multiple dimensions of her personality, he probably finds his spiritual strength, stating, "We are 'taken out of ourselves.'"[117] For Lewis, Sayers is like a gardener who plants a new understanding of gender into his writing life and prepares the road to walk on, while at the same time, Davidman is like a designer who inspires Lewis to depict the completed image of the protagonist of his last novel, Orual.

Unlike Sayers and Davidman, who are contemporaries to Lewis, Julian of Norwich (ca. 1342–ca. 1416) was a medieval author of the fourteenth century. During WWII when Britain was in great social turmoil, Lewis begins reading her *Revelations of Divine Love* (1373). Her mystic experience guides him to similar approaches echoing Christian postmodernism. It is surprising to realize that the medieval writer uses both "word" and "image" in order to seek not only spiritual discovery but also self-recognition.

In his fiction, Lewis creates a world of multi-dimensional perception, especially of female protagonists. He learns this reality through reading Julian of Norwich. Examining industrialized society and the Middle Ages, historian Carole Lee Flinders characterizes modern perception as one-dimensional in contrast to the medieval perception of multi-dimensional. She affirms that modern perception associates visions with irrationality separated from reality, but in the Middle Ages, visions defined reality: "Their concept of the real embraced much that we would now call imaginary."[118]

Both Lewis and Julian of Norwich are British writers from war-torn periods, although they lived in different centuries, the twentieth and the fourteenth. As he is inspired by her philosophical and religious spirits, he repeatedly draws on her phrases in several of his writings, both fiction and non-fiction. In a letter (March 21, 1940) to his brother Warnie, an army officer at the front in World War II, he expresses joy at reading Julian: "in such *a ghastly age?* . . . I have been reading this week 'Revelations' of Mother Julian of Norwich."[119] One month later (April 16, 1940), he writes again about Julian of Norwich to his former pupil, the Catholic monk Dom Bede Griffiths: "Have you noticed how God so often sends us books at just *the*

---

116. Lewis, *A Grief Observed*, 49.
117. Ibid., 102.
118. Flinders, *Enduring Grace*, 84.
119. Lewis, *The Collected Letters II*, 369–70.

right time?" (emphasis added).[120] Lewis seems to suggest that "the right time" for him to read Julian is "a ghastly age" when his life and his country are urgently in need of hope and peace.

Like Lewis, Julian of Norwich lived in a period of social conflicts. Medieval society, political and religious, suffered the great tribulations of two wars: the split within the Catholic Church between Rome and Avignon (from 1378 to 1417) and The Hundred Years' War between the kingdoms of England and France (from 1337 to 1453).[121] She did not rail against the states of disturbance, but instead called people to peace, love, and joy through the writing of a book with no title (1373) (known to later generations as *Revelations of Divine Love*).

In many of his writings, Lewis repeats famous phrases by Julian, such as: "All shall be well."[122] He repeats this statement by Julian of Norwich in order to emphasize the limitation of human capacity: "how little we knew and therefore, how many things one might keep in mind as possibilities."[123] Lewis's quotations including "All is well" are found in several of his writings which cover almost his whole writing career between the 1930s and the 1960s: "The Pains of Animals" (1950) and "Miracles" (1942), *The Great Divorce* (1945), *Reflections on Psalms* (1958), *The Grief Observed* (1961), and *The Collection of C.S. Lewis Letters* (1940, 1942, 1945, 1949, 1955, and 1959). As David Downing states, Lewis is certainly inspired by the mystic philosophy of the anchorite who, for religious reasons, withdrew from secular society.[124]

For the contemporary reader, it may be a great surprise to observe the parallel between the writings of a medieval female and Christian postmodernism. Carole Lee Flinders declares that the medieval female writers including Julian of Norwich share "some of the same personal issues that my contemporaries are."[125]

120. Ibid., 392.

121. In his address to general audience (December 1, 2010), Pope Benedict XVI transmits a message of the divine love and hope based on Julian of Norwich's phrases in *Revelations of Divine Love*: "And all will be well. All manner of things shall be well." Vatican Official Website. The Holy See. Message. http://www.vatican.va/holy_father/benedict_xvi/audiences/2010/documents/hf_ben-xvi_aud_20101201_en.html.

122. Julian of Norwich, *Revelations of Divine Love*, 103–4. It is also repeated in 109, and 111.

123. Lewis, *God in the Dock*, 169.

124. D. C. Downing, *Into the Region of Awe*, 24.

125. Flinders, *Enduring Grace*, xvi.

In her *Enduring Grace: Living Portraits of Seven Women Mystics* (2007), Flinders presents the contemporary philosophy of the female mystics in three parts: 1. they know the limitation of language so they write with both traditional words and subjective expressions, due to their fear that their mystic experience is considered heretical by male society[126]; 2. they write in order to search for not only the Divine being but also self-identity[127]; and 3. they emphasize the fact that God is a genderless Spirit.[128]

Julian of Norwich narrates with word, image, and beyond, an approach Lewis follows. After an illness, she recounts sixteen revelations which she experienced on 8 May, 1373. The first book ever written in English by a woman is nowadays known as *The Revelation of Divine Love*. She reports what God shows to her: the visible nature with her actual eyes and the invisible with her inner sight. However, while writing, the border between her two visions becomes ambiguous.

With her eyes, she sees the bleeding of God's head, "Great drops of blood rolled down from the garland like beads,"[129] while with her inner sight she sees, on her hand, "a little thing, the size of a hazel-nut."[130] Finally she sees not what she sees but what is beyond her inner sight. She is reminded of three things and feels the greatest comfort to know that "God and Lord, so holy and aweful, is so unpretentious and considerate."[131] These three include "round beads as the blood flowed, round herring scales as it spread out, and raindrops from the eaves for their abundance."[132]

As Flinders states, the medieval female writer deconstructs the binary view of categorizing gender in either male or female, and instead proposes postmodernist sexuality in another world: "a breaking down of the traditional polarizing that makes a 'magnificent' maternal figure seem contradictory to us."[133] Lewis, an avid reader of Julian, embodies her imagery into his female characters, especially through Orual.

---

126. Ibid., xvii and 2.
127. Ibid., xviii.
128. Ibid., 4–5.
129. Julian of Norwich, 72.
130. Ibid., 67.
131. Ibid., 72.
132. Ibid.
133. Flinders, 5.

— 3 —

Pre-Historic Magician Awakens in the Modernist Age

That Hideous Strength (1945) (*THS*) is more often discussed in terms of word rather than image. The novel is considered a fictionalized version of Lewis's critical essay on modern education, *The Abolition of Man* (1943), in which Lewis mentions *THS* as a tall tale about "devilry, though it has behind it a serious 'point' which I have tried to make in my *Abolition of Man*."[1] *THS* is, however, worth appreciating for his imaginative taste, not only in word, but also in image. The main characters of *THS* are intentionally and unintentionally conscious of Merlin, the magician of Arthurian legend. Each individually perceives the identity of this old man from their own perspective. Their feedback reveals the contemporary world's moral sensibilities according to their own responses to the ambiguous saga. Although *THS* is generally categorized as science fiction, elements such as Merlin sleeping in the enclosed garden will demonstrate that this novel covers genres beyond this genre, including mythology, theology, philosophy, and gender study.

Merlin presents himself to the reader in limited appearances, and only in the last third of the novel. The reader, however, may have the impression that they have already met him, as his name is often mentioned in all five sections of the first chapter of *THS*. Merlin is first revealed in the female protagonist Jane's dream in section 1 of chapter 1; his name is next

---

1. Lewis, *The Abolition of Man*, 7.

mentioned in the professors' meeting at Bracton College in Sections 2 and 4; Merlin's Wood is remembered by persona "I" in Section 3; and the mythology of Merlin is the topic of dialogue between the two scholars, Jane and her former tutor Dr. Dimple in Section 5. Merlin is a main concern for the other characters, but he is not as obviously introduced as a major player to the reader. He is instead presented as if he plays a minor role. He is considered by the other characters to be dead or asleep in Bragdon Wood or Merlin's Wood—the underground, pre-historic, enclosed garden.

Merlin's ambiguous identity reflects the changing fate of the enclosed gardens. He is depicted in a double garden, both pre-historic and classical (a Renaissance style garden of Bracton College)—the former located within the latter, while the latter is the only way to the former. It also looks as if the classical garden guards the pre-historic man. He first comes up out of the College garden, but ultimately disappears mysteriously into an unknown dimension. The College gardens protect the old man as a gatekeeper might. After Merlin is awakened, the ancient man does not come up in gardens, neither pre-historic nor classical, but in the dark, ploughed field. The dark land of the industrialized society of the twentieth century is associated with death by the female protagonist of *THS*, Jane.[2] The novel ends with the classical and pre-historic gardens finally being destroyed.

Merlin is viewed as a magician by antagonistic groups: St. Anne's, a spiritual successor of Logres (pre-historic Britain) and the N.I.C.E., a technology-based state, (N.I.C.E. is short for National Institute of Coordinated Experiments). The real purpose of Merlin is, however, not obviously known, but gradually revealed, not only to the members of St. Anne's but also to Merlin himself. At the beginning of the story, no one at St. Anne's and the N.I.C.E. knows which side Merlin belongs to, until he is awakened to the modern wilderness.

Dr. Dimple, a member of St. Anne's, supposes that Merlin's *magic* represents what transcends not only mind and matter but also our comprehension.[3] Through the perspective of Dimple, Lewis presents to the reader his interpretation of two types of magic: Renaissance type's and Merlin's that originates in Atlantis. He describes the former as *goeteia*: "the brutal surgery."[4] St. Anne's and the N.I.C.E. regard magic as "Renaissance magic,"[5]

2. Lewis, *That Hideous Strength*, 229.
3. Ibid., 198.
4. Ibid., 174.
5. Schultz and West, eds., *The C.S. Lewis Readers' Encyclopedia*, 260.

which is an attempt to deprive creation from the creator. Even Ransom, the head of St. Anne's, is not sure of the identity of Merlin first, but gradually becomes aware that Merlin's magic is not Renaissance type, but the remnant of what was brought to Western Society from Numinor (Atlantis).[6]

Concerning critical views of Merlin, Martha C. Sammons discusses the meaning of language;[7] Gregory Wolfe analyzes Merlin as the symbol of the wholeness in ancient Britain;[8] Thomas Howard talks on Merlin as a magician not in ancient Britain but in Christian times: "Celt-hood baptized by Christianity";[9] and T. A. Shippery explores Merlin as the polysemy of the novel.[10] Not many critics have discussed Merlin awakening in the garden, but a few who have are David L. Downing, and Doris T. Myers: Downing associates the garden with an earthly paradise;[11] Myer regards Lewis's narrative as the myth of Merlin sleeping in Bragdon Wood. She agrees with Nancy-Lou Patterson, who regards Bragdon Wood as an enclosed garden to reflect an ancient symbol of Paradise.[12]

As to the gardens in *THS*, Sammons discusses the contrasting gardens between St. Anne's and the N.I.C.E., but makes no comments on the gardens at Bracton College or on Merlin; Sarah Larratt Keefer touches upon the etymological study of the word "Edgestow"; and Jared Lobdell analyzes French influence on this work including Arthurian literature. These critics, however, do not comment on the final deconstruction of the enclosed gardens at Bracton College and the extinction of Merlin. An analysis of Merlin in the closed garden will reveal the moral responses of the modern world, and the rehabilitation of sexuality and vocation through the reunion of the broken couple, Jane and Mark, in a re-created garden.

ARTHURIAN LEGEND

Merlin is a complex figure associated with a variety of Arthurian elements. His complexity will invite the reader's participation in interpreting the

6. Lewis, *THS*, 198.
7. Sammons, *A Guide through C.S. Lewis' Space Trilogy*.
8. Wolfe, *Word and Story in C.S. Lewis*, 58–75.
9. Howard, *Narnia & Beyond*, 160.
10. Shippery, "The Ransom Trilogy," 247.
11. D. C. Downing, "That Hideous Strength: Spiritual Wickedness in High Places," 64.
12. Myers, *C.S. Lewis in Context*, 97 n.28.

identity of the old man in the novel of Christian postmodernism. The old man transforms himself in three stages: awakening from a one-thousand, five hundred year sleep in the enclosed garden, reviving again as a savior of the modern world, and finally to extinction into an unknown space.

Unlike the magician in pre-modern times, Lewis re-interprets the image of Merlin as a mythological man awakened within the modernist community, and throws a question to the contemporary reader as to whether the unidentified ancient man is a foe or friend to our modern world.

The mysterious man of *THS* is more often witnessed, discussed, and remembered by someone else rather than speaking himself, except in a dialogue with Ransom, a successor to the twentieth century King Arthur.[13] The complex figure plays a variety of roles associated with Arthurian legends: covering the Druid counselor to Fisher King (a possible healer for the wounded, as Fisher King is considered as the Wounded King in Arthurian legend whose leg injury renders him incapable of moving on his own); war leader Merlinus Ambrosius serving Ransom (the soldier for the Pendragon, although Merlinus Ambrosius bears no connection with King Arthur); a royal subject of pre-historic Britain (Logres); an interpreter, as the double of the bear Mr. Baltitude (the vision dreamer of the dragon's battle with the bear); and a go-between for Jane's reunion with Mark (a prophet of Arthur's marriage to Guinevere).

Other elements of Arthurian legends in *THS* include: mortar and blood[14]; the Dolorous blow; Jane's rejection of maternity[15]; and Merlin's memory of the Anglo-Saxon battle in Badon Hill when Venus came to earth.[16] Merlin in *THS* predicts "the Dolorous blow" by Balin who uses the Sacred Spear, symbolic of the Fall, man against humanity.[17] In the *Post-Vulgate Cycle*, Thomas Malory's Le Morte d'Arthur, and later works based on these, the stroke is delivered by Sir Balin on the thigh of King Arthur. In the ninth century work *Historia Britonum*, the victory for the Battle of *Badon* is attributed to the battle-leader Arthur: the Battle between a force of Britons and an Anglo-Saxon army (probably sometime in the fifth century).

Discussion of its Arthurian features will reveal *THS* as literature of a modern apocalyptic battle. This is how Lewis makes a contribution to

13. Lewis, *THS*, 283–91.
14. Ibid., 230.
15. Ibid., 275–76.
16. Ibid., 321.
17. Ibid., 275.

Arthurian literature by reviving Merlin in the modern age. He draws on multiple sources of Arthurian legend that include French author Robert de Boron's Grail books, *Joseph d'Arimathie* and *Merlin*, as well as Geoffrey of Monmouth's *Vita Merlini* (1150), Chretian de Troyers' *Perceval* (1170–90), and Thomas Malory's *Morte D'Arthur* (1485). David Downing affirms that Charles William's Arthurian books should be included.[18] Walter Hooper evaluates Lewis as a writer of Arthurian literature: Lewis adapts Arthurian elements (including the Fisher King, the Pendragon, Logres, and Merlin) in a clash between a modern totalitarian government and the spiritual kingdom of Logres.[19]

Lewis employs indefinable images of Merlin, and invites each character of *THS* to respond to the old man according to his/her ethics. He benefits from the paradox of multiple representations of the Arthurian legend when he describes the harmony between the supernatural and the natural. One such interpretation is from Geoffrey of Monmouth, who uncovers complicated aspects of Merlin, describing the magician as the son of a nun (divine) and an incubus (demonic), as a Druid wizard in a forest, and also as a war-leader, Ambrosius (Ambrosius or Emrys in Welsh was a war leader of the Romano-British in the fifth century). He suddenly disappears in the medieval romance. His unexplainable disappearance in the legend is depicted in several versions. In Malory's Le Morte d'Arthur (1469), he fades out when he falls in love with Niniane, the Lady of the Lake. Geoffrey of Monmouth and his contemporary writers assert that the wizard never exists during Arthur's reign, while Thomas Malory and later writers, including Robert de Boron, Wace, and Layamon, write about Merlin as chief adviser during King Arthur's reign in poems "Joseph d'Arimathe" and "Merlin."

Lewis integrates complicated images of Merlin into *THS* that morph into multiple forms. He favorably identifies with the pre-historic heritage, the mixture of matter and spirit: "confused."[20] The shape-shifting of Merlin was originally composed by French poet Robert de Boron, who describes the transformation of the magician into a white stag in the forest. Robert de Boron is the first author to give the Holy Grail myth a Christian dimension and give the title Fisher King to Arthur. The old man in *THS* is not a white stag, but first introduced is the head of the mythological man with

---

18. D. C. Downing, "That Hideous Strength: Spiritual Wickedness in High Places," 65.

19. Hooper, *C.S. Lewis: A Companion & Guide*, 233.

20. Lewis, *THS*, 282.

Pre-Historic Magician Awakens in the Modernist Age

a white beard and covered with earth.²¹ Later he appears as a clean shaven interpreter. The bearded face represents pre-historic magical power, while the shaved figure embodies his submission of old magic to the divine entity "Glund-Oyarusa, King of Kings."²² His pre-historic mythology is deconstructed, but his new mission is recreated: "no longer his own man."²³

Merlin in Arthurian romance is not a figure composed by a single writer, but a multi-century product involving multiple writers. King Arthur is generally known to have been introduced to the English reader by Thomas Malory in the fifteenth century. As Norris J. Lacy states, Malory is not actually an original writer of Arthurian literature, but one who selects material from different books, arranges the tales, and presents the life and death of King Arthur to contemporary readers."²⁴

Merlin is therefore a product of numerous good story-tellers, including Malory. Arthur and Merlin were first introduced to Britain in the Latin language by Geoffrey of Monmouth, a Welsh author of *Historia Regum Brittaniae* ("History of the Kings of Britain") around the twelfth century. As the Arthurian scholar Ronan Coghlan states, Geoffrey of Monmouth introduced the first literary creation of the character King Arthur. His French translator, Wace, introduced the idea of King Arthur's Round Table into the literature. On this base, a French poet of the late twelfth century, Chretien de Troyes, built and expanded the tales, and added courtly love into Arthurian literature.²⁵ Merlin is first composed as a young boy-prophet in *The History of the Britons* (around 830 AD), which is traditionally thought to be written by Nennius, a Welsh monk of the ninth century. From Nennius, Geoffrey of Monmouth largely derives his *Historia Regum Britanniae* (c. 1137). To Nennius's Arthurian story, Geoffrey incorporates the episode of courtly love—King Arthur's marriage to Guinevere. To Geoffrey's story, Chretien de Troyes includes Guinevere's affair with the French knight Lancelot. The versions of Norman poet, Wace include the Round Table, the legendary sword Excalibur, and Chretien de Troyes talks about Camelot, Lancelot, and the Holy Grail.

In the version by Chretien de Troyes, Merlin and Arthur are associated with a bear. In *THS*, Lewis adapts this association, focusing on Merlin's

---

21. Ibid., 13.
22. Ibid., 324.
23. Ibid.
24. Lacy, ed., *The New Arthurian Encyclopedia*, 297.
25. Coghlan, *The Illustrated Encyclopaedia of Arthurian Legends*, 14.

relation with a bear. It sounds irrational to the modernist technocrats of the N.I.C.E., however the mysterious relationship signifies not only Merlin and King Arthur, but also the two living creatures between the supernatural (Merlin and King Arthur) and the natural (bear).

By depicting the resemblance between Merlin and a bear named Mr. Bultitude, Lewis emphasizes the essential qualities of nature in the ancient man, in terms of humanity and environment (natural and supernatural). Through this cordial resemblance of the ancient man and the bear, Lewis reveals the assumed reality of human and animal in the un-fallen world, and pictures a possible rehabilitation of the "fallen"[26] world. "Fall" in this context means the broken fellowship with God (biblically called Original Sin). As seen in the story of Adam and Eve (Gen. 3), the separation from God affects not only humans, but the whole natural world: "for the creation was subjected to futility, not of its own will but by the will of the one who subjected it" (Rom 8:20 NRSV).

The harmonious communication between these two living creatures is well-expressed when the bear licks Merlin's hand. The inherent character of Merlin is closely connected with all living things, both natural (the bear) and supernatural (the druid's magic). The druid's face is described as an appearance "full of the patient, unarguing sagacity of a beast."[27]

Lewis employs the supernatural nature of this ancient man to focus on the unnaturalness on the side of the modern female protagonist, Jane. She refuses to participate in procreation of the next generation. Merlin thus mistakes Jane for Guinevere, the legendary queen of King Arthur. The magician is afraid that Jane will similarly desecrate the holy plan to bear a child with her husband, as he believes that Guinevere has thwarted the purpose of God by refusing to have a baby with Arthur. Merlin laments that if Guinevere had not refused to have children with Arthur, their possible progeny should have defeated "the enemies of Logres."[28] He asks Ransom for an order to execute Jane according to the ancient criminal law.

In *THS*, Lewis thus revives the medieval hero Merlin in a modern background by demonstrating the sharp contrast between pre-historic and modern. He adapts medieval thoughts in order to appeal to the post-modern reader, and contributes to the revival of Arthurian literature in the twentieth and twenty-first centuries. A number of versions of Merlin

26. Lewis, *THS*, 284.
27. Ibid.
28. Ibid., 276.

in Arthurian literature were written between the ninth century and the thirteenth century. Although Arthurian legends won many readers during medieval times, the boom was subdued in and after the Renaissance. Lewis, however, appeals to the postmodern reader with the ambiguous identity of Merlin.

THE ENCLOSED GARDEN

The ambiguous image of Merlin in *THS* is in sync with the fate of the enclosed mythological and Renaissance gardens. Lewis demonstrates a harmony of multiple viewpoints, guiding the reader to the gardens not only with traditional motifs from biblical, classical, and early Christian literature, but also with pagan mythological sources. He uses the ambiguous borders to displace not traditional values but the previous interpretations of the texts, and to guide the reader beyond the rhetoric landscape of word and image. Such postmodernist approaches express his doubts about the modernists' dualistic dominance of reason over faith and the supernatural over the natural.

The destruction of the idyllic cosmos is a reflection of materialist values in modern times. In *THS*, Lewis initially presents persona "I" as a guide, taking the contemporary reader to the mythological garden through the classical quadrangles. The purpose of Merlin's Wood is not obvious, at first, even to the persona "I," or to the College, but an analysis of the enclosed gardens at Bracton College will reveal that Merlin and the persona "I" represent the destiny of the gardens and the prediction of the garden recreated.

The persona "I" seems to be sidelined from the main context, but the episode functions to predict that the destiny of Merlin is a reflection of the fate of other characters in *THS*, especially the persona "I." The persona "I" switches roles from a narrator to a character, suddenly speaking to the reader about the enclosed gardens of Bracton College, then has a brief sleep in the garden, until he is awoken. He has no description of sensations in his mind during sleep, but the un-described "dream" works as if it is a story within a story, in order to connect not only the reader and Merlin, but also Merlin and the persona "I."

A vague border exists between the narrator and the persona "I," but his narration connects the two worlds between Merlin and persona "I," and between Merlin and the reader in a story within a story. It is not clear whether persona "I" speaks as character or whether in a vision. In the College gardens, he switches roles from narrator to character, talking directly to the reader about the memory of a pleasant stroll in the garden, but finally finds himself awakened by an unidentified friend.[29] After he is awakened from his dream, he almost fades out of the main story. In his dream, the two characters—the guide and Merlin—appear to be unified.

Persona "I" completely disappears except for one sentence in chapter 16 when he suddenly appears again and expresses his inability to locate the tramp (another ambiguous character): "I have not been able to trace him further."[30] The identity of the friend who awakens persona "I" is not clearly mentioned, either, but this person serves to inspire persona "I" to reevaluate the pre-modern history of Britain: Renaissance, the Middle Ages, and pre-history. One candidate for the identity of the friend is a professor at Bracton College. This is because persona "I" mentions being invited as a guest to the College.[31]

The real identity of the persona "I" is similarly sealed except for a little information: he is not identified as a particular character in *THS*, but is introduced as "Oxford-bred and very fond of Cambridge."[32] One possible candidate is Ransom, former Cambridge philologist and Director of St. Anne's, who might have been invited to dinner at Bracton College.[33] A politician, Lord Feverston, remembering the dinner with Ransom at Bracton College, talks to Mark about the philologist Ransom, a Cambridge scholar, who has "weak eyes, a game leg, and a fair beard."[34] Another candidate would be Ransom's close friend, a professor at Oxford named "Lewis" who works as narrator for the first two novels of Lewis's Space Trilogy, *Out of the Silent Planet* and *Perelandra*. The rest is left open to the reader's interpretation.

The persona "I," of a mysterious identity, has a one hour siesta in the Wood, much shorter than Merlin's one-thousand five hundred year old sleep. In his dream, he envisions four figures that cover four hundred years of British history. Three out of the four are real: Sir Kenelm Digby, William Collins, and George III. The last fourth is a fictional character, Nathaniel

29. Ibid., 20.
30. Ibid., 348.
31. Ibid., 18.
32. Ibid., 15.
33. Ibid., 39.
34. Ibid.

Fox. The persona "I"'s dream proposes to the reader the re-evaluation of past tradition from the perspective of Merlin.

The four figures represent a four hundred year history of Britain in the academic fields of humanities and politics: Sir Kenelm Digby was a seventeenth century Catholic philosopher-diplomat; William Collins was an English poet of the early eighteenth century; George III was the king of Great Britain between the late eighteenth and nineteenth centuries; and Fox is unknown, but Doris T. Myers supposes that he might be a substitute for Rupert Brooke, a poet in Victorian and Edwardian England.[35]

The persona "I" appears mainly in the first chapter of *THS*, and it sounds as if he is interpreting what he sees in his dream. In a mythological story within a story, he envisions the ideal paradise beyond earthly cultures and religions. He highly respects the historical roles of gardens that include the ancient (pre-Christian), the Middle Ages (Catholicism), and the Renaissance (Protestantism) (mainly the years of the English Civil War, 1642–49). In his dream, the persona "I" contemplates the reactions to Merlin's Wood among different social groups. Beside the well in the center of the Wood, he gradually falls to sleep, but is awoken. As it is not easy to distinguish between Alice's dream in Lewis Carroll's *Alice's Adventures in Wonderland* (1865) and her experience, it is not easy to tell between the dream of the persona "I" and his experience. When the old man, Merlin, comes out of the pre-historic cave into the modern wilderness, the character "I" seemingly changes himself into Merlin, and the persona "I" almost disappears.

The persona "I" enters the enclosed gardens that include the classical space of the quadrangles at Bracton College and the mythological wood with a well in the center of Merlin's Wood. In seventeenth century English society, people were pressured to politically categorize themselves as either Roundheads or Republicans. In *THS*, Lewis, however, tells a different story of this period from the perspectives of enclosed gardens in literature, and the gardens—Renaissance, mythological, and recreated. For the walled garden in *The Magician's Nephew*, Salwa Khoddam discusses in an article, "The Enclosed Garden in C.S. Lewis's *The Chronicles of Narnia*" (2006).

The philosophical concept of the garden in literature changes according to the different periods: the Bible (harmonious communication at Garden of Eden), medieval literature (an earthly paradise), and Renaissance (a mixture of the previous ideals). The concept of earthly paradise matters in the garden of any periods. Lewis regards courtly love as an erotic model of

---

35. Myers, 264.

entrance to earthly paradise, equivalent to Tír na nÓg in Irish: "the earthly paradise, Tirnanogue."[36]

Tirnanogue, "Land of the Youth" in old Irish, is widely known as another world in Irish mythology, particularly in the story of Oisin brought to *Tirnanogue* by a beautiful fairy, Niamh. The term is spelt differently: Tirnanogue by Lewis; "*Tir na Nog*" by Miranda J. Green[37]; and "tin a n-Og" by Arthur Cotterell.[38] This paper is based on both Jeremiah Curtin's version of Oisin,[39] and Marie Heaney's one.[40]

The medieval garden is designed according to the traditional notion of an earthly paradise that includes elements such as birds, trees, fountains, and roses.[41] In the thirteenth century French romance *Romance de la Rose*, the narrator or "the Dreamer" uses the technique of describing the enclosed garden as a metaphor of courtly love: "a favorite device of Renaissance poets."[42]

The enclosed garden is derived from *Song of Solomon* in the Bible (Song of Sol. 4:12) (the Septuagint): "*Hortus conclusus* soror mea, sponsa, hortus coclusus fons signatus" ("A garden enclosed is my sister, my spouse; a *garden enclosed*, a fountain sealed up"). The term garden derives from the *Hortus conclusus* in Latin, which means enclosed. According to Derek Clifford, garden is designed to protect the private precinct from public intrusion, and etymologically from yard, which means "an enclosure."[43] He regards the purpose of enclosed garden as "appreciation" among three kinds of medieval garden: the other gardens are for practical purposes, the vegetable and the medicinal.[44]

The enclosed garden is popularly depicted in medieval visual arts.[45] One well known example is a painting of an enclosed garden with a well in the center, titled "The Little Garden of Paradise" by an anonymous German painter, known as the Upper Rhenish Master, in the early fifteenth century.

36. Lewis, *The Allegory of Love*, 119–20.
37. Green, *Dictionary of Celtic Myth and Legend*, 210.
38. Cotterell, *A Dictionary of World Mythology*, 176.
39. Curtin, *Myths and Folk Tales of Ireland*, 231–41.
40. Heaney, *Irish Myth and Legend*, 80–91.
41. Giamatti, *The Earthly Paradise and theRenaissance Epic*, 62.
42. Ibid., 64.
43. Clifford, *A History of Garden Design*, 17.
44. Ibid., 17–18.
45. Giamatti, *The Earthly Paradise and theRenaissance Epic*, 61.

The Virgin Mary and the infant Jesus are pictured in the center with a fountain, a well, and angels in an enclosed, flowery environment. The painting is meant to emphasize Mary's purity and the miracle of the virgin birth. The Bible states that Jesus Christ was conceived by the Holy Spirit, the third person of the Holy Trinity, and given to Mary miraculously and without disrupting her virginity.[46]

The Renaissance garden regards nature as imperfect, so it views it as access to God, not as fellowship with God. Lewis similarly depicts the Renaissance quads of Bracton as the reflection of both an imperfect earth and a perfect heaven. The Renaissance garden is the channel to reach God.[47] The holy concept of garden gradually changes into a mixture of both heavenly and secular worlds.

The fourteenth century garden is no longer a perfect earthly paradise, but the enclosed garden in Chaucer's "The Merchant's Tale" is the reflection of a married couple's betrayal and recovery. In the same way, in seventeenth century writer John Milton's *Paradise Lost*, God's walled garden is a symbol of a blessed but vulnerable couple because Satan is ready to begin his evil work over the wall. As Giamatti states, Renaissance literature uses the same technique of associating the earthly paradise with the garden of this world.[48]

The Renaissance garden of Bracton College in *THS*, represents not only Lewis's deep appreciation for the classical tradition, but also his postmodern concept of limited human construction. The garden inside Bracton College is composed of three quadrangles, each of which is politically and socially associated with seventeenth century England during the Civil War: the Newton Quad (confusion about science), the Republic Quad (controversy on Reformation), and Lady Alice Quad (reconciling the contrast between Catholicism and Protestantism). Each quad is named after a seventeenth century figure, fictional or historical. The gate is designed by the Renaissance architect Inigo Jones. A quad, symbolic of an earthly paradise, is generally composed of a rectangular green field partially or entirely surrounded by building sections. Three quadrangles of Bracton garden are cultivated in a rectangle-shaped space, each walled with mainly buildings—medieval and Renaissance.

---

46. The tempera on wood (26.3 x 33.4cm) is in the Historical Museum at Frankfurt.
47. Giamatti, *The Earthly Paradise and theRenaissance Epic*, 65.
48. Ibid., 64.

The Newton Quad is described as a dry garden of small stones, elaborately designed in the Gothic architectural style: "florid, but beautiful."[49] This contradictory description of the Quad suggests that the Newton is not perfectly comfortable, while not completely rejected. "Newton" reminds the reader of seventeenth century English Protestant physicist, Sir Isaac Newton. He regards the world as regulated under machine-like laws, but he believes that the laws work within the Providence of God, so that humanity is guided by the Creator. His scientific revolution deconstructs the old interpretation of humanity embraced by the previous generation. The Newton Quad of *THS* must represent reconstruction within the deconstruction.

The second quadrangle, "Republic," is controversial, as the silence within is broken by a disagreeable sound. The equanimity of the Republic Quad is disturbed by the noise of an old clock in the chapel within the College.[50] This disturbance is suggestive of the religious disruption in seventeenth century England, as well as the distraction of classical education.

The term "Republic" reminds the reader of three historical figures with complicated backgrounds in both a positive and a negative sense: the Greek philosopher Plato (about 427 B.C.), writer of *The Republic*; the English political leader of the Republic, Oliver Cromwell (seventeenth century); and the English Republic poet John Milton (seventeenth century). In the medieval universities of England, the dialogues between Plato and his master Socrates are acknowledged as the classical foundation of university education. In the Preface to his poetry "Dymer" (1950), Lewis expresses mixed emotions, love and hate, toward Plato's *Republic*,[51] but Plato's *The Republic* provides him with imaginative inspiration. As a scholar Colin Duriez states, "Some forms of Platonism were deeply influential during the medieval period, which was Lewis's great love and which was the object of much of his scholarship."[52]

The second "Republic" figure is Cromwell of the English Civil War, who turned the monarchy of Britain into "the Republic" commonwealth in opposition to the Royalists.[53] Although he possibly destroyed the previous political system according to his convictions, he is also infamously known today as a destroyer of medieval gardens. Derek Clifford regards the Civil

---

49. Lewis, *THS*, 18.
50. Ibid., 18.
51. Hooper, *C.S. Lewis: A Complete Guide to His Life & Works*, 147.
52. Duriez, *The C.S. Lewis Encyclopedia*, 166.
53. Lewis, *THS*, 295.

War as the critical period for the disfiguring of English gardening: the gardens "were destroyed."[54]

The third "Republic" figure is John Milton (1608-1674). He balances multiple views in his epic poem *Paradise Lost* (1667). Although *Paradise Lost* reflects the conflicting social and political climate of the seventeenth century, the ironical structure of the work holds multiple points of view in equilibrium, which torment Satan.[55]

The third quadrangle, Lady Alice, is a reflection not only of Lewis's interest in female writing during the Renaissance, but also his pursuit of a reconciliation of the dualistic conflicts occurring during the Civil War in seventeenth century England. He displays his literary concern about female writers of the Tudor and Reformation periods. Lewis includes several female writers, such as Lucy Harington, Countess of Bedford (1581-1627) and Mary (Sidney) Herbert, Countess of Pembroke (1561-1621).[56] He introduces Mary Herbert as a collaborator on her brother, Philip Sidney's, prose, *The Arcadia* (1580).

The three sides of the Quad surrounded by Renaissance architecture are suggestive of an unsteady social life, but the delicately designed architecture reminds the persona "I" of Lady Alice's spiritually tranquil mind. The quad is agreeably illustrated with a positive contrast between life and death: the green field full of light, "soft and alive"[57] is a serene place, but the quad with a cloister is associated with death as a place of calm contemplation, the memento mori ("do not forget" in Latin). The cloister, or "enclosure" in Latin, is built to separate the world of the monks from the world of the outside. The cloister in the Quad is designed to keep inner tranquility separated from the world outside, while the quad itself is reached through the other passage, symbolic of death: the passage is decorated with urns and busts in memory of dead Bractonians. The persona "I" feels comfortable with both the cloister of the quad and the milieu of the Middle Ages, stating that "The grass here looks very green after the aridity of Newton."[58]

The Lady Alice Quad is the embodiment of Lewis's specific interest in female literature during the Tudor period. Lady Alice is fictional, but she

---

54. Clifford, 94.

55. Giamatti, *The Earthly Paradise and theRenaissance Epic*, 121-22.

56. Lewis, *English Literature in the Sixteenth Century Excluding Drama*, 178, 286, 307, 331-33, 371, 482, and 627.

57. Lewis, *THS*, 18.

58. Ibid.

is possibly a noble woman in the Protestant world of seventeenth century England. When the persona "I" walks in the field surrounded with seventeenth century buildings, he speaks to the reader, saying that "you are in a sweet, Protestant world," while "thinking of Bunyan or of Walton's Lives."[59]

This final Quad is also the embodiment of chaotic Civil War England, as the persona "I" connects the quad with two Protestant writers, Bunyan and Walton.[60] These two names reflect the turbulent minds of the seventeenth century British world, as they were on opposite sides in the Civil War: Walton was a Royalist and Bunyan was an anti-Royalist.

The Baptist preacher Bunyan was imprisoned several times because of his public sermons, as Baptists were prohibited from public preaching. Lewis, however, focuses on Bunyan's repose with God, regarding his imprisonment as spiritual awakening and affirming that without the turbulance, he would not have created *The Pilgrim's Progress*.[61] Although Izaak Walton (1593–1683) is from a different social group to Bunyan, his mind is similarly reconstructed by God. In spite of his turbulent life, he finds tranquility in the river where he spends devotional time before God. In *The Compleat Angler* (1653), he claims the river to be "not only the quietest and fittest place for contemplation, but will invite an Angler to it."[62] Lewis recommends a list of books written between 1400 and 1830, including Isaak Walton, to J.O. Reed who read English under Lewis at Magdalen in 1952.

The fourth side of the Lady Alice quad is a picturesque image of a quiet earthly paradise that includes a row of elms forming a wall, the sound of running water, and the cooing of birds. The entire Bracton garden is kept tranquil from outside conflicts for a limited amount of time.

Merlin represents the double world of the seventeenth century architect Inigo Jones (1573–1652): both Renaissance and pre-historic. The pre-historic man, Merlin, while asleep, is protected by the Renaissance gate, while the magician comes out through a pre-historic construction of stones: "a pile of loose stones."[63] Inigo Jones is well-known for his appreciation of both classical Renaissance architecture and ancient construction. He is famous for not only his introduction of the Palladian movement to Britain, but also for his conclusions regarding the pre-historic Stonehenge

59. Ibid.
60. Ibid.
61. Lewis, *Selected Literary Essays*, 152.
62. Walton, *The Compleat Angler*, 40.
63. Lewis, *THS*, 224.

construction. According to Derek Clifford, the Palladian movement is an Italian Renaissance architectural style related to the Roman ideas of harmonic proportions.[64]

The Renaissance garden temporarily serves to protect the mythological Wood from the destructive effect of the modernist world. In *THS*, the fictional gate designed by Inigo Jones is described as the only way to the mythological Wood. Lewis focuses on this architect, repeating his name several times: "the gate was by Inigo Jones"[65] and "through the Inigo Jones gate..."[66]

Since Inigo Jones's gate works as the bridge that joins the pre-historic world and the Renaissance, the Bragdon Wood similarly serves to mirror two gardens: the classical ideology of the enclosed garden and the mythological cosmology of an earth-centered religion. Although the mythological garden is called Merlin's Wood, the forest does not look like an uncultivated ground. The natural space appears more like a classical garden except for the mythological man asleep underground. Lewis describes the space with traditional images, associating the garden with a well, sheep, and green trees enclosed by a high wall from outside. Lewis discusses his concept of traditional gardens in *Allegory of Love*.[67]

The persona "I" or narrator of *THS* reevaluates the history of Merlin's Wood and witnesses the change of meaning between "sacred" and "profane." He observes the contradictory effects of the four hundred year old wall between the seventeenth (Elizabeth I's reign and the Civil War) and the twentieth centuries. During the Renaissance period, the Wood is enclosed by a wall to protect the "sacred" society from the "profane" Wood: "all wakes, May games, dancings, mummings, and baking of Morgan's bread."[68] Society of the seventeenth century is so frightened of the pre-historic effects that they are compelled to build a wall to separate the outside, or "sacred" humanism, from the inside, or "profane" pre-historic Wood. In the twentieth century, however, the Renaissance wall ironically works to protect the inside (the savior Merlin as "sacred") from the outside (mechanized

---

64. Clifford, 18.
65. Lewis, *THS*, 19.
66. Ibid.
67. Lewis, *The Allegory of Love*, 119–20.
68. Lewis, *THS*, 20.

modern world as "profane"). The persona "I" feels in awe of the holy when approaching Bragdon Wood.[69]

Through depictions of the gardens at the College, Lewis emphasizes the harmonious relationship between classical education and mythology. He means that classical tradition similarly serves not to abandon the prehistoric elements but to protect them. The persona "I" remembers one scholar of Bracton College who risks his life to protect the Wood when Cromwell is about to destroy it. The classical garden serves as a temporal medium to the eternal entity, reflecting a shadowy paradise of Renaissance culture and classical education. The shadowy world acts as if it is a gardener who takes care of our imagination for the true garden.

The fate of the garden unexpectedly ends in double steps: Merlin ascends into the wild open field of the twentieth century (section 5 of chapter 17), and the gardens of Bracton College are catastrophically destroyed by earthquake, flood, and riots. The destruction of the university town of Edgestow, including Bracton College, is described in detail from the perspectives of three characters: the narrator who reports Henrietta Maria's smashed east window in the Lady Alice Squad; Mrs. Dimple (wife of Dr. Dimple) who is evicted from her garden; and the sub-warden of Bracton College, Dr. Curry, who talks with a ticket collector.

Lewis contrasts two ladies to reflect the peaceful cosmology of two worldviews between Henrietta Maria (history) and Lady Alice (fiction), and between Catholic Maria and Protestant Alice. The harmonious illustration of the two is Lewis's proclamation for the basic doctrines of Christianity and resistance to discuss the differences between Christian denominations. He expresses this stance in *Mere Christianity*, his book of Christian apologetics based on a series of BBC lectures: "ought never to be treated except by real experts."[70]

When the east window is broken by riots, the spiritual legacy of temporary peace is damaged: "a splintering of glass . . . and a shower of stones. . ."[71] Historically, Henrietta Maria, the daughter of the king of France, Henry IV, was married to Charles I of England (1600–1649). In *THS*, a Catholic lady, Henrietta Maria, has her name cut with a diamond into the east window inside the Quad of Lady Alice, which is associated with "a Protestant world."[72]

69. Ibid., 18.
70. Lewis, *Mere Christianity*, Preface, VIII.
71. Lewis, *THS*, 91.
72. Ibid., 18.

The quiet Quad is, however, disturbed by noises from a construction site outside, indicative of the mechanized modern society.

Another noise is Mrs. Dimple's wrath over her eviction from her beloved garden, which is ruined by the modernist state group N.I.C.E. The destruction of her garden is suggestive of the death of Mother Earth as her nickname, Mother Dimple, suggests. She loves the trees in the garden so deeply that she calls each tree name as if they are her own children: "the beech," "the plum," and "the poplar."[73]

Except for Mark, the only survivor of the catastrophe at Bracton College is subwarden Dr. Curry, who lacks empathy for the victims of the disaster, abdicating any responsibility for the university town. He is only concerned with his own social promotion, so he attempts to take this opportunity for administrative success as the new warden. He does not care for the victims, even when he hears the station master speaking about the disaster: "Sir, I'm afraid you'll find nothing of Bracton College."[74]

In the last chapter, Lewis uses the epithalamium as a literary form of "baptized eroticism."[75] He depicts Jane going to restore herself and also to re-unite with Mark. The epithalamium is a medieval poem sung for a bride on her way to the wedding room. Epithalamion, the Bridal Chamber in Greek, (*epithalamium* in Latin) originally means a wedding hymn sung in classical Greece outside the bride's room on her wedding night. The tradition of poetry believed to have begun by Sappho was revived by Renaissance poets including Sir Philip Sidney, Spenser, Donne, and Ben Jonson.

In *THS*, Lewis revives the custom of epithalamium. Similar to a bride of the epithalamium going to the wedding room to meet her bridegroom, Jane heads toward the lodge where Mark awaits her. "Baptized eroticism" is a term coined by Thomas Howard to mean such Lewisian eros. In *The Four Loves* (1960), Lewis defines eros as sexual desire from the Goddess of Eros, as well as an emotional bond with others. In the garden, Jane has not only her eros healed, but also the bond with her partner restored.[76]

The epithalamium is a literary form of Christian poetry that depicts agape-love with the love-lore of pagan mythology. The epithalamium, or the erotic-mythical story, is one of Lewis's life-long literary themes. He

---

73. Ibid., 75–76.
74. Ibid., 372.
75. Howard, *Narnia and Beyond*, 189.
76. Lewis, *THS*, 124.

regards Bishop Ennodius as a poet of epithalamium.[77] Ennodius was a Pavia poet in the fifth and sixth centuries.[78]

In *THS*, a modern version of the epithalamium, the female protagonist Jane rehabilitates not only the broken relationship with her partner Mark, but also restores her own identity. In the last chapter, Jane is described as walking to the lodge in the cottage garden of St. Anne's. She hopes to reconcile her broken marriage with her husband. Just as the cottage garden was formed in the nineteenth century when Britain was searching for a new national identity, so Jane is to have her true self restored, and to have her damaged relationship with Mark healed through the garden recreated.

ETHICAL RESPONSES TO THE PRE-HISTORIC MAGICIAN

The identity of Merlin is ambiguous, but the other protagonists of *THS* individually make a quest for him. Just as King Arthur's knights seek the Holy Grail, all the main characters of *THS* search for Merlin and his identity. An analysis of the seven responses to the old man from each character will demonstrate the individual moral values in *THS*: Elwin Ransom (Fisher-King), scholars of the N.I.C.E. (Mark and Wither), Double Merlin (Mark and the tramp), the treason of intellectuals including Dr. Dimple, Merlin himself, and the modernist couple (Jane and Mark).

Elwin Ransom embodies the ambiguous borders between fact and fiction but points to an understanding beyond limited human language. The owner and head of St. Anne's manor, as well as a linguist at Cambridge, is not willingly to desire for a literal translation of the Indian Sura's signs, but receives the message as an inheritance from Ransom's sister that includes only her family name "Fisher-King" (suggestive of the wounded king in Arthurian legend), but also a mission from her friend, Sura. Even though his knowledge of Sura is limited, he receives Mrs. Fisher-King's will without knowing its significance completely, and waits until the time that he understands it to mean the coming of Merlin.

Neither Mrs. Fisher-King nor Sura appear as characters in the main story of *THS*. Their names are mentioned only in one paragraph, but their legacy is influential enough to affect the rest of the characters, especially

---

77. Lewis, *The Allegory of Love*, 85.
78. Ibid., 77.

Pre-Historic Magician Awakens in the Modernist Age

Jane. The last of the four messages by Sura is connected to her: "a seer."[79] The third is related to St. Anne's: "a company"[80] around Ransom and watch for danger to strike. The rest of the messages are predictions regarding the end of the world: a great danger is hanging over the human race just before the end, and the danger coming to "a head" in Britain.[81]

Through the term "Sura," Lewis probably suggests a universal virtue respected worldwide, like "Tao." He adopts Tao as the value for "the Way" when he discusses the universally respected law in *The Abolition of Man* (1943). By Sura, he must mean "holiness" and "goodness." The word "Sura" is, according to Lewis scholar Kathryn Lindskoog, etymologically a god in Sanskrit, a good angel in Hindu, and is the name of each chapter of the Koran.

In *THS*, Ransom takes up the spiritual mission which his sister receives from the Indian mystic Sura. With Sura, Lewis presents a vague border between fact and fiction. Sura (fiction) has a possible connection with Sundar Singh (historical). Kathryn Lindskoog views a synchronicity with the Indian Christian missionary, Sundar Singh (1889–1929), who may have influenced Lewis in several ways.[82]

Similar to the fictional Indian mystic, the historical Indian mystic finally disappears to a place unknown to the reader. Lindskoog claims that Lewis possibly read a biography of Sadhu, *The Sadhu: A Study in Mysticism and Practical Religion*, by B. H. Streeter and A. J. Appasamy. David Downing similarly states that Lewis carefully marks passages on Singh's mystical vision of Christ and underlines a number of Sadhu's sayings.[83]

Lindskoog assumes that Lewis must have heard the well-known name of Sundar Singh when he was a student of University College in 1920 while Sadhu was at Oxford. In *THS*, Denniston, a member of St. Anne's, emphasizes the name of the Indian mystic Sura with his use of the definite article when speaking to Jane about the Indian mystic as a commonly known fact, "the Sura."[84]

Two social scientists of the N.I.C.E., Mark Studdock and his boss John Wither, have opposite responses to Merlin and his words. The two

---

79. Lewis, *THS*, 112.
80. Ibid.
81. Ibid.
82. Sundar Singh is believed to have died in the foothills of the Himalayas in 1929.
83. D. C. Downing, *Into the Region of Awe*, 104.
84. Lewis, *THS*, 112.

modernist scholars, in the beginning, share the concept of language, believing that it exists as "being" but has no "meaning." As his name "Wither" suggests, his mind "withers," or falls into decay, because of his long-term association with superior evil beings or "fallen eldila" (fallen angels). His speech and thinking ability are destined to wither or become vague. Dr. Wither, who represents the N.I.C.E., refers to "fallen eldila" (fallen angels) as "macrobes," ironically meaning superior beings, even though "macrobes," or microbe in the singular, is a bacterium causing disease.

The two scholars represent a destructive modern education that emphasizes the words of language but despises its image. Dr. Wither "interprets" what Merlin speaks into Latin, but never comprehends what the old man means. Merlin actually says in Latin to mean that: "those who have despised the Word of God, from them shall the word of man also be taken away."[85] Wither disdains the worth of image as if he invited a linguistic curse on himself. He always thinks vaguely and speaks only with abstract words.

The Cartesians of the N.I.C.E. fail to discern the difference between the two types of magic, the Renaissance-type's and Merlin's, but view the latter through their conquering nature and controlling humanity: "Nature is a machine."[86] The Edwardian building of the institution represents the modernist thought of Cartesianism that boasts of the victory of humanity over nature. The French palace of Versailles was designed by Cartesian, Louis Le Vau (1612–1670). Lewis academically knows about Versailles from his brother, Warren, a scholar of French history. The original garden of Versailles has been said to embody Cartesianism because it confines the nature within the rule of geometry.

Lewis writes that magic in the Middle Ages is like familiar furniture at home "like knight-errantry,"[87] but the magic of Renaissance as goeteia, which may be as familiar as the neighborhood, but not to be tolerated in the household.

In *THS*, Lewis contrasts the modernistic minds of the two scholars, Mark Studdock and John Wither, through their paradoxical reactions to abstract works of art, and questions the rational awareness among modernistic readers. Counter to Wither's expectation, the pictures on a wall make Mark undergo an existential experience through aesthetical appreciation,

---

85. Ibid., 224.
86. Ibid., 200.
87. Lewis, *English Literature in the Sixteenth Century*, 8.

until he is aware of a value of "something normal."[88] This occurs in three steps: from depression, to dryness or thirst, and finally to a realization of "water." He is depressed with "a meaning,"[89] aware of sensitive feelings of dryness or thirst, and finally the realization of spiritual "water."[90] The unusual works finally awaken him to a new awareness of objectivity.

For the behavioral psychologist Wither, everything created on earth is a machine for controlling the human mind: not only Merlin's magic but also works of art. The scholar uses paintings to test Mark's commitment to the N.I.C.E. These works are intended by the modernist organization to force Mark to lose his moral sensibility until he abandons the power to judge for himself.

This process is similar to the sense of dryness in T.S. Eliot's poem "The Wasteland," in which he uses dryness to suggest the emptiness of modern thought. However, Mark is made to have more thirst for water than the poet in "The Wasteland." He longs for a quality to represent objectivity (moral absolutes): "vision of the sweet and the straight."[91]

Confined to a coffin-shaped room, Mark feels thirstier for the straight and untwisted. No specific reference to any particular artist is described, but there are some allusions to Dada and surrealist works. Some of the strange paintings that Mark is forced to look at include a man "with corkscrews"[92] and a young woman's mouth "overgrown with hair."[93] The descriptions remind the reader of the men with pegged arms in *Republican Automatons* (1920) by German Dadaist painter George Grosz (1893–1959), and the female nude body in *The Menaced Assassin* (1926) by Belgian Surrealist painter Rene Magritte (1898–1967).[94]

Contrary to Wither's perception, both works actually reflect the artists' opposition to modernity as a machine. Wither's malicious loyal test for Mark paradoxically works to awaken the young scholar's sense of ethics to the existence of something or someone straight and honest. The touchstone for Mark is when he is ordered to step on a painting of a life-size crucifix.

88. Lewis, *THS*, 184.
89. Ibid., 183.
90. Ibid.
91. Ibid., 184.
92. Ibid., 295.
93. Ibid.
94. Concerning the discussion of Mark and contemporary artists, refer to my 2005 paper "Awoken and Integrated: *That Hideous Strength* and *The Abolition of Man*."

The desecrating action of stepping on the image makes him feel powerless before the image. Although he has no belief in Christianity, he at least understands that the image of the work is the representation of Jesus Christ on the Cross. Contrary to the N.I.C.E.'s aim to control his humanity, he comes to realize that the picture of the cross represents something straight.[95]

Through the reactions of Wither and Mark, Lewis raises again the criticism against modern education through his comparison of two prisoners, Mark and the tramp. Even though these two men share the same cell, both are ignorant of the reason that they are being held captive, and also of the fact that the tramp has been mistaken for the real Merlin. Mark is philosophically transforming himself through a dialogue with this fake Merlin/tramp—a genuine communication—which serves to prepare Mark to meet the real Merlin.

Through his comical but existential dialogue with the fake Merlin/tramp, Mark is aware of something opposite to his sensibilities. The scholar views the world with rational thought (word), but fails to detest the objective facts that belong to the tramp in the same cell. He is not able to identify the background of the pauper whose life is completely unfettered by modern civilized society. The rationalist, however, finds the fake Merlin/tramp filled with a deep joy of life: "gusto was the most striking characteristic."[96] He unexpectedly develops a friendship with the tramp; they enjoy a private conversation or "tête-à-tête"[97] like children who are at play or enjoying a picnic.

Mark remembers "the realm of childhood"[98] through his talk with the fake Merlin/tramp, who acts on his own preferences, however childish they may be. Although he makes no moral judgments about things, he at least eats, drinks, and speaks as he wishes. Mark realizes in the "children playing" that the tramp has no vanity: "no more power or security."[99] Contrary to the N.I.C.E.'s original plot to appeal to vanity, Mark begins to doubt what the technology group claims as "objectivism."

Through the transforming values of Mark, Lewis reveals the spiritual wilderness of modernism. The scholar, as a product of modern education, learns to listen to the tramp who physically lives in the wilderness but

---

95. Lewis, *THS*, 333.
96. Ibid., 282.
97. Ibid., 310.
98. Ibid.
99. Ibid.

spiritually enjoys his wild life. He expects the tramp to talk in a logical and chronological way, but the wild man talks not as Mark expects. The tramp talks as he himself wishes. Mark comes to pay attention to not only what the tramp says, but also how he feels. He is aware of the significance of both word and image through communication with the tramp.

Lewis uses satirical comedy as a way to persuade the rational reader to understand multiple perspectives. He comically illustrates the ridiculous dialogue between Mark and the tramp, Mark's remorse about life, and exposes the ridiculous behavior of the N.I.C.E., that lacks the ability to distinguish the real pre-historic Merlin from the fake Merlin/modern tramp. The modernist group is satirically fooled by the uneducated tramp, even though the pauper has no intention to deceive the technocrats. The real Merlin humorously interprets the language of the tramp, unknown to the N.I.C.E. As scholar Terry Lindval states, Lewis believes that "satire could be a proper vehicle for persuading a skeptical audience."[100]

The N.I.C.E mistakes the fake Merlin for the real one, in the same way that they do not distinguish between the head of the executed murderer and the divinity. They worship the separated head of the condemned criminal, Alcasan, based on their belief that "Nature is something dead—a machine."[101] Merlin's double (the tramp) is finally made by the N.I.C.E. to dress in robes as a Doctor of Philosophy.[102] When Merlin and the tramp are introduced to all the guests in the dinner room of the N.I.C.E as Dr. Ambroisius and his interpreter, the difference does not matter to the technocrats.

The N.I.C.E. scholars speak to Dr. Ambroisius in several languages—Latin, French, and Welsh—without knowing that the old man understands English. Despite their comical and vain attempts to manipulate the tramp, they somehow find a Basque monk (the real Merlin) as interpreter for the fake Merlin/tramp. The real Merlin acts as if he is interpreting what his double speaks, but actually the double is enchanted by Merlin's spell and speaks an unknown language, as the real Merlin wishes.

Lewis demonstrates his opposition to dualism in academic circles in the depiction of not only the N.I.C.E (scientific state), but also Jane's former tutor, Cecil Dimple. The professor of Arthurian literature, Dr. Dimple,

---

100. Lindval, *Surprised by Laughter*, 357.
101. Lewis, *THS*, 283.
102. Ibid., 331.

accuses these dualistic scholars of committing "*Trabison des clercs.*"[103] "*Trabison des clercs*" means literally "Treason of the clerks" in French, used in *THS* to mean an accusation against scholars for their dangerous passions in academic research. The phrase comes from French philosopher Julien Bendan's "*Trabison des clercs*" (1929). The U.S. title "Treason of the Intellectuals" directly communicates Lewis's denouncement of the educated class. Benda's influence on Lewis has not been widely discussed, but Jared Lobdell makes a comparison of *La Trabison des clercs* with Lewis's essay *Rehabilitations and Other Essay*.[104]

Dr. Dimple is guilty of "*Trabison des clercs*" in the same sense that the N.I.C.E. does not suppose that "anyone would act on his theory."[105] He accuses the N.I.C.E. of a separation between thought and theory. Even though he criticizes the modernist group, he has to agree with a scholar-friend at St. Anne's, Arthur Denniston, who concludes that all scholars are acquitted "Trabison des clercs" because "none of us is quite innocent."[106] Included among "all" is not only the N.I.C.E., but also Dimple himself.

As a scholar of Arthurian literature with a special interest in Merlin, Dimple is ashamed of too lightly using the phrase "the Dark Ages."[107] He simply regards the magician as a supernatural creature who is beyond the conceptual borders of being "good" and "evil"[108]: "He's not evil, yet he's a magician."[109] During a night tour with Denniston and Jane, however, he realizes that he has not understood the holistic reality of the magician in the "Dark Ages." The Dark Ages are usually considered to be the time between the fall of the Roman Empire and the high Middle Ages,[110] but Dimple regards the "dark pit of history" as the time of the "'Pre-Roman' or 'Pre-British.'"[111]

Dimple seeking Merlin in the dark wilderness leads to his realization of Merlin with both word and image. His academic research is connected

---

103. Ibid., 370.

104. Lobdell, *The Scientification Novels of C.S. Lewis*, 130.

105. Lewis, *THS*, 370.

106. Ibid.

107. Ibid. 230.

108. Ibid., 30.

109. Ibid., 29.

110. Second edition, 1989; online version November 2010. http://www.oed.com:80/Entry/47295. Earlier version first published in *New English Dictionary*, 1894.

111. Lewis, *THS*, 230.

Pre-Historic Magician Awakens in the Modernist Age

with his personal experience of entering into a different dimension, as if he is passing from "a waking into a phantasmal world."[112] He envisions all of Britain suddenly rising up "like a solid thing."[113] He sees British landscapes rewinding or in a temporary reverse motion: from Christian, back to Roman, pre-Roman, pre-Britain, and pre-historic.[114]

Although Dimple has pursued a career of academic research on Merlin and the Dark Ages, he regards the magician as an allegorical character of abstract ideas, not as a living natural force who could be incarnated in this world. He does not accept the story of the old man as fact until he looks for the magician in the dark field: "they had not really believed in Merlin till now."[115]

The identity of Merlin is ambiguous because of his paradoxical nature: he is both a savior and a sinner; he suddenly appears and disappears. The old man is confusing to the reader as well as to Merlin himself. Merlin misunderstands the purpose and reason for his awakening into the modern age. It is initially unknown, but gradually revealed, that he has two missions: one is to save the world with his pre-historic magic, as Ransom speaks to Merlin: "only one man . . . could still be recalled: You"[116]; and the other is to save his own soul.[117]

The members of St. Anne's fail to identify Merlin, assuming that the sleeper may be on the side of the enemy—the N.I.C.E. Director of St. Anne's, Ransom, later tells Merlin that "you would be on the side of the enemy."[118] Merlin similarly misunderstands his own parachronic mission. His notion needs redeeming and reconstructing, because he misunderstands that peace should be restored by the rulers on earth, and that he is awakened to heal the wounded ruler, Ransom.

The ancient magician assumes that he is a healer for Ransom, but comes to realize that the modern King Arthur will not be healed on earth, but must return to Venus where he is wounded. This happens when Ransom kills his former colleague Professor Weston in the second book of the

---

112. Ibid., 229.
113. Ibid., 230.
114. Ibid.
115. Ibid., 229.
116. Ibid., 288.
117. Ibid., 286.
118. Ibid.

Space Trilogy, *Perelandra* (1943). Lord Feverstone (Dick Divine in *Perelandra*) suggests to Mark that the murderer is Ransom.[119]

It is certain that Merlin is awakened in order to rescue the modern world from destruction, not as a gallant fighter as he wishes to be, but as an interpreter working in the background. He effaces himself when his old interpretation of himself is deconstructed, and is humbly self-deprecating when his concept of "me" drops in his encounter with Glund-Oyarsa (equivalent to the Creator God): "he was no longer his own man."[120] His mistaken sense of modern civilization is modified by Ransom, who explains to the magician the fatal danger of dualism:

> The machines, the crowded cities, the empty thrones, the false writings, the barren beds; men maddened with false promises and soured with true miseries, worshipping the iron works of their own hands, cut off from earth their mother and from the father in Heaven.[121]

Lewis does not specify the reason for Merlin's disappearance, but presents different accounts of his ambiguous last scene through the narrator, the character "I," and Jane. Thomas Malory describes Merlin with his fall into a deep sleep in *Le Morte D'Arthur* (1469), but Lewis's story of Merlin ends with a man asleep or "dead and yet not dead."[122] The narrator of *THS* knows the fact that Merlin disappears, but does not realize when he does. He finds Merlin fading out after the old man releases the imprisoned at the N.I.C.E., including both animals and human beings: "No one had seen him go."[123] The persona "I" here suddenly appears again and lastly in the text, describing how Merlin goes, but cannot tell to where he disappears: "I have not been able to trace him further."[124]

These are the last two witnesses to see Merlin disappear. The last mention of his name in the novel is when Jane sees him in a dream. He looks to her as if he is deconstructed into dust: "he'd fall to pieces the moment the powers let him go."[125]

---

119. Ibid., 39.
120. Ibid., 324.
121. Ibid., 290.
122. Ibid., 229.
123. Ibid., 348.
124. Ibid., 348.
125. Ibid., 359.

Pre-Historic Magician Awakens in the Modernist Age

Just as the wounded King Arthur is healed on the island of Avalon, so too is Ransom healed back on the planet of Perelandra. As twelfth century author Geoffrey of Monmouth describes King Arthur in a double metaphor of ruler and magician, Lewis likewise creates the story of Ransom with a double image of Arthur and Merlin. He does not specify the place to which Merlin disappears, but hints to the whereabouts in a picture of the magician as a duplicate of Ransom. The two men look like the two sides of the same coin, disappearing almost simultaneously. Like the bleeding King Arthur, the final destination of the bleeding director is evidently mentioned as he is brought back to a place with the double image of Perelandra (Venus) and Avalon: "the Third Heaven, in Perelandra. In Aphallin (Avalon), the distant island."[126] David Downing regards the double image of Perelandra as mythological integration of paradise.[127]

Mythologically, Aphallin (*Avalon* in Celtic) is the site where the injured King Arthur is healed. Aphallin in *THS* reflects an integration of mythology and the Bible, as the island of Aphallin in Perelandra is a place where not only King Arthur, but also the biblical figures Enoch, Elias, Moses, and Melchizedek are found. Jared Lobdel analyzes the relation between Aphallin and Scripture. Martha C. Sammons supposes that Lewis may connect his alternate names Abhalljin and Aphallin with the root word apple.[128]

The disappearance of Merlin is related to Jane's restored communication ability. She sees two visions of Merlin, but reveals contrasting reactions to the images. She has no one to talk with when she has her first dream of the old man awakening, while she has a community with which to share the last vision of Merlin. She talks to her two female friends at St. Anne's (Ivy and Mother Dimple) about the illusion of the old man receding.[129]

The identity of Merlin is totally unknown to the modernist scholar couple, Jane and Mark. The self-effacing experience, as if going through death, paradoxically brings the stalemated couple to a recreation of their marriage through each encounter with the old magician Merlin. The couple is just married but already almost divorced. Not only their marriage but

---

126. Ibid., 367.

127. D. C. Downing, "*That Hideous Strength* Spiritual Wickedness in High Places," 66.

128. Sammons, *A Far-off Country: A Guide to C.S. Lewis's Fantasy Fiction*, 327 and 369.

129. Lewis, *THS*, 359.

also their vocations are stalemated. Merlin's magic, however, brings a self-awakening experience to Jane and Mark.

Jane questions her modernist worldview when she sees the mythological Merlin in a dream. The question deconstructs her rationalist concept of marriage and vocation. She unconsciously becomes suspicious of reasoned thinking through her unusual vision of Merlin and her encounter with a mysterious "Person" (with a capital letter).[130]

When she meets this Person in the garden at St. Anne's, she realizes the Person is her creator. She describes her life as a person (in lowercase) made by the Person (capitalized). The person makes her "a made thing"[131] in the Person, just like "in the moulding hands. . ."[132] She gives up herself, and makes herself deconstructed.

Unlike the Renaissance quads of Bracton College, the cottage garden at St. Anne's is a homely place, with vegetables, flowers, and a greenhouse. Even though Freud associates the garden with the female body from the perspective of the male,[133] the cottage garden reminds Jane of joy for both genders. It brings the rationalist woman to a re-comprehension of sexuality and vocation that "the beauty of the female"[134] is the joy to both the female and the male.

Jane is frustrated by the deadlock in both her academic life and her married life, as she contradicts herself between rationalist conviction and un-rational vision. Although she rejects her own sexuality, she attempts to write a dissertation on the poet John Donne and sexuality entitled "Triumphant Vindication of the Body."

The title of Jane's dissertation is not clearly comprehensible, but as Thomas Howard presumes, the title is possibly suggestive of Jane's rejection of motherhood. She rejects having children with Mark in order to pursue her scholastic career.[135] Gregory Wolfe believes that Lewis is not moralistic to Donne's passion, but this does not affect his use of Donne in *THS*.[136] Lewis describes Jane as an atheist in belief, but who expects the wedding vow before God to be true. He possibly has in mind *A Vindication*

---

130. Ibid., 315.
131. Ibid., 316.
132. Ibid.
133. Freud, *A General Introduction to Psychoanalysis*, 130.
134. Lewis, *THS*, 60.
135. Howard, "The Catholic Angler," n.p.
136. Wolfe, "Essential Speech," 71 n.15.

of the Rights of Woman (1792), the book by the eighteenth century British feminist Mary Wollstonecraft. She claims equal education for males and females.

Jane pretends to write: "I must do some work."[137] By work, she means the doctoral thesis on Donne, but she lacks the desire to write any further. It seems that she fails to grasp Donne's adaptation of double expressions in sacred verses (*agape*) beneath the facade of secular lyrics (*eros*). John Donne was a popular choice for the modernist student of literature in the first half of the twentieth century, as T.S. Eliot reevaluated the conceits in Donne's metaphysical poetry. Donne compares his depression to a female mummy captured by a man: "Hope not for mind in women; at their best, / Sweetness and wit they are, but mummy, possess'd."[138] A mummy is physically dead, but spiritually alive, while Jane is physically alive, but spiritually dead. Like a reverse mummy, she hopelessly repeats a line from John Donne's poem "Love's Alchemy."

Jane's idea of "religion" is quite different from "a Person."[139] In order to write about John Donne, Jane is intellectually curious about religion, but keeps her distance from a genuine belief in God. In the term "religion," Jane is possessed by her female fear of being treated as "an object of barter . . ."[140] Her ambivalent attitude toward religion is reflected in the invisible inner voices pressuring her to choose either a religion or John Donne. The voices are heard from inside of Jane herself: "How much better you will now understand the Seventeenth-Century poets!"[141]

Jane uses Mark as a way to boost her lost passion for work, expecting the marriage to inspire an understanding of *agape* through a sexual relationship, *eros*. On the contrary, she instead gains not what she wishes for, but solitude, as if she is the poet in "Love's Alchemy." Jane may have been seduced to exploit her spiritual experience for the sake of her research on John Donne. The poet seeks an elixir that turns all metals into gold, but in vain. Like this poet, Jane fails to pursue her writing.

Mrs. Dimple triggers Jane to deconstruct her mental obsession with work. Jane gets Ransom's kiss upon her lips and his words in her ears,

---

137. Lewis, *THS*, 7.
138. Donne, *The Poems of John Donne*, 22–23.
139. Lewis, *THS*, 315.
140. Ibid.
141. Ibid., 316.

suggestive of her humble attitude in accepting her sexuality.[142] Writing about Donne, paradoxically, allows Jane to face the limitations of language. Doris T. Myers regards Jane's choice of Donne as her preoccupation with language of the ideology.[143]

Lewis regards John Donne as paradox of the form of argument.[144] A casual question by Mrs. Dimple causes Jane to realize that she is doomed as a writer. She is disturbed by Mother Dimple's simple question about a kiss. By kiss, Dimple probably means an affectionate greeting, but Jane perhaps accepts the question in a deeper dimension and interprets it as a rejection of the intellectual mind: "That indeed is the question."[145]

Mark is similarly possessed by the modernistic motto of language as a machine. He lacks the imagination to consider Jane's traumatic mind on eerie visions, but excessively longs for words of admiration for his professional ability among the inner group of the N.I.C.E. As a socialist, he uses language as an instrument to convey information or facts for practical purposes. Just like Jane, he regards marriage as an automatic system to fulfill his desires for power or title. Unlike Jane, who tries to write with both word and image, social scientist Mark writes with only word. Writing does not help him to deconstruct and thus understand himself. He must wait for the supernatural intervention of Merlin.

Through his depiction of Mark, Lewis warns of the danger of a modern education lacking ethics. The socialist learns rationalistic thought from "modern" education. Mark does not mind even writing fake articles for major newspapers in Britain in order to instigate riots in the college town of Edgestow. He is coerced by the N.I.C.E. to fabricate the stories without knowing that this is a spiritual battle between angels (eldilas in *THS*) in space. He is also ignorant of the fact that the N.I.C.E. is under the control of a fallen angel who attempts to alter the nature of mankind through pride and greed inherent in the N.I.C.E. Although the acronym N.I.C.E. (the National Institute of Coordinated Experiments) sounds "nice" or amicable, this agency of technocrats is devoid of the morality to judge whether or not it is a nice language. It is, ethically, not a "nice" place.

Mark is a product of a modern education that finds statistical information more real than reality. His education has the effect of making what

---

142. Ibid., 251.
143. Myers, 99.
144. Lewis, "Donne and Love Poetry in the Seventeenth Century," 110.
145. Lewis, *THS*, 28.

he reads and writes more real to him than the things he sees. Statistics about agricultural laborers are the substance: "any real ditcher, ploughman, or farmer's boy, was the shadow."[146] Lewis has regard for both tradition and science, but opposes modernist thought through his depiction of Mark as a monster of modern education: "His education had been neither scientific nor classical—merely "Modern." The severities both of abstraction and of high human tradition had passed him by. He was a man of straw, a glib examinee in subjects that require no exact knowledge."[147]

Through their encounter with Merlin, Mark and Jane undergo a philosophical transformation. The magician works to change their concepts of ordinary things, such as home, work, and partner, into something different. It is as if he is an alchemist who attempts to convert base metals, or usual material, into elixir or gold. Jane becomes curious to know a most ordinary person, her partner Mark, when she accepts her own sexuality, while Mark effaces himself through his aesthetic experience in modern visual works.

Jane and Mark accept the spiritual heritage of King Arthur as their vocation—vocation for "man, made in God's image,"[148] as Dorothy Sayers states. Mark changes himself when he recovers an objective sense of morality through the appreciation of abstract paintings. He reconsiders his marriage with Jane not as a booster, but as a context for communication.

RECREATED GARDEN

The reactions to mythological figures in the garden reveal a clash and integration of multiple perspectives between the supernatural and the natural. Lewis uses the cottage garden to inspire the modernist couple to identify themselves anew. Jane's old interpretation of "obedience" is destroyed through her encounter with the light of the Person (the earthly Venus as a shadow of the heavenly Venus) in the garden at St. Anne's, while Mark feels guilty about damaging his wife through interpreting medieval stories of garden. Contact with the Person in the garden changes Jane's concept of sexuality. By the "Person," Lewis means all myths, and by sexuality, he means the relation between all created things on the earth and all things

---

146. Ibid., 57.
147. Ibid., 109.
148. Sayers, "Why Work?," 89.

in Heaven: everyone is feminine in relation to what is above "beyond all things is so masculine."[149]

The mythological entities work to restore communication between Jane and Mark. The mythological characters include not only Merlin, but also "the Person" and Ransom. These three collectively represent the Trinity of God, the Son, and the Holy Spirit. In pre-historic and classical gardens, the mythological magician Merlin acts as a guide, a prototype of the Holy Spirit; "the Person" in the cottage garden is nearly equivalent to the Creator; and Ransom, the owner of St. Anne's, represents a paid ransom, similar to Jesus Christ's and a lord like King Arthur.

Ransom in *THS* represents both King Arthur and Jesus Christ. Ransom capitalized is King Arthur, while "ransom" in lowercase is biblically associated with Jesus Christ who gave himself as a ransom on the Cross. The term ransom is from the Greek word "Antilutron," meaning "an equivalent price." This concept of equivalent value is, biblically, an absolute law: "for as all die in Adam, so all will be made alive in Christ" (1 Cor. 15:22 NRSV). This is the fundamental story of the Cross: Jesus's ransom for Adam satisfies justice as he paid the equivalent price—a perfect life for an imperfect life: "Christ Jesus, himself human, who gave himself a ransom for all" (1 Tim. 2:5–6).

In order to inspire Mark and Jane to go for a self-effacing and self-seeking adventure, the three mythological entities, Merlin, Ransom, and the "Person," collaborate themselves with the biblical metaphor of the Trinity.

Mark's deep regret is narrated through retelling two romances: *Ereck and Enide* by twelfth century French writer Chreatian de Troyes and *Romance of the Rose* by thirteenth century writer Guillaume de Lorris. Lewis describes Mark's remorse by using key words from medieval stories: "the hedge," "the roses," and "that fenced garden."[150] By roses, he means Jane, and by hedge, her humanity. Mark is ashamed of being a trespasser who does not notice the hedge, but plucks the roses, tearing them into pieces and crumpling them.

Lewis focuses on the individual transformation of the couple, Jane and Mark, by narrating the retold romance of *Ereck and Enide* to the contemporary reader. In a medieval romance, a lady is typically depicted as being seated at the center of an enclosed garden with roses, protected from being intruded on over the hedge. However, the lady in *Ereck and Enide*

---

149. Lewis, THS, 313.
150. Ibid., 379.

is not quietly seated. As the garden enclosed by the air is an expression of Ereck's egoistic love, so Mark's egoistic love involves his intrusion over the hedge. As Ereck is suspicious of Enide's love, he makes an adventurous journey with her. However, the modernist couple, Jane and Mark, do not act together, but rather individually undertake different adventures under the invisible guidance of Merlin. Although Enide is prohibited from communicating by speaking out of love for Ereck, she breaks the rule to warn to him of an approaching danger, resulting in a successful journey.

Lewis emphasizes each couple's process to discover their self-identities, Mark's failure to comprehend Jane's spiritual gift as a visionary dreamer, and the simultaneous rehabilitation of both vocation and sexual relationship. Jane is not prohibited from communicating, but is faced with a communication barrier. She experiences the limitation of human language as a writer and as a wife. She fails to write the thesis and to love her husband. However, in her extreme misery, she unwittingly becomes aware of a hereditary power of seeing "real things"[151] in her dreams, and it is this power that breaks her communication barrier.

Jane mistakenly accuses Ransom of sexism as she has a prejudice against men. Through a debate on sexuality with Ransom, Jane questions her own modernist concept of binary selection—man or woman, work or marriage—but is still confused by his concept of sexuality, because he attributes the cause of her losing Mark to her failure to try "obedience."[152] By obedience, she means blind submission, but he means a dance: "obedience and rule are more like a dance than a drill—specially between man and woman where the roles are always changing."[153] As he serves as the "Pendragon" ("dragon's head" in Celtic) of St. Anne's, she identifies Ransom as a sexist who is against women as if a male head ruled over the female body. She feels "annoyed" and "ashamed" to see a female member of St. Anne's "courtsying" to Ransom.[154]

To Ransom's evaluation, Jane responds from four perspectives: in the first she is receptive to Ransom, in the second she is disgusted with the first Jane, in the third she is emotionally unknown to herself, and in the fourth

---

151. Ibid., 64.
152. Ibid., 145.
153. Ibid., 147.
154. Ibid., 139.

she is joyous.[155] These divided and multiple minds enable her to recognize "the Person" or the earthly Venus who stands in the garden at St. Anne's.[156]

The garden is equivalent to the Person as an invisible shape or "a boundary"[157] for Jane and Mark to cross. For Jane, it is Ransom's comment on sexuality, "obedience" as dance, and for Mark, it is accepting Jane as a personality. Jane is mysteriously charmed by the Person to be awakened in the garden of St. Anne's, while Mark is enchanted by the magician Merlin to be asleep and awakened in prison. The prisoner encounters the same "Person" of the garden at St. Anne's. Merlin deconstructs the old concept of pre-historic and classical gardens, while the Person recreates the new image of gardens through a story of the recreation of the married couple.

The boundary for Mark is a test of whether or not he can depend on Jane, whose personality is filled with both femininity and masculinity. Through a fear of death while in prison, he, for the first time, can think of Jane, imagine her happiness, and consider himself a foolish intruder into Jane's life as if into an enchanted garden: "which he could not enter but could have spoiled."[158] When Mark takes up the challenge as his test, he encounters the Person or earthly Venus in the garden at St. Anne's where he feels guilty for damaging Jane, like a trespasser over "that fenced garden."[159] He restores the aesthetic sense of sexuality in a room at the cottage in the garden: "with food and wine and a rich bed."[160]

Merlin's relationship with Jane and Mark is biblically associated with the creation of Adam and Eve. The Scripture tells us that God created Eve while Adam slept (Genesis 2: 21–22). Just as Adam is asleep, suggestive of death, during the creation of Eve, so too is Mark asleep/dead while Jane is re-created. Mark is charmed to sleep by Merlin, while Jane is given a new life by the Person (Venus) in the garden of St. Anne's: "'Surge, miselle,' (Get up, wretched boy) he said, helping Mark to his feet."[161]

Although God directly brings Eve to Adam, Merlin indirectly connects Jane and Mark. He sends a written message to Mark via a member of St. Anne's, Denniston. The memo informs Mark that Jane expects him:

155. Ibid., 148–49.
156. Ibid., 315.
157. Ibid.
158. Ibid., 244–45.
159. Ibid., 379.
160. Ibid., 380.
161. Ibid., 225–26.

"Your wife awaits you at the manor at St. Anne's on the hill."[162] Merlin acts through the community of St. Anne's: Jane and Mark are re-created through the simultaneous guidance of both the human communication of Denniston, a scholar of St. Anne's, as well as the spiritual guidance of Merlin, the Person, and Ransom.

When Mark and Jane are newly inspired by Merlin, the modernist couple individually reconsider their married life, no longer regarding it as an automatic tool to restore lost passions for social success and profession, but as a context for a harmonious relationship. They are presumably challenged by accepting their vocations as a heavenly gift, Jane being a successor in the role of King Arthur and Mark in the role of her companion, similar to Merlin. The couple is rehabilitated vocationally and sexually through their encounter with gardens in the shape of Merlin, Ransom, and the Person.

---

162. Ibid., 226.

— 4 —

Medieval Paradise
East, West, and Beyond

The Voyage of the Dawn Treader (*VDT*) (1952) is a contemporary *mappa mundi*, a depiction of not only the medieval romance of sailing to the west, but also the imram (old Irish tale) to the west. This proposition of multiple interpretations of directions will reveal C.S. Lewis as a novelist of Christian postmodernism in the sense that he uses the postmodernist literary approach of simultaneously revealing to the reader multiple directions in the contemporary world and embracing the supernatural guidance of God, who transcends human interpretations. Based on Charles Huttar's proposal of imram as a voyage to the ultimate goal beyond any earthly direction, east and west,[1] and Mary Zambreno's adaptation of medieval desires for multiplicity, this paper will further their viewpoints and reveal *VDT* as a modern *mappa mundi*, an illustration of each voyager's pilgrim course and beyond, in a comparison of *VDT* with the medieval romances for the east and imram for the west.

C.S. Lewis revives the medieval imagination counter to the general perception of the Middle Ages as undeveloped and modernity as the successful result of rational thought, as Matthew Innes redefines the medieval time as the revived marginalization after the Classical era (Greek-Rome).[2] Just as multiple images of the magician Merlin asleep in the garden re-

---

1. Huttar, "'Deep Lies the Sea-longing' (1)," 5.
2. Innes, *Introduction to Early Medieval Western Europe, 300–900*, 7.

vealed in chapter 3, the multiple directions of the ship the *Dawn Treader* are a reflection of the postmodernist sensibility in *VDT*. In the third book of the Narnian series, although it is popularly known as a children's fantasy, Lewis writes to overcome any inhibitions in the minds of both children and grown-ups.[3] He is referring to the limitation not only of humanity, but also the human language and the literary genre.

The voyagers of the *Dawn Treader* depart for "the Utter east,"[4] but ultimately return to the west, toward the land of Narnia, except for Reepicheep and the children.[5] Reepicheep is the only one who goes beyond the furthest utter east. The three children return to their own world, neither east nor west. In the contrasting directions of east, west, and beyond, Lewis suggests that the other world lies in neither human direction, but transcends the contradictory elements of limited human language.

Other distinct postmodernist strategies in *VDT* are the notions of the Kingdom of God, the undulations of the ship, and the transforming self-identities of the voyagers. The Kingdom of God in *VDT* is depicted not as having a political purpose, but with a spiritual reason for a voyage in the past, a desire for the self-changing challenge of the voyage in the present, and a longing for another world in the future. According to *A Dictionary of the Bible*, "The kingdom of God" is not to be equated with a human Utopia, nor the rule of a political sovereignty.[6] The sea journey illustrates three time zones (past, present, and future) which are, individually, Lewis's multiple interpretations of the Kingdom of God: sea-faring people, search for missing friends, and longing for Aslan's Country.

Lewis focuses on the positive aspects to describe the changing situations throughout the voyage, as the ship is swallowed, drifted, and attacked by the ocean surges. The swallow, drift, and attack of the ocean, and their resulting movements of the ship, are used to reflect both living in a world of ambiguous values in our time and the change in Lucy's awareness of self-identity as a woman. Lucy, Queen of Narnia, who engages in many voyages, is the contemporary woman, socially and culturally challenged. Just as multiple values confuse the modern world, so the Narnian ship, the *Dawn Treader*, including the voyagers, is at the mercy of rolling, pitching,

---

3. Lewis, *On Stories*, 48.

4. Lewis, *The Voyage of the Dawn Treader* (*VDT*), 3

5. Lewis does not italicize the definite article "the" when it is used for the name of the ship, for example, "the *Dawn Treader* was the finest ship he had built yet" (*VDT* 30).

6. Browning, *A Dictionary of the Bible*, 844–47.

and swelling, as well as lulling of the wind. Lucy finds herself comfortable on the moving boards, rather than frightened by the billowing motion of the ship: "the motion of the ship did not worry her."[7]

In medieval romances, the limited geographical directions get blurred in meaning between geographical "east" and imaginative "west," until the two ideas are integrated. In *VDT*, Lewis employs such medieval values in order to write a story of another world beyond. In the literature of the Middle Ages, navigators sail east to find paradise in and beyond the east, which is overflowing with wealth and luxury. Among the medieval stories concerning the quest for the east are the collections including Alexander Romance, *The Letter of Prester John* (1165), and *The Travels of Sir John Mandeville* (circulated in the fourteenth century). In contrast to the east, the Irish medieval stories of voyaging, "Imram," concern the quest toward the west. *The Navigation of Brendan* (circa AD 800) is widely known as the typical "Imram,"[8] an old Irish voyage tale of Saint Brendan and his companions. The old Irish word "Imram" is usually translated as a "voyage" tale. In the old and Middle Irish narratives, travelers reach another world, supposedly located on islands in the Western ocean.[9]

In *VDT*, the immediacy of God's Kingdom is reflected by the voyage of the *Dawn Treader* in three ways, past, present, and future: respectively King Caspian's vision of the Narnians to be "sea-faring folk,"[10] his intention to look for friends missing in the Eastern Seas, and his knight Reepicheep's dream to find Aslan's country at the eastern end of the world.

King Caspian X decides to look for the seven missing lords who have been deposed by his Uncle Miraz. Not forgetting to save the missing friends, Caspian tells the nation to become "sea-faring folk once more."[11] After the death of Caspian's father, Caspian IX, Miraz rules Narnia as Lord Protector to support his young nephew, but Caspian later discovers that his father was assassinated by Miraz and that the seven lords loyal to his father have been exiled from Narnia.

King Caspian's mission is to seek out the seven lords, but Reepicheep has an even nobler goal. This knight desires to find Aslan's Country at the very eastern end of the world, always reciting a Dryad's poem: "There is the

---

7. Lewis, *VDT*, 26.
8. McKillop, *A Dictionary of Celtic Mythology*. n.pag.
9. According to McKillop, "Imram" is sometimes spelled "Immram."
10. Lewis, *VDT*, 30.
11. Ibid.

Medieval Paradise

utter *East*."[12] Aslan's Country is the home of the Great Lion Aslan, who is a central character in *The Chronicles of Narnia* series, although he does not always appear in the story. This heaven-like place is described as a series of mountains located beyond Narnia's rising sun at the eastern edge of the world.

VDT is a modern imram formulated from both Christian tradition and pre-Christian sea travel mythology: the former includes *The Voyage of Saint Brendan* (circa the ninth century), or "Naomh Breandan (*Navigator Brendan* in Irish)"; and the latter is the journey metaphor of *The Voyage of Saint Brendan*, likely modeled after what is classified as pre-Christian imrama: *The Voyage of Bran* (possibly written in the eighth century) and *The Voyage of Mael Duin's Boat* (composed around the eighth century and written in Irish around the tenth century).

The Voyage of Saint Brendan was one of the most influential books in medieval Europe. The old story is about a monk, Brendan, who was historically active around the sixth century and in mythology renowned for his legendary journey in a coracle, a small boat made of wickerwork, to "The Promised Land."[13] The narrative of Brendan is an oral history later recorded by Irish monks around the ninth century. Philip Sheldrake views the Brendan voyage to North America as the literary fruition of Ireland in the Middle Ages, although historically the Vikings may have arrived in the area earlier.[14]

A possible link has been suggested between *VDT* and *The Voyage of Saint Brendan*, but the literary link connecting the two tales has yet to be analyzed in detail. Walter Hooper speculates that Lewis had *The Voyage of Saint Brendan* in mind when he wrote a rough sketch of *VDT*.[15] David C. Downing elaborates on the literary influences on *The Chronicles of Narnia* not only from Saint Brendan, but also the biblical book of Revelation in addition to other literary sources.[16] Salwa Khoddam has also discovered the same motif as *VDT* in the story of Saint Brendan,[17] while Charles

---

12. Ibid., 31.

13. O'Meara, trans, *The Voyage of Saint Brendan: Journey to the Promised Land*, 67.

14. Ibid., 62.

15. Hooper, *C.S. Lewis: A Companion & Guide*, 403.

16. D. C. Downing, *Into the Wardrobe*, 48.

17. Khoddam, "The Enclosed Garden in C.S. Lewis's *The Chronicles of Narnia*," n.p. Khoddam also suggests reading the unpublished paper on the same motif by D. C. Downing which was presented at Oxbridge in 2005.

Huttar finds a parallel between J.R.R. Tolkien and Lewis in their way of using inherited myths, *The Voyage of Saint Brendan* being an example.[18] In this paper, a comparison of *VDT* and *The Voyage of Saint Brendan* will demonstrate Lewis's postmodernist approaches to the Kingdom of God and his wish to rehabilitate a longing for the other world beyond imperfect humanity.

THE IMMEDIACY AND FUTURE OF THE KINGDOM OF GOD

In *VDT*, Lewis gives a full description of the paths taken by each of the five groups of main characters travelling in multiple directions. The reader is reminded of an intricate liaison which may stir a sense of awe and eternity leading to an understanding of the Kingdom of God. The track of each protagonist's movement is not visibly discernable, but the interlacing image of their different trails arouses a "numinous" sensation in the reader, as if the presence of a divinity is felt from the intricate patterns of Celtic spirals. The term "numinous" feeling is a religious composite which Rudolph Otto defines as "daemonic dread."[19]

The five units of protagonists include the personified ship, *Dawn Treader*, that circles between east and west; the three British children, Lucy, Eustace, and Edmund as a collective company, who infiltrate the world of Narnia; the talking mouse/knight, Reepicheep, who makes a direct advance to the utter East; the two *VDT* story-tellers who unpredictably jump between fact and fiction; and lastly, Aslan, who makes epiphanic manifestations in multiple forms: cave wall, bird, sheep, lion, door, and voice.

The network of the characters' paths causes the reader an indescribable perception, in the same way Lucy feels at the World's End. The female protagonist in *VDT* is so filled with a mysterious sense that she cannot explain it in words, but instead paraphrases it in an image, "a dim, purple kind of smell,"[20] and she is silent as her happiness is beyond description: "too happy to speak."[21]

---

18. Huttar, "'Deep Lies the Sea-longing' (1)," n.p.
19. Otto, *The Idea of the Holy*, 45.
20. Lewis, *VDT.*, 206.
21. Ibid., 30.

On the surface, all of the characters seem to have equal voices, but Aslan, the true central character in *The Chronicles of Narnia*, surreptitiously orchestrates the whole of the cosmos, including the reader's world.

The Dawn Treader

The Narnian voyage is characterized by both a longing for antipodes as well as numinous sensations. The ship, the *Dawn Treader*, navigates to antipodes of east and west in a different style from either east or west in traditional voyages of the Middle Ages. In the Brendan imram, the ship sails westwards for the paradise of Tir na n'Og, the land of youth in Irish, while medieval romances from the continent navigate east to find their imaginative paradises, including "Indie," "Catai," and "Jepang." The *Dawn Treader* circulates between the east and the west, contrary to King Caspian's wish to sail beyond the utter East for the Country of Aslan where the son of the Great Emperor exists. As Thomas Cahill writes, Europeans of the Middle Ages had a desire for antipodes due to various cultural contacts with the eastern world, including the Islamists (the seventh to fifteenth centuries), the Tatars or Mongols (the thirteenth century), and *The Travels of Marco Polo* (the fourteenth century).[22]

As a scholar of medieval literature, Lewis adapts these colliding factors to appreciate a desire for another world beyond reality. The contrasting directions in *VDT* are considered as his literary approach to stir a longing for another world. The repetitive traveling pattern of Brendan's imram causes contrasting qualities of the daunting and the fascinating. A mysterious composite, similarly evident in the modern imram, *VDT*, reminds us of the contrast labeled by Rudolf Otto as "daemonic dread."[23] The German philosopher compares the numinous feeling to the religious development produced during the long pauses in German composer Johann Sebastian Bach's church Mass music: "the holiest, most numinous moment in the Mass..."[24]

This numinous sensation of *VDT* is similar to the consciousness produced by the triple spiral of a Celtic pattern. Philip Sheldrake associates the cyclical quality of the pattern with the liturgical motion of Brendan's

---

22. Cahill, *Mysteries of the Middle Ages*, 264.
23. Otto, *The Idea of the Holy*, 45.
24. Ibid., 85.

voyage, asserting that the Irish monk's course represents the link between reality and another world: "beyond the experience of everyday life."[25]

Charles Huttar connects the imagery of sunrise in the East with the resurrection of Christ.[26] He states that Christ is symbolically associated with "the sun" of righteousness: "But unto you that fear my name shall the Sun of righteousness arise with healing in his wings; and ye shall go forth, and grow up as calves of the stall" (Mal. 4:2 KJV); and the Apostle John calls Jesus Christ the true Light: "That was the true Light, which lighteth every man that cometh into the world" (John 1:9). Paul compares the dawn with the immediacy of the Kingdom of God: "The hour has come for you to wake up from your slumber . . . Rather, clothe yourselves with the Lord Jesus Christ" (Rom. 13:11–14).

The *Dawn Treader*, however, navigates in one direction, east, while receiving guidance from not one star but from multiple "stars," including Coriakin, Ramandu, and his daughter. Unlike the biblical account of the Magi, travelers from the east guided westwards by one special Star to the infant Jesus, modern travelers are guided by multiple stars suggestive of the contemporary world.

Reepicheep

Reepicheep, one of the voyagers, functions as an integrated image of both myth and Gospel. As the destiny of Christ is prophesized and fulfilled in the Bible, the fate of the mouse-knight is mysteriously predicted by a Dryad, or mythical Irish tree spirit, whose song inspires him to seek the utter East. The depiction of the mouse on a coracle going up the waterfall is suggestive of both Irish martyrdom and Christ's Crucifixion. There are two types of Irish martyrdoms, Green and White. Green Martyrdom is leaving behind the pleasures of human society and White Martyrdom is leaving the homeland of Ireland, never to return.

The fate of Reepicheep is not exactly described in the story, but his destiny is predicted by two mythological characters: one is a Dryad and the other is Star Man Ramandu. When the mouse/knight is born, a female spirit of the tree predicts that the baby will seek the utter East. Due to the Dryad's poem, Reepicheep willingly receives the Star Man's message as a

---

25. Ibid., 53.
26. Huttar, "'Deep Lies the Sea-longing' (1)," n.p.

Medieval Paradise

personal oracle: someone will have to be left behind in the utter East to break the enchantment holding the lords in oblivion.

The last scene with Reepicheep reminds the reader of the ascensions of two biblical prophets: Elijah (2 Kings 2:8) and Enoch (Gen. 5:24), in addition to Jesus Christ (Acts 1:9), are described in the Bible as disappearing alive into the Heavens. Just like them, Reepicheep disappears from this world. He moves not in the medieval way as he originally expects, the visible world dropping like a cataract at the end of flat land, but instead advances in a rising line. The valiant mouse unhesitatingly devotes his whole life to finding Aslan's Country in the utter East. David Downing associates Reepicheep with the Arthurian Legend for the Holy Grail.[27] Although Reepicheep is witnessed by the three outsiders—Lucy, Edmond, and Eustace—paddling his coracle and being lifted up the sides of the waves, his last destination is not clearly indicated. It is, however, indirectly suggested by the narrator: the mouse is at Aslan's Country.

Just as Elijah and Jesus are biblically associated with the image of water, so Lewis connects the waves (waterfalls) with "the Cross" of Christ. In *The Great Divorce* (1945), Lewis writes the personified waterfall as if it has been crucified: "like one crucified."[28]

The last motion of Elijah, a prophet of Samaria in the ninth century BC, is his miracle of pouring out water in sacrifice on Mt. Carmel (1 Kgs 18:32-35). The prophet is taken up into the Heavens after he divides the water to the right and to the left: "Then Elijah took his mantle and rolled it up, and struck the water" (2 Kings 2:8, NRSV). The humanity of Jesus Christ is depicted by his self-immersion into the waters of baptism, while his divinity is depicted by his control over water when he walks on it (Matt 14:22-23) and turns water into wine as a symbol of blood (John 2:1-11). David Downing associates Reepicheep with Elijah and Enoch who were taken up into heaven without dying.[29]

Just as the Israelites believe the words of the prophets regarding the Messiah's coming, Reepicheep is inspired by the prophecy of the utter East from a Dryad. Lewis makes repeated references to the mythological Dryads in all seven books in *The Chronicles of Narnia*. They are able to assume physical bodies similar to human form.[30] Each Dryad is spiritually tied to

---

27. D. C. Downing, *Into the Region of Awe*, 137.
28. Lewis, *The Great Divorce*, 49.
29. D. C. Downing, *Into the Region of Awe*, 137.
30. Lewis, *Prince Caspian*, 170-71.

one particular tree, and if that tree is cut down, that particular Dryad will fall down, die, and disappear.[31]

The Dryad's prophetic, poetic song fills the mouse/knight with desire for the East. The short poem is composed of six lines in rhyme. Each ending of an "ee" sound emphasizes the close connection between Reepicheep and the utter East:

> Where sky and water *meet*,
> Where the waves grow *sweet*,
> Doubt not, *Reepicheep*,
> To find all you *seek*,
> There is the utter *East*.[32] (emphasis added)

The story of Reepicheep is a parallel to the pre-Christian story *The Voyage of Bran*, as both protagonists are set on their respective voyages by a female voice.[33] In *The Voyage of Bran*, one of the earliest Irish imrama (plural of imram in Irish), Bran and his followers make a sea journey to the Isle of Women and attempt to return home.[34] Unlike the old imram, the last destination for Reepicheep is not a place limited by gender: Bran returns to the earthly homeland, Ireland, while Reepicheep returns to a heavenly homeland, possibly Aslan's Country beyond human construction.

Through his quest for Aslan's country, Reepicheep embodies the synthesis of both myth (image of water) and history (word of prophecy). This character, guided by the Dryad's voice, is finally lifted up upon the waves, possibly to Aslan's Country. The *VDT* narrator is convinced that Reepicheep is the true dawn treader in Narnia and that the courageous knight might possibly be alive at Aslan's: "he came safe to Aslan's country. . ."[35] From the historical perspective of Narnia, Reepicheep is considered to live his whole life to fulfill the Dryad's prophecy.

Two Story-Tellers

The two story-tellers of *VDT* are not directly involved with each other, but their lives seem to be blessed by reciting the same story of the modern

---

31. Lewis, *The Last Battle*, 26.
32. Lewis, *VDT*, 22.
33. Meyer, ed. and trans., *The Voyage of Bran, Son of Febal, to the Land of the Living*, 2.
34. Cotterell, *A Dictionary of World Mythology*, 148.
35. Lewis, *VDT*, 268.

Medieval Paradise

imram as truth. Their paradoxical roles reflect Lewis's concept of Gospel in which he believes that myth comes true. Lewis affirms that the myths of pagan gods, risen from the dead, became historical fact when God was incarnated in the body of Jesus Christ.[36]

One story-teller is the persona "I," who acts both as a narrator and a character. His ambiguous roles that blur between fact and fiction, is another example of the embodiment of Lewis's notion of a Gospel in which myth is beyond reason and thought. This narrator is involved as a character in the story on only one occasion. The interaction between the three children and the narrator is mentioned in the last chapter: "*said I*, 'was it so sad?'" (emphasis added).[37]

The other storyteller is the sailor Pittencream. This minor character deserts the ship at the Lone Islands, goes to live in a different country, Calormen, and tells tales of the voyage of the *Dawn Treader* until he believes them himself. Calormen is an empire to the south of Archanland and Narnia[38]: "you may, say, in a sense, that he lived happily ever after."[39]

The cowardly man deserves criticism for his "inability to deal with reality,"[40] but he should be worthy of telling the truth about the voyage as a representation of the Kingdom of God. His tale seems to work as mythology—oral history as a tool of the truth, the roots of which are unknown in our age. With the exception of the false story of his courageous role, he conveys the truth of the voyage of the *Dawn Treader* which successfully fulfills the three missions of living as sea-faring people, searching for missing souls, and reaching the World's End. Paul Ford associates Pittencream with someone who is pitiful or a pittance.[41] He also introduces Thomas W. Craik's parallel between Pittencream and Pittenweem (a fishing village in Fife, Scotland) and with Macbeth's "cream-fac'd loon" (Act V, Scene 3) as Pittencream hangs back from volunteering for the adventure. He embodies images of both pity and adventure.

---

36. Lewis, "Myth Became Fact," 63–67.

37. Lewis, *VDT*, 265.

38. The term "Calormen" means men from a warm land: from the Latin "calor," meaning heart and the English "men" (Ford 92).

39. Lewis, *VDT*, 238.

40. Ford, *Companion to Narnia*, 315.

41. Ibid., 31.

Three Latecomers

In both imrama three people come late for the voyage, but each of the latecomers is individually judged. In *The Voyage of Saint Brendan*, three monks move within the same biblical world, while in the modern version, *VDT*, three children travel through different dimensions between the fictional world and the reader's world. They join the voyage from halfway beyond the modern world, but disembark the ship just after arriving at the utter East, and finally return to the reader's world. Just like the *Dawn Treader*, the visitors move in a circular motion, to finally return through time and space. The modern latecomers enter a new dimension in Narnia where people, similar to the medieval imagination, believe in a flat earth—the round earth is just a hypothesis. In chapter 15, King Caspian shares the Narnian fairy-tale about a round earth, confessing to the three visitors from the real round earth his long-time dream to see a different world: "If only I had the chance."[42] Caspian's dream comes true in *The Silver Chair* (1954).

Transportation to Narnia as well as the encounter with Aslan are unpredictable—the children are unpredictably transported to the *Dawn Treader*—but both sides welcome the reunion, except Eustace. The uncertainty of when to make the journey reveals that choice of time is not within the control of the characters on either side. The unpredictability of Aslan's appearance to the other characters suggests that the great lion is equivalent to a divine being, like Melchizedek. A king and priest, Melchizedek appears out of context in the Old Testament, mysteriously identified as the King of Salem and Priest of God Most High, with "having neither beginning of days nor end of life" (Heb. 7:3 NRSV).

The voyage is associated with two kinds of journey: those seeking an earthly adventure aboard the *Dawn Treader*, and those on a life trip to paradise, which individually responds to the Kingdom of God, past, present, and future: Eustace's encounter with Aslan in the present; Edmund and Lucy's developing relationship with Aslan in the past, present, and the future; and Reepicheep's possible entry into Aslan's Country, a dimension beyond time and space, in the future. From Aslan's point of view, the discussion of the three late-comers' transformation will reveal that the children are not latecomers, but just on time in Narnia to undergo a spiritual growth through navigation and through each encounter with Aslan.

---

42. Lewis, *VDT*, 251.

Medieval Paradise

The modernist boy, Eustace, embodies the spirit of nineteenth century society. Thomas Carlyle imaginatively regards the spirit as the "young Ismael." Ismael, Abraham's first son in Genesis 21, discovers himself in a wild desert: "howling with savage monsters."[43] In his imaginative autobiography, *Sartor Resartus* (1836), Carlyle states that the young Ishmael represents "self-help" in order to comply with his fear of the mechanized universe. Laura-Jane Meas affirms that this fear makes Ishmael react negatively to people who tend to converse with imaginative words.[44] The modern "Ishmael," Eustace, makes fun of his cousins who talk about Narnia. In the first chapter of *VDT*, the sinister boy deliberately attempts to provoke his cousins, Lucy and Edmund, while they enjoy talking about their memory of Narnia in front of a painting of a sailing boat. They are reminded of Narnia by looking at the boat.

Lewis fills the reader with multiple perspectives through describing not only the misery of Eustace, who discovers himself in a wild desert, but also his transformation from human-monster to dragon-monster and finally to human-boy. Just like young Ishmael, the rational thinker Eustace reacts in a similar way to his cousins who remember their days in Narnia. He teases them about it, thinking that they were making up a false story because he is "too stupid to make anything up."[45]

This agnostic monster constantly feels intimidated by being prone to failures of logic and reason. A prisoner of self-affirmation, which he never quite recognizes himself to be, he feels superior by enclosing himself inside a cocoon of in-communication with others and an inside unconscious abnormality of loneliness and powerlessness.

Eustace takes a negative attitude toward his cousins because of his disinterest in humanity as well as his hidden desire for communication. He assumes a contradictory attitude toward his "balmier" cousins[46]: he is indignant with their talk about Narnia, which he interprets as stupidly imaginative, but he cannot ignore them. Through communication with Lucy and Edmund, the monster boy is unexpectedly made to feel a hunger for something which he lacks but longs for. It is a kind of charity and compassion which he never records in his diary. He keeps a diary to find fault

---

43 Carlyle, *Sartor Resartus*, 250.

44. Meas, "The Nineteenth Century 'Disappearance of God': Perceptions of God in Hardy and Hopkins," 2.

45. Lewis, *VDT*, 5.

46. Ibid., 6.

with others, recording his evaluation of others in simple numbers as in an academic record. He speaks with abstract words, in a similar fashion to Dr. Wither in *THS*.

This modernist boy needs two kinds of help: one is supernatural intervention to change his self-recognition, the other is human support from Edmund. The modern Ishmael cannot change himself with self-help simply because he has a wish for change. The rationalist boy lacks the ability to realize his real desire as he undergoes three supernatural experiences: once when entering Narnia, next transforming himself into a dragon, and finally conversing with the great lion, Aslan.

Eustace reacts differently to each supernatural experience, from complete rejection and confusion to gradual change from hesitation to acceptance. He rejects accepting his three-dimensional experience as fact when he is drawn inside the painting of the sailing vessel. When transformed into a dragon, he lacks the self-understanding of being "a dragon" because he has no experience of reading old tales. When he meets the lion, he mysteriously hears "his" voice speaking—not audibly, but at the bottom of his heart, and he is not sure of the source of the voice.

The metamorphosis of Eustace, from "monster" to a new born "boy," is shown by the different voicing styles which are indicated in his diary. His diminishing selfishness is expressed by a monologue spoken from the perspective of Eustace, but his salvation is expressed through a dialogue with Edmund, who acts as a compassionate listener and a supporter who stands by to help him restore his self-identity.

Navigation on the *Dawn Treader* provides Edmund with deeper communication not only with himself, but other people, as well as with Aslan. Edmund grows spiritually by facing his past bitter experiences rekindled by the sight of the stone knife which reminds him of his past treachery in the previous story of *The Lion, the Witch and the Wardrobe (LWW)*. Through the voyage, the old traitor Edmund learns how to love Aslan and other people through supporting Eustace. When he joins the *Dawn Treader*, he is not completely aware of the ultimate purpose of the journey but gradually comes to understand as the voyage progresses. He tells Eustace that: the ship is sailing to "Aslan's country."[47]

Edmund grows by loving other people, as demonstrated in the exchange of empathetic dialogue with Eustace. Edmund uses the technique

---

47. Ibid., 125.

of "empathetic listening,"[48] when communicating with Eustace. Empathetic listening is, according to *The Dictionary of Personality and Social Psychology*, an ability to understand "another person's emotional experience."[49] One basic principle is to help one connect cognitively by a process of active listening in which what is thought to be heard is repeated back to the person to make certain it is understood. The other basic principle is to ask how the person feels about the situation. Whereas sympathy is "feeling for someone," empathy is "feeling as someone."[50]

Edmund can empathize with Eustace because he has had the same experience as the traitor. He can feel as Eustace does because of the regret over his own past sins against Aslan. In the first book of the Narnian series, *LWW*, Edmund deeply regrets betraying his family, Peter, Susan, and Lucy, to the White Witch in exchange for his desire for Turkish Delight. He gives great thanks to the Great Lion Aslan, who sacrifices himself to the Witch in order to redeem Edmund.

A remorseful heart transforms Edmund into a good listener. He is ready to compassionately listen to the new traitor, Eustace. Edmund lets Eustace choose where to talk: "anywhere you like. . ."[51] He cares for both the body and soul of Eustace by having him sit on a rock and express the joy of meeting again: "I am glad to see you."[52] He humbly manifests an understanding of his cousin's traumatic feelings: "You must have had a pretty beastly time."[53] He encourages Eustace to talk freely about his mysterious experience with the Lion, without interrupting him: "'Fire ahead,' said Edmund."[54] He patiently listens to him, waiting for him to finish his story: "with considerable patience."[55] He is more concerned about identifying how Eustace feels, taking into consideration how the boy wants to talk: "Is that all right now?"[56]

The dialogue allows Eustace to confess his doubts about the Lion. Although his cousin exposes negative feelings toward everything in the

---

48. Harre and Lamb, eds, *The Dictionary of Personality and Social Psychology*, 91.
49. Ibid.
50. Ibid., 92.
51. Lewis, *VDT*, 120.
52. Ibid.
53. Ibid.
54. Ibid.
55. Ibid., 121.
56. Ibid., 120.

world, including Aslan, Edmund does not reject these doubts. Eustace is finally able to make an apology for his past wrongdoings to Edmund: "I'd like to apologize. I'm afraid I've been pretty beastly."[57] After listening to Eustace, Edmund finally presents his own interpretation about the great Lion—that Eustace has met Aslan in the actual world: "you've seen Aslan."[58]

This empathetic dialogue leads to Eustace's essential question about Aslan: "'what do you think it was, then?'"[59] This question motivates Edmund to confess the secret of his own past mistake: "Between ourselves. . . . You were only an ass, but I was a traitor."[60] He adds his own conviction that Aslan knows him. The personal experience by Edmund makes Eustace ask the last question: "who is Aslan? Do you know him?"[61] Edmund shares his witness of salvation: "He is the great Lion, the son of the Emperor-beyond-the-Sea, who saved me and saved Narnia."[62]

Deep regret for past wrongdoings makes Edmund grow in wisdom, allowing him to ethically discern right from wrong. His remorse is once again tested when he sees the stone knife on Aslan's Table on Star Island. The knife reminds him of his past sins against the great Lion, Aslan, who was killed by the White Witch to redeem Edmund: "more and more uncomfortable."[63]

Edmund's growth is revealed in his meeting with a mysterious woman on Star Island. He tries not to let himself be blinded by her obvious beauty, because of his previous bitter experience with the White Witch in *LWW*. He, instead, cautiously but politely, tries to identify the woman: "things aren't always what they seem."[64]

Contrary to the allegorical role of the male-oriented medieval imram, Lewis depicts the complex nature of both men and women in *VDT*. The modern imram illuminates self-discovery in both males and females in contemporary society. Lewis shows not only Edmund's negative lesson from the White Witch and the positive lesson from Lady Star, but also

57. Ibid., 125.
58. Ibid.
59. Ibid.
60. Ibid.
61. Ibid.
62. Ibid.
63. Ibid., 221.
64. Ibid.

Medieval Paradise

Lucy's self-seeking voyage as psychological metamorphosis, similar to the "alchemical" process.

Lucy serves as the light of hope to the hopeless, making the invisible visible, but she suffers an inferiority complex about appearance similar to the monopod-dwarves on the Invisible Island.[65] The invisible dwarves function as a virtual image of Lucy.[66] Both are so confused about their ambiguous values of life that they misjudge self-image: the dwarves are physically invisible, while Lucy is spiritually invisible. The dwarves hate their appearance because they see themselves as ugly, so much so that they place themselves under a curse of invisibility. The male dwarves make themselves physically invisible as they misunderstand the role of self-identity: they are invisible not only to themselves, but also to others.

Lucy reconsiders her distorted image of herself by liberating the monopod-dwarves. She works, through reading a magic book, as if she is a magician. She is able to make not only the dwarves visible, but also the real image of herself. She is the liberator of the invisible dwarves, as well as herself. When she breaks the curse on them, her gift of light works to reveal not only the unique bodies of the dwarves, but also her hidden self-image. After their curse is broken, the dwarves are disappointed to see reality. They do not look as attractive as they expected—they are one-footed men like mushrooms. Lucy, however, has a different opinion. She sees the dwarves as "rather nice,"[67] because their jumping feet seem to her evidence of happiness and they are "perfectly contented"[68] with their lives. She concludes that their happy life is more important than their contradictory debates on appearance, even though they constantly express opposing opinions.

Until reaching the eastern edge, Lucy is troubled by the two conflicting natures in her mind. Reading "the Magic Book" on the Invisible Island works not only to release the dwarves from the curse of invisibility, but also to make Lucy's hidden inferiority complex visible. While reading aloud, she realizes that she has two selves inside her mind but has not yet faced up to her true self. Although she is faced with her true self by reading the magic book, she is not completely comfortable with the opposite principles inside herself.

---

65. Ibid., chapters 9–11.
66. Ibid., chapter 11.
67. Lewis, *VDT*, 182.
68. Ibid., 184.

On the water of the Eastern Sea, Lucy sees her divided selves integrated as if she is baptized by water. Water baptism is a symbolic burial in Christianity, by which the new Christian declares that they have died and are now beginning a new life in Christ. Lucy undergoes a similar process of death and life in the eastern water: "death" in her encounter with the Sea People, and new "life" through her meeting with the Sea Girl. In the water, she has an awakening experience as if she's seen the reflection of two natures integrated.

Lucy experiences, again, both death and life when she is on board the ship in the utter eastern sea. She almost loses consciousness when she is absorbed by the mysterious view of the Sea People in the water. She is, at the last minute, saved by a male voice when she is "leaning so long on the rail in one position."[69] She finds her arm goes figuratively "dead," while in Greek myths, the male sailors find themselves physically "dead" in a shipwreck. She is, however, awoken by a voice of her brother Edmund: "What are you staring at, Lu?"[70]

The divided personalities are healed through Lucy's encounter with the Sea Girl in the eastern sea: Lucy acts as a light (an alchemist-healer) and the Sea Girl as a shadow (the object of being healed). Unlike the other voyagers, she has the privilege of "only one short glimpse"[71] of the Sea People. She fears the other Sea People, but welcomes one of them, the little Sea Girl. As soon as Lucy meets that girl, she likes her and feels the girl likes her: "they had somehow become friends."[72]

Lewis creates the Sea Girl based on the Sirens of Greek mythology, but retells the fatal story of male sailors from a new angle, sailors both male and female. In Greek mythology, the Sirens lure sailors to shipwreck on the rocks with their hypnotic female voices. Lucy is lured not by a female voice, but by an enchanting view of the Sea People's hunting party, both male and female.[73]

The two girls, Lucy and the Sea Girl, are described as "opposite to one another"[74]: Lucy from above and the Sea Girl from the sea below. However opposite they are in dimension, they connect very deeply emotionally in

69. Ibid., 248.
70. Ibid., 247.
71. Ibid., 254.
72. Ibid.
73. Ibid., 247.
74. Ibid., 256.

that instant.⁷⁵ The fateful meeting of the two girls reminds the reader of Lewis's significant relationship with his best friend, Arthur Greeves, in Ireland.⁷⁶ The encounter between two girls like seems to be both the first and last time that she sees the girl at the utter East. There is, however, a suggestion that she is always with the girl: "There does not seem to be much chance of their meeting again in that world or any other."⁷⁷ This suggests that the two personalities are harmonized within her.

Lucy's search for self-discovery reveals the spiritual challenge of our modern world, in which the male and female are disintegrated at opposite poles. In Jung's terms, the opposites are called the anima, the female aspect present in the collective unconscious of men, and the animus, the male aspect present in the collective unconscious of women. Lucy is lost among the opposites created by an inferiority complex caused by her sister's beautiful appearance, her classmates' partiality, and her brothers' hierarchical attitudes. Her true self is discovered through a psychological metamorphosis similar to the alchemical process. Her meeting with the Sea Girl is the harmonization of two natures within herself: light (as an alchemist-healer) and shadow (as the object of being healed).

Lewis describes this self-transforming process with Jung's concept of Paracelsus—the integration of alchemy and healing. According to Jung, Paracelsus (1493–1541) was a Renaissance alchemist-healer who joined the two concepts—alchemy and healing—and explained the conflicting elements in transition through the depiction of two combined tales: the French legend of Melusine and the Sirens of Greek mythology.

Melusine is a feminine spirit of water in sacred springs, who has healing power. She is usually depicted as a woman who is a serpent or fish.⁷⁸ In *Psychology and Alchemy* (1944), Jung introduces the integration of animus and anima in Fig. 132,⁷⁹ the woman with a fish body in Fig. 157,⁸⁰ and the Melusina on the tree in Fig. 257.⁸¹ He states that Paracelsus regards the

---

75. Ibid.

76. Lewis, *Surprised by Joy*, 151–52.

77. Ibid., 255.

78. The most famous literary version of Melusine tales was compiled by the fourteenth century French poet Jean d'Arras into a collection of "spinning yarns" as told by ladies at their spinning. The tale was translated into English c. 1500.

79. Jung, *Psychology and Alchemy*, 259.

80. Ibid., 305.

81. Ibid., 459.

philosopher's stone as a light to show Christ. Just like Paracelsus, Lucy tries to make the philosopher's stone into the light. As if she is an alchemist, she makes visible the hidden identity of the monopod-dwarves and that of herself. As the light of hope, she can heal any injury instantly with a magical cordial, a heavenly gift from "Father Christmas."[82] She cures the injured Edmund, Narnians in the battlefield,[83] the wounded Reepicheep at the Battle of Beruna,[84] and also the seasick Eustace.[85]

As the mirror of Lucy, the Sea Girl is a perfect healer living in the sweet-tasting water of the utter East; the sweetness is suggestive of eternal life. Lucy sees the anima of herself in the Sea Girl. Her inner self is spiritually integrated with the Sea Girl into one full personality. The two girls are physically separated, but spiritually connected, as their union in the future is suggested.

Narnian Voyager of Christian Postmodernism

The combination of two contradictory goals in *VDT*, an ultimate goal and an earthly destination, embodies the approach of Christian postmodernism. The three children on the last island is similarly the embodiment of two conflicting worldviews, myths integrating with Scripture.

The journey of the three visitors from the *Dawn Treader* to the last island, "Lamb Island," is a depiction of both Green and White Irish Martyrdoms, as well as the biblical resurrection. The Green Martyrdom of Ireland is the medieval Irish monks leaving behind the pleasures of human society for the sake of their honor to retreat to a lonely place, while the White Martyrdom is leaving of their homeland, Ireland, in order to reach another country with the Christian message, but never to return home. As Thomas Cahill states, the Green Martyrdom was a solution for the Irish who had no Irish martyrs in their early history of Christianity, or no Red Martyrdom by blood.[86] Columcille was an Irish monk of the sixth century who founded a monastery on the Island of Iona where *The Book of Kells*, an illuminated manuscript Gospel book in Latin, together with Celtic knots, was made.

---

82. Lewis, *The Lion, the Witch, and the Wardrobe* (*LWW*), 111.
83. Ibid., *LWW*, 193.
84. Lewis, *Prince Caspian*, 223.
85. Lewis, *VDT*, 36.
86. Ibid., 283.

Medieval Paradise

The three voyagers similarly leave their community, the *Dawn Treader*, change onto a small boat, representing White Martyrdom, and walk into the water from the boat to a lonely island, representing Green Martyrdom, where they find a lamb preparing breakfast for them. The story of meals at the waterside is biblically associated with those of Jesus Christ after His Resurrection (John 21: 9–12). As the disciples recognize Him, so the three children finally see the lamb transformed into Aslan.

VDT keeps balance in the unbalance in the sense that each character individually takes a different course, reflecting the multiple values of our time, but they all share a longing for Aslan's Country. Although the main characters temporarily share the same experiences on board the *Dawn Treader*, each individually travels in a different direction and moves through a different route: Caspian X and his men go to the east to look for the missing lords, but come back to the west to break the enchantment over three sleeping lords; Reepicheep enters into a different dimension; Pittencream runs away from the voyage but unintentionally makes a mythological contribution; and the three latercomers, Lucy, Edmund, and Eustace, join the voyage at the halfway point of the journey and return to their world.[87]

The voyagers have limited information about the east, even though they are excited about the mission. The ship departs toward the east without knowing the exact course they should take and which way to go in their search for their missing friends. As King Caspian and his voyagers have no information about the eastern sea, they have to depend on rumors and legends about the sea ahead, which they can only gather from fishermen. One fisherman talks about Aslan's country beyond the end of the world, which he has heard from his father. The information gathered sounds unreliable for navigation, but spiritually encouraging to the reader because they are reminded of the islands visited by St. Brendan and his companions: "the islands inhabited by headless men..."[88]

The *Dawn Treader* is a medieval sailing vessel, without the modern navigation tools of map and compass. In spite of such insufficient information, King Caspian is not hesitant about sailing forward because of his oath to the nation and Aslan, as well as Reepicheep's noble ambition. He decides to clear the port of Doorn Island: "I have an oath,"[89] and "what could I

---

87. Lucy and Edmund will never return to Narnia, but Eustace will come back again later (as in *The Silver Chair*).

88. Lewis, *VDT*, 67.

89. Ibid., 77.

say to Reepicheep?"[90] As the voyage progresses, the voyagers unexpectedly receive magical support from another world that includes the three children from the modern world, the real stars (Coriakin, Ramandu, and his daughter), and Aslan in different forms (rock, bird, and light).

Spiritually, Lucy is a kind of priest who conveys petitions to God. She supports the other voyagers in the same crisis by praying to Aslan. She shouts for help when all the voyagers become desperate on the Dark Island: "Aslan, Aslan... send us help now."[91] Magician Coriakin on Invisible Island produces a magical map of the Eastern Ocean for Captain Drinian. This map drawn on parchment looks like a three dimensional picture of the medieval mappa mundi (picture map): the first maps made "without Magic."[92] The Star Man Ramandu informs the voyagers of the way to break the enchantment over the sleeping lords as if he is a prophet of the Old Testament talking about the savior. His daughter gives, like the Holy Spirit, rest, peace, and help to the four lords (the three sleepers in addition to Lord Rhoop who is saved on Dark Island). As she is not given a particular name, she is called "Lady Star" by the author.

All of these courses are combined to produce a heavenly destination. The motif sounds similar to the repetition of a Celtic design in *The Book of Kells* in Lewis's homeland. This complex design is the expression of Christian symbolism in a longing for the Kingdom of God. Each character in *VDT* is a depiction of mesmerizing stories similar to the pattern of *The Book of Kells*, while sharing a longing for Aslan's Country. The repetitive theme is the expression of what David Downing calls "balance in the unbalance."[93] Downing focuses on Lewis's literary stance, by adapting T.S. Eliot's poetry *Four Quartet*, revealing that Lewis is willing to use "decentering strategies at the operational level, while rejecting self-canceling denials about the possibility of 'a still point in the turning world.'"[94]

THE EAST, THE WEST, AND BEYOND

VDT is a spiritual adventure to another world beyond east and west: a composite of both a medieval sea romance and an imram pilgrimage. Medieval

90. Ibid.
91. Ibid., 206.
92. Ibid., 194.
93. D. C. Downing, "C.S. Lewis among the Postmodernists," n.p.
94. Ibid.

Medieval Paradise

consciousness in Europe lies within an imaginative circle; Jerusalem in the east being at the center of the universe. Just as in the east the sun rises, so the same direction is associated in this story, as the title *The Voyage of the Dawn Treader* suggests. The voyagers are supposed to go in the same direction—east—as the ship's name also indicates: dawn as the first light before sunrise, and to tread is to walk. Irish literature about voyages, on the contrary, head to the west beyond the sunset. Far to the west beyond the edges of the map, the imram seeks Tir na nOg or "the Land of the Young" in Irish. An analysis of medieval literature will reveal that *VDT* is a story of navigation heading for another world beyond the east and the west.

Eastern Paradise

Lewis equates earthly paradise in the remote East to the medieval Alexander romance.[95] "Alexander romances" are a body of legends about Alexander the Great. An Alexander romance is an account of the career of Alexander the Great, or Alexander III, based on an historical core but consisting, in the main, of fictional elements.[96] In his book on medieval literature, *The Discarded Image* (1964), Lewis claims that the romance is the basis of the *mappa mundi* (a medieval map of the world in Latin) and Prester John's country.[97] The book refers to medieval sources including the *mappa mundi* (which Lewis spells as mappemounde) and Prester John.[98] Analysis of the medieval books which underlie the Narnian voyage will reveal that the significance of the "east" is not limited to that particular direction.

Although Alexander the Great is a historical figure, Alexander romance is not limited to a history of Western Europe, nor is it a story situated in the Middle Ages. Since the time of Alexander the Great, the romance has undergone numerous translations and revisions into a flexible form of literature. In medieval England, Alexander romance was popular, even referred to in Chaucer's *Canterbury Tales*. Based on George Cary's *The Medieval Alexander* (1956),[99] Lewis states that *The Alexander Romance* was

---

95. Lewis, *The Discarded Image*, 67.

96. Gagarin and Fantham, eds., *The Oxford Encyclopedia of Ancient Greece and Rome*, 62–64.

97. Lewis, *The Discarded Image*, 144.

98. Ibid., xxxiii.

99. George Cary's monograph, a revised version of his dissertation, *The Medieval Alexander* (1956), is the major foundation for study of Alexander in medieval writing.

written before the year 500, and Latinized in the twelfth century as the *Iter ad paradisum*.[100]

The Alexander Romance is part of several collections of legends concerning the adventures of Alexander the Great. The unknown author of the story is referred to as Pseudo-Callisthene. The Latin version serves as the source for many of the medieval Hebrew Alexander romances.[101] Medieval geographical knowledge of the east expanded with the campaigns of the Crusades, commercial voyages, and the pilgrimages. One example is Franciscan missionaries who visited China during the Yuan Dynasty in the thirteenth century, and another is *The Travels of Marco Polo* written by Rustichelo da Pisa based on the stories told by Marco Polo, who visited Asia in the thirteenth century.

In a similar way to Alexander romance, Lewis expresses a longing for another country in the east by highlighting Prester John's country and the paradise in the remote east beyond. He reads the English version of *Letter of John Prester* by Richard Eden, the sixteenth century translator in England, who accounts for another country beyond Prester John's as a place in Africa considered to be "the earthly paradise."[102]

Prester John is a legendary figure of the east from the medieval period. He is considered a descendant of one of the Magi, the three biblical wise men or kings from a place far from Europe. Their country is believed to be located somewhere far to the East and reigned by a Christian ruler. It is not specified where the Magi came from. It might not be a single country, but rather multiple countries. The Magi are actually a group from another country who visited Jesus and brought to him three gifts: gold, frankincense, and myrrh. The Gospel of Matthew mentions that the Magi came "from the East" to worship the Christ "born King of the Jews" (Matt. 2:1–12 NRSV). Although the story does not specify the exact number of visitors, the three gifts have led to an assumption that there were three men.

Prester John's Letter (*The Letter*) was popular in Europe in the twelfth century. *The Letter* composed of copies of a letter from this priest-king was

---

Regarding the sources of the Alexander legend, Alexander scholar Emily Rebekah Huber depends on Cary's catalogues in his book which Lewis read. General sources for Alexander in literature have been compiled by Huber (University of Rochester) at "The Medieval Alexander Project (MAP)," http://www.lib.rochester.edu/camelot/Alexander/alexgen.htm

100. Lewis, *The Discarded Image*, 144.
101. Cary, *The Medieval Alexander*, 118–42.
102. Lewis, *The Discarded Image*, 67.

Medieval Paradise

originally addressed to the Byzantine emperor Manuel Comnenus. However, the work is known today to have been a fictitious account which originated in Western Europe. Its author is thought likely to be a Westerner and not an Asian. The author's purpose for writing the book remains unclear. The important message of the letter is that a lost kingdom of Nestorian Christians still exists in Central Asia. At the time of the conflict caused by the Crusades, it was considered by medieval society that "Prester John" would come to the aid of Christians in the West. This fictional letter describes a paradise-like land overflowing with opulence and splendor, as well as rather strange but wonderful inhabitants. Medieval people must have believed that there were such beasts and monsters, including the monopods or creatures with a giant foot, beyond the realms of their own communities.

Lewis's idea of the monopods probably came from reading the legends of Prester John, and also looking at the drawing of Sciapots, a people with one giant foot, in the Hereford Mappa Mundi. Brian Sibley presumes that Lewis may have underlined the monopods' appearance on drawings of the one-foot dwarf from the medieval map in Hereford Cathedral.[103] In chapters 9–11 of *VDT*, the Monopod-dwarves are described as living with the magician Coriakin on a small island in the far eastern ocean, near the edge of the Narnian world. The dwarves have one three-foot-long leg with a large foot attired in a boat-shaped shoe. When they sleep, each dwarf lies on his back with his foot in the air, creating a mushroom-like shape.

The explorers of *Prester John*'s legend discover the unusual creatures in the east, while the Narnian voyagers re-discover the value of the unusual inhabitants in the east. King Caspian's mouse/knight, Reepicheep, re-interprets the single foot of the Monopods as a natural raft. He gives them on-the-spot training on how to use their foot. Reepicheep is a good educator in drawing forth the potential of his students. He patiently instructs, guiding them with a show-and-tell lesson by paddling himself in his own miniature coracle boat until the creatures get interested in their hidden abilities.

As the Prester John legend emphasizes the east, *The Travels of Sir John Mandeville*, is another contributor to the significance of "east." Paradise is not limited to the east in *Prester John's Letter*, as Mandeville also places paradise not only in Prester John's country, but also other locations such as Abissinia, in what is modern-day Ethiopia. Lewis writes that Mandeville puts paradise "beyond Prester John's country."[104]

---

103. Sibley, *The Land of Narnia*, 86.
104. Lewis, *The Discarded Image*, 144.

John Mandeville is the first writer to introduce the myth of Prester John to European readers. *The Travels of Sir John Mandeville* was compiled by Mandeville in fourteenth century England, being attributed to "Sir John Mandeville," the name claimed by the compiler. This text is part of a book of purported travels, published between 1357 and 1371, which presented a series of picturesque fables about the east.

In chapter 30 of *The Travels of Sir John Mandeville*, the compiler describes the affluent estate of Prester John as a paradise. Originally written in Anglo-Norman French, the accounts were translated into many languages and became popular during medieval times. These stories fascinated the Europeans, as did the stories of Marco Polo, and the book was often used as a reference. It is said that Christopher Columbus was influenced by this work when planning his voyage of the discovery of the Americas.

The medieval map of the world, *mappa mundi*, looks useless from the perspective of a twenty-first century sailor, but the vision of the unique map is not for practical navigation, but represents the cartographer's longing for the Kingdom of God. Medieval people knew that maps of the world, generally called T-O or tripartite maps, were of no use for navigation, but the *mappa mundi* served to motivate voyagers to depart for unknown destinations in the east. Lewis assumes that the medieval map is not practical, but voyagers with the *mappa mundi* must have been encouraged to venture east: "They are not going to steer by it."[105]

The Narnian map of the Eastern Ocean is similarly incomplete, but it is inspiring to the voyagers heading eastward. The magician Coriakin makes a magical three dimensional map of the Eastern Ocean by asking Captain Drinian to detail their voyage. The captain's memory of the journey graphically appears on magical sheets of parchment. As the map is a result of Drinian's limited information, coastal lines out of his sight are obscurely pictured or not included. Coriakin is not so omniscient as to be able to imagine seas and lands further east: "the Magician could tell them nothing about seas or lands further east."[106]

On the medieval T-O maps, paradise in the east is marked as "mappa mundi." Lewis uses the *mappa mundi* in his comparison of the medieval illustration of earthly paradise to "a jewel" and to "the noble art of cosmography."[107] The T-O maps place east at the top, hence the term

---

105. Ibid., 144.
106. Lewis, *VDT*, 194–95.
107. Lewis, *The Discarded Image*, 144.

"orienting"—a map from the Latin word "orients" for east. "Jerusalem" is placed at the center and "the Garden of Eden" is imagined beyond the east. The T-O maps are one of the four types of *mappae mundi* (plural of mappa mundi). The words derive from the Latin words for medieval European maps of the world: *mappa* meaning cloth or char, and *mundi* meaning the world. T-O maps illustrate the habitable portion of the world. The land masses are surrounded by the ocean, which is illustrated as a circle (an "O") and is divided into three portions by a "T"-shaped channel. These three divisions include the continents of Asia, Africa, and Europe.

The image of "east" during the Middle Ages is variable depending on social, cultural, and religious upheavals, especially with the failure of the Crusades. For Europeans, direct contact with new cultures, especially Islamic values, spurred contrasting emotions, in which curiosity and fear were mixed. The mixed feelings among medieval minds probably affected the expansion and revision of the legends of *Prester John*.

Western Imram

During an Imram, an adventurous Irish voyager sails west. St. Brendan, the protagonist and hero of the Irish medieval voyage literature, *The Voyage of Saint Brendan* (*VSB*), heads for "the Blessed Island," the earthly paradise in the west. Lewis, however, asserts that the real motivation for St. Brendan heading west lies in his search for the imaginative country of "Cathay": "Explorers sailed west to find rich Cathay."[108] He finds the imram neither confined to east nor west, but another world beyond earthly destinations.

St. Brendan is a legendary Irish saint of the fifth century from South West Ireland. His voyage is described to have gone west across the Atlantic in search of "the Blessed Island." *Navigatio Sancti Brendani*, the Latin version of the story of *St. Brendan*, was popularly read in the eleventh century. The earliest extant version of *VSB* was recorded circa 900 AD. The story includes not only the Christian narrative, but also narratives of natural phenomena and fantastic events and places, which appealed to a broad audience among medieval readers.

Lewis discovers an interesting attempt to locate any practical knowledge about the destination which Brendan may have acquired beforehand.[109] As Lewis states, it is certain that he had read "the interesting attempt" in

108. Ibid., 146.
109. Ibid., 144.

Land to the West (1962) by British historian Geoffrey Ashe. Lewis, however, seems to indicate that such empirical information was only of secondary importance to that of longing for an unknown country. He affirms that the success of the sea journey was not simply technical knowledge as it "may not have been completed by the saint himself."[110]

About ten years after Lewis passed away in 1963, British explorer Tim Severin succeeded in reproducing the legend of Brendan for the twentieth century world. In his non-fiction account of the trip, *The Brendan Voyage* (2000), he details building a small boat with wood and leather in the same way as Brendan, and setting sail from the west coast of Ireland in 1976. He was originally motivated by a practical investigation of *VSB*. However, when his wife Dorothy expressed puzzlement over the very detailed and realistic descriptions by Brendan, his motivation altered.[111] As Tim Severin was motivated by Dorothy's idea, Lewis would repeat his conviction as usual: "Even if such knowledge existed, it has no general influence on the medieval mind."[112]

Severin's success, however, inspired modern minds to reconsider the imram, *VSB*, which had long been ignored as a delusion. The comparison of two seafaring heroes, *VSB* translated by John J. O'Meara (1976) and *VDT* (1952), will reveal the voyage to be neither to the east nor west, but beyond—the world of Christian postmodernism.

In *VSB*, Brendan is warmly welcomed by the Invisible, while Caspian and his company, in *VDT*, become the target of attack by the Invisible. The medieval Invisible are friendly to the Irish monk and his Christian thoughts, while the modern Invisible are hostile to the multi-cultural voyagers, especially to their female visitor. The contemporary Invisible are opportunists who care little about the sacrifice of the female character, Lucy.

Brendan and his companions are led by the Invisible hands to the quasi-Eucharistic table with a fair linen cloth and a fresh loaf of bread. Caspian and the voyagers of the *Dawn Treader* are similarly feasted by the invisible people at the magician's estate. However, unlike the solemn and serene atmosphere at the dinner for Brendan and his companions, the banquet for Caspian and his company is interrupted by disruptive sounds. The invisible in the modern imram is a reflection of the feelings of uncertainty

---

110. Ibid.
111. Severin, *The Brendan Voyage*, 2.
112. Lewis, *The Discarded Image*, 144.

Medieval Paradise

and unease in the world of multiple values: "The meal would have been pleasanter if it had not been so exceedingly messy..."[113]

In the two voyages, the numbers three and seven are used symbolically with respect to the significance of their respective missions. Ethelbert W. Bullinger states that three and seven denote perfection: "Three denotes divine perfection; Seven denotes spiritual perfection."[114] During the seven year voyage, Brendan and his friends make repeated visits to the same islands on every one of the three religious seasons of Easter, Christmas, and Epiphany. In *VDT*, the combination of three and seven coexists within an ambiguous system.

Three children encounter Caspian again *three* years after the first meeting, but when the *three* siblings do not act together, each individually undergoes a spiritual metamorphosis via a private conversation with Aslan. *Three* years pass from when King Caspian sits on his kingdom throne, but just one year in the Pevensies' world. Time passes differently between Narnia and the reader's world. Lucy and Edmund have a reunion with Caspian, but not even one minute has passed in the twentieth century world.[115] Three lords out of seven are asleep on Star Island for *seven* years, but when Lord Rhoop joins the three earlier seafarers, four lords in total wait for the *Dawn Treader*. The numbering of *VDT* (a question of what among the Narnian series is the first or the third) is a hot academic debate. Peter Schakel argues that the different numbering gives the reader a different imaginative experience.[116]

In both the medieval and the modern imram, the main world seems to be in parallel and interlaced with another world. Between the two dimensions, there is one ambiguous and invisible boundary. The boundary looks more like a continuum. In Brendan's world, there is no clear separation between Ireland and the Promised Land, except for fog. Brendan goes through this element without noticing that he moves between the real and the supernatural. Both co-exist side by side along one continuum in the fog of Brendan's world.

The painting of a ship serves in *VDT* as the ambiguous sequence. The image in the frame is all but forgotten by the modernist owner, Eustace's

---

113. Lewis, *VDT*, 156.

114. Bullinger, *Number in Scripture*, 107.

115. Paul F. Ford presents a comparison of Narnian and earth time in *Companion to Narnia* (454–55).

116. Schakel, "The 'Correct' Order for Reading the Chronicles of Narnia?," 101.

mother, Alberta. She is not pleased with the artwork which she originally receives as a wedding present. Since it has been put away in the attic, to her the gift is invisible. The small object limited by a frame seems insignificant to her son, Eustace. The rationalist boy cannot believe what he sees, even though he empirically observes waves breaking out of the frame. He is so overcome with a panic that he tries to smash the frame, but finds himself standing in the sea: "waves rushing up to the frame as they might to a rock."[117] Although the painting of the ship is spiritually invisible to him, he physically moves between his world and another.

In both voyages, water is used to estimate the voyagers' sense of morality: the Soporific Well for the medieval monks (*VSB*) and the Death Pond for the modern companions (*VDT*). Both sets of voyagers are ignorant to the extent of their greediness. This results in them putting their lives in danger, both physical and spiritual. However, Brendan, the leader of the medieval navigators, is capable of asking God for rescue from the dangerous water, while Caspian, leader of the modern voyagers, fails morally to discern whether or not the water is right or wrong. The critical leadership of the modern voyage represents the confusing direction of the modernist rulers.

On Well Island, the Irish voyagers are challenged by water. Brendan's companions underestimate the weakness of human nature, thinking little of Brendan's warning against avarice. The disciples drink water as they wish and go to sleep. This sleepiness is a reflection of their failure to control aggressive desires: "Some of them drank one cup, others two, and the rest three. The last were overcome by a sleep of three days and three nights; others by a sleep of two days and two nights"[118]

The Narnian navigators are similarly enchanted, but by water that turns anything that anyone touches into gold. On Golden Water Island, which is later renamed "Death Water," they can see, deep in the water, the golden statue of a man who is actually the missing Lord Restimar. The two kings of Narnia, Edmund and Caspian, are overcome by their greed for gold and fight to claim the island for their own. This is a parallel to the story of King Midas in Greek mythology, a man so greedy that he wants to turn everything he touches into gold.

---

117. Lewis, *VDT*, 18.
118. O'Meara, trans., *The Voyage of Saint Brendan*, 33.

Medieval Paradise

At the last minute, Brendan prays to God to protect his companions.[119] Unlike Brendan, the Narnian leaders, Edmund and Caspian, are incapable of remembering Aslan at this most critical moment. Aslan, instead, appears just in time at this juncture to rescue them from fatal danger. Lucy is the first to notice Him: "Nobody dared to ask what it was. They knew it was Aslan."[120] The modern world is spiritually so numb that people are deprived of the power to communicate with God. In the time of eschatology, the end of the world, God must act first.

In the two imrama, a sharp contrast exists between the doomed and the blessed. The medieval tale presents the differing fates of two exiles living on separate islands, damnation in the case of apostate Judas and blessing in the case of the sufferer Paul. The modern imram contrasts two public servants of Narnia, the red-tape Governor Gumpas and the truthful deportee, Lord Bern. Although the medieval servants, Judas and Paul, are aware of the reason for their harsh lives, it is not clear whether the modern servants are faithful until King Caspian arrives on the island. By this depiction of the modern "servants," Lewis asks which servant awaits the king's return. The modern imram reminds the reader of Jesus's parable of a good steward in the Scripture: "Blessed is that slave whom his master will find at work when he arrives" (Luke 12:34, NRSV).

In *Brendan's Voyage*, two possible human destinies, eternal life or eternal damnation, are presented in contrast, through the two lives of Judas and Paul. Brendan and his group find Judas sitting unhappily on a cold, wet rock in the middle of the sea, and discover that this is his respite from Hell on Sundays and feast days. The Irish monk protects Judas from the demons of Hell for one night. Next they find an island where Paul the Hermit has lived a perfect monastic life for sixty years. He wears nothing but hair and is fed by an otter.

In the Narnian adventure, the corrupt Governor Gumpas is dismissed and replaced by Lord Bern, who is one of the missing lords. Gumpas is commissioned to serve as a steward of the Lone Islands under the Kingdom of Narnia. He is not the owner, but the governor, of this Narnian territory. He conducts his mission poorly by ruling the islands in a very nonchalantly bureaucratic fashion. He is not pleased to welcome the arrival of the real owner, King Caspian of Narnia.

---

119. Ibid., 33.
120. Lewis, *VDT*, 144–45.

The main voyagers in both stories come back to their original points of departure, their respective earthly homelands of Ireland for Brendan, Narnia for Caspian, and Britain for the three children. These earthly hometowns, however, function as a transit point en-route to their final adventure to the heavenly homeland. All the modern voyagers ultimately return through their earthly homeland to the heavenly homeland in the last book of the Narnian series, *The Last Battle* (1956).

Brendan sails eastward back to Ireland, while Caspian and his seafarers head west to Narnia, and the three children return to the space and time of the readers. Throughout his voyage to an earthly paradise in the west, Brendan's faith is challenged, but he is able to train himself to overcome spiritual temptation and to deepen his contact with God. He finally goes to the heavenly homeland peacefully through his earthly home country. The three children also end their lives peacefully at the end of *VDT*, but not in the last volume of the *Chronicles of Narnia*, *The Last Battle*. The children meet sudden death through a train accident. Their fate reflects the defects of the mechanized age of spirits in modern civilization and the imperfection of humanity. They ultimately go to Aslan's Country at the end of the Narnian series, but their final destination is not narrated in *VDT*.

In both imrama, visiting islands is the expression of a voyager praying to God, connecting the wandering pilgrimage tradition with ascetic inner self-discipline. The voyagers, in both *VSB* and *VDT*, sail for a Land of Promise, visiting mysteriously attractive islands while overcoming spiritual and physical damage from severe weather at sea. The Irish monk, Brendan, repeatedly encounters the same people (the steward and Jasconius) circling around the same islands (the Island of Sheep and the Paradise of Birds) during the same religious seasons of Easter, Christmas, and Epiphany. Although the *Dawn Treader* repeats the motif of sailing from island to island, the modern voyagers discover different people on different islands, reflecting the multiple values of contemporary times. In *VSB*, repetitive motion is a feature of Brendan's journey—one characteristic of the monk's voyage is visiting the same islands, encountering the same people in the same season, and circling around the same islands. The monastic and ascetic world of four saints is valued: St. Enda, St. Ailbe, St. Paul the Hermit, and St. Peter. The repetition is especially emphasized in and after chapter 15, titled "The Island of Sheep, Jasconius and the Paradise of Birds Again."

In a similar way to the labyrinthine movements of the five main players of *VDT*, Brendan's repeated movements bring to mind mesmerizing

Medieval Paradise

Celtic designs. As John Anderson states, the cyclical quality of Brendan's voyage reminds the reader that "The ineluctable rise and fall of human existence is rendered salutary when Brendan achieves his goal and arrives at the Promised Land of the Saints."[121] Sheldrake associates the layers of concentric circles with idealized models of the universe, a microcosm of the macrocosm, and an image of Creation.[122]

The medieval gifts from heaven directly involve biblical associations. Unlike Brendan's biblical world, the Kingdom of God is not directly mentioned in the modern imram, but the modern gifts are narrated as a reflection of the harmony of myth and the Gospel story of God incarnated in Christ. Brendan is offered two gifts at the end of his journey, stone and fruit, which are associated with Jesus Christ (1 Peter 2:4) and the Holy Spirit (Gal. 5:22). At the end of *VSB*, Brendan discovers these precious gifts of stone and fruit, both visible but spiritual. The stone is associated with Jesus Christ as the stone of stumbling: "The stone the builders rejected has become the chief cornerstone" (Ps. 118:22 NRSV), and "Everyone who falls on that stone will be broken to pieces, but he on whom it falls will be crushed" (Luke 20: 17–18); while the fruit is associated with the Holy Spirit as the qualities of character God grows inside the life of genuine believers: "But the fruit of the Spirit is love, joy, peace, patience, kindness, goodness, faithfulness" (Gal. 5:22).

The gifts for the Narnians are indirectly introduced to the reader through a re-telling of the classic fairytale *Sleeping Beauty*. In *VDT*, the woman plays a more active role than in the traditional imram. The woman is sleeping in the fairytale, while she is not sleeping in *VDT*, but rather the three men are. The prince kisses Sleeping Beauty, but Prince Caspian is to be kissed *by* Lady Star. She will kiss Caspian if he comes back from the East, breaks the spell on the sleepers, and awakes them. Lady Star encourages Caspian to complete his mission, and protects the three sleepers until he comes back to break the curse of the sleeping enchantment.

A bird is God's direct answer to the medieval monk Brendan's prayer, while God's revelation is suggested in the metaphoric expression of nature in *VDT*. In both voyages, angelic birds guide the pilgrimages and disclose the divine secret to the travelers. In the medieval imram, a bird talks with Brendan in a human language. He feels awestruck by the mysterious sight

---

121. Anderson, "The Voyage of Brendan, an Irish Monastic Expedition to Discover the Wonders of God's World," 273–74.

122. Sheldrake, *Living Between Worlds*, 54.

of a tree covered with white birds, and implores God to reveal the reason for this mystery. One bird flies to prophesize his fate to find the Promised Land or "what you cherish in your heart."[123] All the birds in the tree, beating their wings against their sides, start to sing and worship God in human words: "A hymn is due to thee, O God . . ."[124]

It is unlikely that it matters whether the tool for conveying meaning is a language or not, but seems to be more important that the meaning of the message is understood. Though the strong sweet voice of a bird sounds like words, no one on the *Dawn Treader* understands them. To Captain Drinian and Lucy, however, the meaning of the bird's message is communicated in a mysterious way. The captain hears no words from the angelic bird, but understands that the bird seems to be a good nautical rudder to guide the ship out of a dark labyrinth. In these dire straits, Lucy sees a beam transforming itself into a cross-like shape and then into an albatross. The bird seems to be whispering a message which sounds like Aslan's voice saying, "Courage, dear heart."[125] An albatross-shaped bird sounds to Lucy like Aslan's voice speaking to her.

Colin Duriez describes the long maritime tradition of the guiding albatross as a harbinger of good fortune, as featured in Samuel Taylor Coleridge's "The Rhyme of the Ancient Mariner."[126] Paul Ford associates the Albatross with Christ,[127] and Christin Ditchfield connects the bird with the Spirit of God.[128] The Holy Spirit appears in the form of a dove in the New Testament (Mark 1:10–11).

Through the symbol of a bird, Lewis emphasizes not the outer structure of the words, but the inner meaning, parallel and interacting with the framework. On Ramandu's island, white birds flying out of the sun sing in a language which no one knows and make everything white, all shapes blurred. To Edmund, it is the most exciting event of the entire journey.[129] The song makes the whole crew know that they "come to the beginning of the End of the World."[130]

123. O'Meara, trans., *The Voyage of Saint Brendan*, 21.
124. Ibid.
125. Lewis, *VDT*, 201.
126. Duriez, *A Field Guide to Narnia*, 167.
127. Ford, 5.
128. Ditchfield, *A Family Guide to Narnia*, 137.
129. Lewis, *VDT*, 222.
130. Ibid., 223.

Medieval Paradise

THE NATURAL WORLD

The fusion of myth and Christianity as well as humanity and natural features is in particular indicated in the utter East, (which Lewis also calls "the Lily Lake" or "the Silver Sea"[131]), where humans are in harmony with animals, natural landscapes, and the spiritual realms. The Narnian navigators moving within an ambiguous boundary is like a pilgrimage to a Christian site built on earlier pre-Christian religious ground. Philip Sheldrake exemplifies three Christian sites culturally connected with pre-historic holy places offered to the god of light: Mont Saint-Michel in France, St. Michael's Mount in Cornwall, England, and Skellig Michael in Kerry, Ireland.[132] He introduces especially Mount Saint-Michel as having a continuity of association with pre-Christian sacred places: "a Celtic burial mound!"[133]

The ambiguous continuity in *VDT* begins with the painting of a sailing ship stored in a room of Eustace's house. The painting interconnects this world and another world. Through this aesthetic channel, the children are invited into another world beyond the visible landscape, Narnia. This world" in *VDT* is used in a dual sense: this world, the reader's world vis-à-vis Narnia, and this world, the Narnian world vis-à-vis Aslan's Country. In chapter 1, Lucy and Edmund, in this world, are described as looking at the painting of the ship, looking along the picture, and finally thinking deeply of Narnia. If the aesthetic experience works as faith in Narnia, the adventurous voyage is a participation in the community of Narnia.

The painting is an iconographic fusion of the material and the spiritual: it is made of physical materials, while it represents a spiritual world. The fusion of this world and another world is similar to the iconography of the traditional Orthodox Church and its religious works of art, most commonly from Eastern Christianity. In *VDT*, Aslan's Country is beyond this country of Narnia, which is in turn beyond this world on earth.

The earthly paradise in the utter East is depicted with a metaphor from natural forces, which reflects Lewis's concept of Christian postmodernism, in that there is a world beyond the human language of word and image. Near the utter East, different features of the creation are intermingled in essence between light and water, as well as between light and living flesh. In the final stage of the *Dawn Treader*'s voyage, the Last Sea is divided into two

---

131. Ibid., 257.
132. Sheldrake, *Living Between Worlds*, 20.
133. Ibid.

zones: the sea near the utter East and the Last Sea of the utter East. Near the utter East, the voyagers are provided with the signs of the Last Sea—mysterious opportunities to drink light and to glance at it. The Narnian voyagers drink not only the drinkable light but also look at the brightness of the sun without blinking. Their bodies are changed and made more suited for entering the unknown territory in the utter East.

Lewis claims that the whole of creation is good and that God is to be experienced in the natural world. He highlights his affinity for humanity and natural features as he agrees with the psalmists who regard God as the provider for the whole natural world. He finds, in Psalm 104, both lions and leviathan (or whales) in the same cosmos.[134] The earthly paradise in *VDT* is described with the loveliest emotions of joy, excitement, and tranquility.[135] The Last Sea is like the mythological land of youth. The water in the Last Sea looks dazzling and tastes stronger than wine. After drinking the water from the Last Sea, no one wants to eat or sleep or speak. Some of the older sailors regain youthfulness. Everyone on board is filled with joy and excitement.[136]

The end of the world is described using metaphors from natural features that include whiteness, ice, lilies, and the Arctic. The voyagers see something white which looks like ice, prompting Captain Drinian to steer the ship clear of it. Lewis changes the fatal motif of white ice into the hope of life, but the depiction reminds the reader of the historical tragedy of the *Titanic* in 1912. The *Titanic* sank as it struck an Arctic iceberg. Lewis must have heard the sound of the ill-fated ship's construction as he was still in Belfast until 1911. The Titanic was built at the shipyard in Lewis's home town of Belfast, Ireland. The ship construction began on March 31, 1909 and required three years for completion.

The whiteness in *VDT* shines like the brightness of the Arctic, but it is not a reflection from the ice but from the lilies in bloom. They are a kind of lily but not the same kind as those in Narnia, because they lie too deep in the water. Lucy finds it hard to describe the smell of the "lilies," but finally explains with contradictory words including "sweet" and "wild."[137]

The white "lilies" are not clearly identified in the text, but the whiteness suggests humbleness which echoes the stricture of the narrow gate in the New Testament: "Enter through the narrow gate" (Matt. 7:13 NRSV).

134. Lewis, *Reflections on the Psalms*, 112.
135. Ibid., 255.
136. Lewis, *VDT*, 256.
137. Ibid., 260.

Medieval Paradise

Just as people are required to humble themselves to pass through this narrow gate, the three children move themselves from a big ship to a small boat. The change of vessel size from the *Dawn Treader* to a coracle is a necessary process of humbling oneself.

As white ice prevented the *Titanic* from sailing further, the ice-like whiteness prevents the Narnian ship from advancing further. The three children and Reepicheep abandon the big ship to go forward in a small boat, but the whiteness prevents the small boat from advancing as well. Finally, the smallest voyager, Reepicheep, is able to go forward in a little coracle. As he has prioritized Aslan's Country throughout his life, he is allowed to ride alone through the whiteness, the symbolic narrow gate to the Heavens: "where I go on alone."[138]

Unlike Earthly paradise depicted with a metaphor from natural forces, Aslan's Country is indescribable as it is beyond the human construction of language. The female protagonist, Lucy, uses a metaphor from nature to describe the Last Sea, but not Aslan's country beyond the Last Sea. She is overwhelmed by the sublimity of the heavenly breeze, so Aslan's country is literally and figuratively indescribable beyond the human construction of language. Lucy compares the Last Sea to something visible, a smell and musical sound. All Lucy can say is "it would break your heart."[139] Lewis urges the reader to equip their physical eyes with water from this earthly paradise, the Last Sea. The reader can see Aslan's Country with their newly equipped eyes as if they are wearing new glasses to see Heaven opened.

Aslan's Country is not directly described in *VDT*, but suggested through the three visitors' perspectives: "No one in that boat doubted that they were seeing beyond the End of the World into Aslan's country."[140] The three outsiders and Reepicheep are able to see a range of mountains beyond the waves and the sun. It means that they actually do not look at the mountains, as they similarly understand that they are not seeing the mountains in this world. The mountains are described not as a realistic representation of "mountains" in this world, as no one remembers seeing any sky. They feel as if they were looking at the mountains in a different dimension: "And the mountains must really have been outside the world."[141] With the enormous

---

138. Ibid., 267.
139. Ibid.
140. Ibid.
141. Ibid., 266.

height of the mountains in Aslan's Country, Lewis expresses the limitation of human beings and the human awe at the vastness of deep space.

In the depiction of the Last Sea, Lewis emphasizes the harmony of landscapes, both visible and invisible. He presents his ecological concept of nature, claiming a deep relationship with human and natural landscape in the local community. Humanity is so limited that we have to depend "on soils and weather"[142]; even so, the voyagers have to humbly give themselves up as the ship is prevented from advancing by the whiteness in the Last Sea. In his essay *Reflections on the Psalms,* Lewis defines invisible nature as "the local alter" and "God."[143] The reader is awe-inspired by the mountainous vastness in Aslan's Country and by the mysterious movements of the spiral courses, parallel and interconnected, in which the five units of protagonists travel both east and west—and beyond the directions of this world. As Lewis suggests, we should act practically to know both natures intertwined, visible and invisible, and to expect a harmony of myth and the Gospel, just as we fear and love the Lord as "an utterly concrete Being."[144]

A sea voyage is a solitary experience similar to Israel's exile in the wildness, but this solitude rehabilitates the broken humanity of Eustace and the complex nature of Lucy, as well as developing spiritual growth in Edmund. Compared with the medieval imram, Lewis further uses the mysticism of the natural world to incorporate the two paradoxical concepts of mythology and Christianity. He thus demonstrates not only his belief in the Gospel as a Myth which becomes a Fact, but also his literary conclusion that Aslan's country is indescribable in human words. Beyond this, he narrates the adventure in the *Dawn Treader,* and the beauty of "the smell"[145] and "the musical sound"[146] of "a breeze"[147]: the story of East, West, and Beyond.

---

142. Lewis, *Reflections on the Psalms,* 350.
143. Ibid., 356.
144. Ibid.
145. Lewis, VDT, 265.
146. Ibid.
147. Ibid.

5

Re-Writing Mythology
Greco-Roman and Norse

In his last novel, *Till We Have Faces: A Myth Retold* (1956) (*TWHF*), C.S. Lewis creates a world of Christian postmodernism beyond the stereotypes of Greco-Roman and Norse mythologies. *TWHF* is rarely read by the general reader, even though it is rated as the best book of Lewis's fiction, not only by critics, but also by Lewis himself.[1] *TWHF* is generally discussed as a retold story of Greco-Roman myth with the main focus on Psyche as the sufferer, but from her sister Queen Orual's point of view, this is a retelling of both Greek and Norse mythologies. Her modernist paradigm of the righteous is deconstructed and reconstructed through transition from the traditional Greek story of Eros and Psyche into the Norse legend of Orual, Psyche, Ansit, and Bardia, and into the mythology of the gods, dead and resurrected.

Queen Orual rationally accuses the mythological gods of unfairly stealing Psyche, complaining as if she is the Norse god Loki who charges other gods, including Odin, with unjustly having him bound. Through the writing of two letters, the female protagonist deconstructs, then reconstructs, her interpretations of what she writes and discovers her own "face" or self-identity as the title suggests. However, her last word, "might," is ambiguously suggested and leaves its interpretation to the reader. Lewis creates a literary world of Christian postmodernism through Orual's writing.

---

1. Schakel, *Imagination and the Arts in C.S. Lewis*; and Myers, *Bareface*.

Queen Orual logically writes two letters of complaint to the Greek (whom Orual assumes as the reader) to claim her own righteousness, but illogically ignores the four tremors involving three women including herself and the prophetic voice of Captain Bardia. The first three include the echo of Psyche's swaying in the breeze, the beat of Orual's writing with a pen, and the vibration of Ansit's spinning with a stick. These sounds gradually deconstruct the Queen's concept of justice. The four work together to make her abandon herself before a superior being. The divine being is, in the beginning, not clearly identified but, in the end, is vaguely associated with Christ as Orual speaks to the Person indicated by "Lord" capitalized.[2]

Few critics discuss Orual's writing from the perspective of Christian postmodernism, but Lewis's focus on the reader is explored by scholars Kath Filmer and Doris T. Myers, while Orual's rewriting of the stories is discussed by Mara E. Donaldson and Joy Alexander. Filmer views not only a fusion of identities of Orual as author, protagonist, and reader, but also a projection of the Anima, the female element of the male.[3] Myers and Donaldson make no particular comment on Orual's last word, but Myers's conclusion is that the purpose of *TWHF* is to abolish the view of myth.[4] Donaldson compares Lewis's concept of logos and poiema to Ricoeur's concept of narrative time. Lewis's literary technique of speech is similar to Joy Alexander's assumption: she presumes that Lewis must have applied the same technique of speech shaped for Aslan to Orual, though she makes no particular comments on Orual's last word "might" and Arnom.[5]

These scholars do not explore Lewis's ambiguous expressions between fact and fiction, but others, such as Carla A. Arnell, notice that Orual's last word "might" is an important factor,[6] but ignore the last undecipherable "marks" at the end of the second letter. Karen Rowe discusses Orual's reconciliation with Psyche, but Ansit and Bardia are excluded. Thomas Howard highlights Arnom as the last narrator. Although he gives no particular reason for the priest's involvement in the story as the second narrator, he alludes to the priest who has a different opinion of Orual to the readers.[7]

---

2. Lewis, *Till We Have Faces* (*TWHF*), 308.
3. Filmer, *The Fiction of C.S. Lewis: Mask and Mirror*, 113.
4. Myers, *C.S. Lewis in Context*, 210.
5. Alexander, 48.
6. Arnell, "On Beauty, Justice, and the Sublime in C.S. Lewis's *Till We Have Faces*," 31.
7. Howard, *Narnia and Beyond*, 237.

Re-Writing Mythology

Lewis presents his postmodern interpretation of how to read *TWHF*, but he asserts that a story is not exclusively created by the author. In his letter to Clyde Kilby (Feb. 10, 1957), he distinguishes the author's intention and other possibilities, possibly the reader's, regarding *TWHF* as a retelling of Greek myth involving Psyche as an instance of Christian soul by nature and Orual as that of human affection in its natural condition. However, he goes on to write in the same letter that an author "doesn't necessarily understand the making of his own story better than anyone else."[8] This statement is taken as his respect for the reader's interpretations, provided the reader respects the author's intentions and also his authorial passion to help the reader to take their reading "seriously" and "whole-heartedly."[9]

In *TWHF*, Lewis retells a story from Greco-Roman mythology to express his concept of the transcendent world of the Gospel. He spends more than thirty years seeking a literary form for *TWHF* until he crystallizes the idea of Psyche (logos) into form (poiema). Through his search for the form for *TWHF*, he demonstrates the harmony of logos and poiema through postmodern literary approaches that include subverting, ambiguous ending, multiple perspectives, unconventional assumption, obscure roles of protagonists, and meta-narrative or a story within a story.

By mythology, Lewis means the Gospel as the fulfillment of pagan myth. He interprets the Gospel as Mythology (capitalized) reflected in pagan mythologies. As he recalls in a letter to friend Arthur Greeves (Oct. 18, 1931), he is fascinated by the sense of longing for another world through his reading of mythologies. He compares the stories of the Pagan poets (human) to the story of the Gospel in which God expresses Himself through a human being, Jesus.[10]

Many critics refer to the impact of Norse mythologies on Lewis's concept of another world, but few have made a literary analysis of mythological influence on his fictions. Daniel Warzecha's research (2008), however, discusses the eschatological impact of the Norse gods on *The Chronicles of Narnia*, but it excludes *TWHF*. An analysis of *TWHF* from the perspective of both Greco-Roman and Nordic mythological impact will contribute to the further understanding of Lewis as a novelist of Christian postmodernism.

---

8. Lewis, *The Collected Letters III*, 830.
9. Lewis, *An Experiment in Criticism*, 11.
10. Lewis, *The Collected Letters I*, 977.

RETELLING GRECO-ROMAN MYTHOLOGY

Lewis culminates the myth of Psyche from the viewpoint of the anti-traditional woman, Orual, who is not beautiful, but is ugly and egoistic. Through the confession of this female protagonist, he demonstrates the fruit of literary composition in which poiema is fermented into form. *TWHF* seems to finish with Orual's last word—"might,"[11] but in the concluding paragraph, the story actually ends with Priest Arnom's memo of Orual. His modernist worldview is the key to unlocking what the last word "might" suggests. The concluding paragraph of *TWHF* consists not of Queen Orual's words, but Priest Arnom's report of her death and his speculation that she breathed her last breath while writing the second letter. He concludes that her letter is left unfinished. The analysis of her last word from the viewpoint of Priest Arnom reveals that Lewis is a Christian postmodernist writer.

Orual's changing viewpoints are integrated into her rewriting and reading of the first letter. The shift in her self-recognition develops in three steps: the rational approach of writing a complaint against the gods in the first letter; the kinesthetic experience of reading the first letter, both silently and aloud; and the aesthetical appreciation of narrative stories through a series of picturesque images in the second letter.

Lewis adopts the retelling of stories as a literary technique by which he extracts the essence of myths through the process of retelling myths. He consciously uses a story within a story by retelling Greco-Roman myths, such as the story of Cupid and Psyche from *The Golden Ass* of Apuleius and the account of the Greek mythological Queen Demeter's search for Persephone in the Eleusinian mysteries. Orual intentionally hides her face in a veil to avoid encountering not only herself, but also other people and the gods, until the last moment of her life, as suggested by the title of the book. In the end, she seems to leave the final words to the reader, finishing her story in mid-sentence with an auxiliary verb: "might."

To express the concept beyond word and image, Lewis employs the mysteries of Eleusis related to the mythology of Demeter, the goddess of agriculture and fertility. Demeter's daughter, Persephone, is seized by Hades, the god of death, and taken to his underworld kingdom. Eleusis was an ancient Greek religion in which drama was assumedly staged to allow

---

11. Lewis, *TWHF*, 308.

integration with divine beings beyond this world. As Karen Rowe states, Apuleius was a teller of the tale, not the original writer.[12]

Lewis describes Orual's experience of writing and reading as a parallel of the mythological themes of death and life. He uses the recurring keynote of the pagan myth—death and resurrection—and applies the term "myth" to Christianity, regarding the Gospel as God's myth, as he states that "stories happen in actual human history."[13]

Lewis affirms that readers come closest to having an imaginative experience that "incarnates" the abstraction of death, life, and "God is love"[14] when they read, or "taste" as Lewis phrases it, the story of myth. He uses the novel as a tool of truth in the same way as mythology. Thomas Howard writes that the difference in method between myth and novel lies in the appearance: it depends on the place of the real action, inside for a novel and outside for a myth. He compares an alpine "peak" to the feeling of "exaltation."[15]

By entering Orual's story, Lewis initially operates within her worldview, and then retells her perspective from within the second letter. Finally, he reveals the incompleteness of Orual's story, moving beyond her terms to tell his own story. This approach sounds similar to a literary method proposed by Curtis Chang to communicate the gospel to people of the postmodern-challenged epoch.[16]

At the end of Orual's first letter, Lewis focuses on her death and life by adapting the postmodernist approach of a story within a story. He includes three mythological stories together within the story of the old priest in Essur: Apleius's story of Cupid and Psyche, Lewis's story of Orual and Psyche, and the old priest's story of Talapal and Istra.

The old priest in Essur narrates to Orual the myth of the goddess Istra, relating that Talapal is jealous of the beauty of Istra and so sacrifices her to a mountain brute. He tells this story as mythology, but Orual interprets the jealous Talapal as herself and the goddess Istra as Psyche. Just as Lewis tells the story of Orual and Psyche as a retold version of the Latin *Metamorphoses* by the Roman author Apuleius, the priest's story likewise becomes Orual's.

12. Rowe, "Till We Have Faces: A Study of the Soul and the Self," 140.
13. Lewis, *The Collected Letters I*, 18.
14. Lewis, *God in the Dock*, 66.
15. Howard, *Narnia & Beyond*, 162.
16. Chang, *Engaging Unbelief*, 24–26.

The old priest, one of three priests whom Orual encounters in her life, reflects pagan mythology. The other two include the priest of Ungit, representing the theistic mind even though he is a priest of pagan religion, and the new priest of deistic nature, Arnom.

In the narration by the old priest in Essur, Talapal is like Aphrodite in Greek mythology, or Ungit in Orual's world, and Istra is Psyche. Talapal's son, Ialim, loves Istra and takes her to his secret palace. Ialim, referred to as the West Wind in Greek mythology, is similarly called "West Wind" in Orual's world. He is also called "the Brute." The old priest in Essur lives in a thatched house behind the temple where there is the image of a woman carved in wood on the altar. Although the goddess Istra in exile reminds the reader of Psyche, the head of the image covered with a black scarf looks like Orual's face hidden by a veil.

Lewis writes *TWHF* based on Apuleius's *Metamorphoses*, which includes the tale of Cupid and Psyche. It is not certain of whom Orual is envious in the beginning, but the Roman story clearly begins with Venus's envy toward a beautiful girl, Psyche. The Roman goddess Venus, known as Aphrodite to the Greeks, tells her son Cupid, known as Eros to the Greeks, to use his golden arrows so that Psyche will fall in love with a vile creature, the first person she sees when she awakens. Cupid accidentally scratches himself with his arrow and he himself falls in love with Psyche. In both versions, the West Wind carries Psyche away to a palace where she is attended to by invisible servants. In the darkness, the bridegroom, West Wind/Cupid/Eros, invisible to Psyche, meets her every night. He demands that she never light any lamps since he does not want her to know who he is until the time is right. Enraged with this news, the Venus of Greek mythology places a curse on Psyche, preventing her from meeting a suitable husband. Orual similarly prevents her sister Psyche from living with her husband.

In both versions, Psyche is urged, by her sisters, two sisters in Greek mythology and Orual in *TWHF*, to betray the West Wind so that she is exiled to search for her lover. In the Greco-Roman versions, Psyche lights a lamp after the West Wind sleeps, but as a drop of oil falls, it wakes him, so he flies away. Psyche is punished for her disobedience and also for Venus's anger over the injury to Cupid. In Lewis's version, he focuses on the role of the reader as the key factor for Orual to transform herself: not Psyche's glance at the West Wind but Orual's glimpse of him is emphasized. Orual sees his face in the darkness, but she cannot accept the empirical fact as truth, finally leaving the judgment to the reader: "You, who, read my book, judge. Was it so?"[17] Lewis provides no detailed information of how Psyche lights a lamp, but instead focuses on the spiritual impact of the glimpse on Orual. She threatens Psyche to follow her by attempting to kill herself Psyche to follow her by attempting to kill herself with a dagger, and ultimately gives Psyche the crucial choice of love to either Orual or the West Wind.

In the Greek and Latin versions, Psyche and her sisters are described as sharply separated personalities, while Lewis draws an ambiguous border between Orual and Psyche. In the first letter, he emphasizes the different characters of Orual and Psyche, but in the second letter, he shows the merging of the two. In the story within the story, Orual shares the hard labor with Psyche, who is punished to wander with Orual. In both versions, Psyche is given four ordeals: ordered to separate the mixed grains in a large basket before nightfall, then to retrieve the golden wool left in a field by a flock of golden sheep, next to bring back water flowing from a rock cleft impossible for any mortal to attain, and finally to get a box of beauty from the Roman goddess of the Underworld, Proserpina, Persephone to the Greeks.

The union of two worlds is expressed through the marriage of Cupid and Psyche in Greek mythology, but Lewis creates harmony with the illusionary merging of Orual and Psyche. In the myth, Ceres, the Roman goddess of agriculture, Demeter to the Greeks, advises Psyche that she must call Venus. Psyche attempts to throw herself off a high tower to go into the Underground, but the tower prevents her from falling. Jupiter calls a council of the gods and declares that it is his will that Cupid marry her. In Lewis's version, Psyche does not fall to the Hell, but is instead punished by being forced to wander in this world. In the first letter, she wanders alone, but in the picturesque illusions of the second letter, she walks with Orual.

In both versions, jealousy is the reason for sending Psyche into exile. In *The Golden Ass*, Venus, the Goddess of Beauty, is jealous of Psyche's beauty. Psyche's sisters, envious of her beautiful palace, deceive her into distrusting her bridegroom, Cupid. Although Psyche in Greek myth is passively chosen for exile by Venus and by her sisters, Lewis describes Psyche as a woman who chooses her own destiny: Psyche voluntarily chooses the punishment of wandering alone.

Orual is jealous of her beloved sister Psyche because Psyche's palace is invisible and because of her inability to control Psyche's ability to see visions. Her failure to share Psyche's happiness makes Orual feel angry toward her

17. Lewis, *TWHF*, 173.

because Psyche can know what Orual does not know through her visions. Orual attempts to test her sister's love by forcing Psyche to choose either her husband's happiness or Orual's. The choice for Psyche is either that she should lose trust in her husband or that she should lose Orual to suicide.

Psyche's reason for choosing sacrifice is because her love for Orual is greater than for the West Wind. Psyche is penalized on Orual's behalf through choosing the punishment for her sister. She sacrifices herself and goes into exile as punishment for Orual. Orual is the one who should have been disciplined for her own egoistical love. She instead hides her true personality both from herself and from others, with her face veiled for another forty years. She must suffer the loss of face to herself and to others.

In the final scene, there is a striking contrast between the two versions. Apuleius ends the myth with a single perspective in which Psyche and Cupid are married under the rule of Jupiter. In *TWHF*, Orual's metamorphosis is the key theme. She plays multiple roles as a protagonist: the writer of two letters, the reader of what she writes, and the first person narrator. The last role is usually interpreted as trustable by the reader, but not probable.

In the conclusion of *TWHF*, Orual changes herself from a single self-view of an ugly woman, Ungit, to a harmony of both Orual and Psyche. The transformation is suggested by her monopoly of multiple roles to the abandonment of self: male, female, writer, reader, narrator, character, queen, and warrior. With the final word, "might," she can similarly be united with the divine being if she abandons herself and unites with Psyche. She wishes to find Psyche in Eleusis, but realizes that the ideal place is impossible to find in this world.[18]

By using her writing experience, Lewis reflects Orual's mythological journey of death and life. Her struggle to fulfill word and image in a literary form is her goal for true self-recognition. As she tries to put her angry words, or logos, into a letter of complaint, poiema, in Part 2, she comes to see visions in which the writer of letters, Orual, acts simultaneously as a character within the story of Psyche. While writing the two letters, she experiences the duality of logos and poiema. The writing experience makes her realize that there is something wicked within. She does not think herself selfish, as she finds it easier to observe her natural, though unpleasant, love toward her sister Psyche.

In a similar way to Lewis, nineteenth century artists engage in retelling the myth of Psyche. Counter to the unpleasantness of rationalism,

---

18. Ibid., 281.

atheism, and evolutionism, writers of the Victorian age write to forget the harsh reality of the outer world. They re-write the old tales of Greek myths into a Pre-Raphaelite's longing for the inner world. These writers include Walter Pater and William Morris. Walter Pater rewrites the myth of Psyche in chapter 15 of *Marius the Epicurean* (1885) and William Morris writes "May" of *Earthly Paradise*.

Lewis gives praise to the literary technique of both of these writers, but he takes a different approach for his contemporary reader. In his letter to Greeves (Jan. 10, 1932), he expresses his amazement over the close association of Christianity because of the beauty of Pater's works.[19] In a letter to his brother (Jan. 17, 1932), Lewis likewise expresses his excitement at reading Pater's *Maius the Epicurean*: "the epicurean-aesthetic business."[20]

As a reader of Morris, Lewis similarly admires the English author as a witness of truth, though he finds Morris "unwilling."[21] Lewis discovers death lying at the root of Morris' whole subject, and wonders why Morris paints the Earthly Paradise.

Unlike Pater and Morris, Lewis creates Orual as a reflection of unpleasantness in modern society. She rationally writes a letter of complaint to justify herself and to demand fair judgment. As the main narrator, except in the last paragraph, she writes and re-writes while reading both silently and aloud what she has written down. In her second letter, she comes to realize herself through a series of picturesque images of Greek mythologies. In the end, her solid belief in the elevation of enlightenment over faith is deconstructed. The reader is led not to reject her irrational demand, but to show compassion for her miserable experience with the gods. Even though readers empathetically agree with her, they are faced with a fatal dilemma: to believe what she ultimately writes or what Arnom reports.

Contrary to a focus on the beauty of the spirit of Psyche, twentieth century writer Lewis emphasizes the gradual shift of perception of the modernist protagonist from wicked desire to self-abandonment. He describes how exclusively Orual occupies Psyche's time and space in the name of affection through the devouring of her materialistic love. He integrates the two elder sisters of the Greek version into one ugly queen, and recreates the entire story from the Queen's perspective through the literary form of the writing of two letters. Re-writing the first letter, Orual recreates a new

19. Lewis, *The Collected Letters II*, 34.
20. Ibid., 41.
21. Ibid., 34

story by extracting the essence of the narrated one. What she does as a writer is the integration of content and form. Mara E. Donaldson regards the process of Orual's changing viewpoints between the two letters as the union of logos and poiema.[22]

Lewis starts with the known style of the myth of Psyche, but moves beyond the myth. Orual writes of giving Psyche a lamp so she is able to see her husband's face against his will, but Lewis tells his own story through Orual's second letter, in which Psyche brings back beauty from the land of death as a symbol of salvation. As Wayne Martindale comments, Orual learns that the most fearful thing for her is "the Beautific Vision—to see God face to face."[23]

For Lewis, the text consist of both form and meaning, but modern theorists isolate both the meaning of words and the form. Lewis defines "poiema" as what the readers do and "logos" as what is done by the author. He affirms that the reader can embrace "various imaginations [poiema] at a tempo [logos] prescribed by the author."[24] Poiema is not "an autonomous thing," but "the result of what the author has intended."[25] In poetry/image, he sees the two parents of the story as logos, the poet's opinion and emotions, and poiema, the organization of words that the poet chooses.

Lewis distinguishes between the two parents in the writing of every poem. He states that the mother is "the matter," or the mass of experience (the thought inside the poet), and the father is the pre-existing form (epic, tragedy, and novel). "The matter inside the poet wants the form: in submitting to the form it becomes really original, really the origin of great work."[26] As Bruce Edwards affirms, the modernists detach the text from author and reader, as if the text is "a reflection of oneself" or "only about itself" and "corresponds to nothing in the 'real world.'"[27] Lewis would claim that "a poem is 'both Logos (something said) and Poiema (something made).'"[28]

---

22. Donaldson, "Orual's Story and the Art of Retelling," 169–70.
23. Martindale, *Beyond the Shadowlands*, 129.
24. Lewis, *An Experiment in Criticism*, 133.
25. Ibid., 62.
26. Lewis, *A Preface to Paradise Lost*, 3.
27. Edwards, *A Rhetoric of Reading*, 64.
28. Ibid., 61.

Re-Writing Mythology

ORUAL AS WRITER AND RE-WRITER

TWHF is a story of Orual's spiritual metamorphosis through her struggle to write the letters. Writing is, to her, a painful process in which she undergoes both surgical treatment and childbirth. Viewed individually, the two ways connote different concepts of death and life in the dazzling illusions which she sees in picturesque images in the second letter.

The operation, not by knife but by pen, probes deep into Orual's subconsciousness and locates what motivates her to write what she writes. The delivery in birthing language—"labor"—requires the undergoing of intellectual and mental pain in the process of endlessly detecting words. After writing the first letter, she feels a faint change in her awareness—the change drawing near unnoticed. She expresses the indescribable impact of writing on her mind in the beginning of the second letter: "It was a labour of sifting and sorting, separating motive from motive and both from pretext...went on every night in my dreams..."[29]

Writing becomes, for Orual, a comprehensive experience that includes all elements of her practical, mental, and spiritual life: she supposedly starts writing the letter, railing against the gods for stealing her sister, but in the end she finds herself not accusing, but being accused. Through writing, she undergoes not only the playing of multiple roles—narrating, writing, and accusing—but also finds her roles finally reversed: being narrated, being reported, and being accused.

Orual monopolizes all perspectives: a writer/reader, narrator/character, accuser/accused, soldier/queen, and victim/offender. Throughout her life, she controls what everyone owns, but finally abandons herself through death. Her death is declared by the new priest, Arnom, and her corpse is an object seen by him. The readers are allowed access to her narrative world only through what she writes with her egoistic mind except in the last paragraph on the declaration of her death.

After writing the first letter, Orual decides to rewrite it. Penning this letter causes her to re-realize what she needs to write again. While reading the first letter, she decides to rewrite the second. During the second letter, she recognizes the fact that her love for Psyche is provoked by her desire for possessiveness, and that jealousy is her actual motivation for urging Psyche to look at her husband. She thought that she was jealous of Psyche, but actually she was jealous not of Psyche, but of the West Wind, who, in

---

29. Lewis, *TWHF*, 256.

her eyes, stole Psyche's love. The West Wind, Cupid in Greek mythology, is referred to in the story as "the Brute . . . , Ungit herself or Ungit's son, the god of the mountain."[30]

The two activities of writing and re-writing (which also includes reading), become integrated in the life of Orual and create a world in which the writer can simultaneously be a reader. The reader Orual comes to see three interpretations of what she writes: firstly the original letter of complaint which she writes in the first letter; secondly the letter that she repeatedly reads aloud; and thirdly the letter that she reads silently. Instead of rejecting the multiple images, Orual as reader finally accepts all three views. Orual as character collaborates with Orual as reader, and finally captivates the truth through both activities of writing and reading.

The first letter ends with Orual's dissatisfaction at having no response from the gods. Writing is, for her, an expression of protest against the god Ungit, as well as a means of rejecting her ugly personality. The ugliness is similarly identified with Ungit, a deformed version of Aphrodite. Just as she avoids looking at herself in the mirror, she also rejects facing the reality of her hidden personality, as implied by the veil hiding her face.

Confessing by pen enables Orual to recognize that she is among the dead. In the second letter, she finds herself associated with "death" in such images as falling down the dark cave, the land of death, and the underground. In the hellish depths, she sees an illusionary picture of herself walking in the desert and bringing a container of water from the land of the dead to Ungit. Although Psyche in Apuleius's version is saved by the voice of the mountain, Orual is persecuted not only by the mountain voice, a black thing coming out of a crack in the mountain, but also by the ghosts on both sides, antagonistic and allied.

However, by rewriting, Orual achieves beauty through and beyond death. She sees the golden rams of the gods on the opposite bank of a river of death. She walks through the river, a symbol of death, to get the golden flock, a symbol of beauty. In the river, she resolves to die, which she earlier feared to do at the River Shennit, but she is not able to die in the way that she wished.

Re-writing serves as a mirror for Orual to see an image of self-sacrifice: the story of both her search for Psyche and Psyche's departure for death and return from exile. Orual wishes that she could go to Eleusis to die and live

---

30. Ibid., 48.

again, as in Greek mythology where Demeter and her daughter Persephone are the goddesses based in Eleusis: "how could I go there?"[31]

Unlike Apuleius's separation between Demeter and her daughter Persephone, Lewis presents a unified image of mother and daughter in one protagonist, Orual. While re-writing, Orual is in a dream in which she experiences both death and life. She tries to rescue Psyche (life) as if she were Demeter who searches her daughter Persephone, while she falls into the hellish underground (death), just like Persephone, Queen of the Underground.

Re-writing brings to Orual the vision of another world that transcends life and death in this world. In the dream, she sees her father, though they are both dead. Her ghost-father takes his ghost-daughter to a dark shallow cave at the bottom of a hole. This constrained place is similar to Virgil showing Dante around Hell and Purgatory in *The Divine Comedy*. This place, suggestive of Hell, makes her feel so suffocated that she is afraid that both of them might be buried alive. She, however, comes to realize that there is no need to worry; her father is already dead, and she herself is also dead in the dream. She, however, feels a fear of death for the first time.

The ghost-father brings Orual in front of a mirror and forces her to look at herself. Her father, when alive as the King of Glome, is described as a man of cruel disposition—tyrannical, oppressive, and violent. Although she fears his short-tempered nature, he unexpectedly forces her to stand before the reflection of the disastrous face of Ungit. She is not able to avoid looking at her ugly face, so she cannot help acknowledging her destructive personality. Although she believes that the gods are to blame, she becomes gradually and painfully aware that she is the deformed god, Ungit, as if she were a queen spider who rules Glome like a web and devours men's lives caught in the web: "That ruinous face was mine."[32]

Re-writing is an action causing Orual to enter an ambiguous zone in which it is hard to discern dream from reality. She is incapable of ascertaining whether or not she is in a dream.[33] In the ambiguous zone, her awareness awakens from slumber. Waking up is not an easy experience for Orual: "which is the truer."[34]

---

31. Ibid., 281.
32. Ibid., 276.
33. Ibid., 283.
34. Ibid., 276.

By rewriting, she can see a reverse image of the world. In the pastures of the gods on the opposite bank, symbolic of Heaven, she is knocked down by golden rams that stampede over her. She is, unexpectedly, able to accept the rush not as a destructive sign, but as divine rapture. The rushing rams feel like the gods' anger when looking on from outside the pasture, but she finds herself in the midst of bliss when looking from inside.

For Orual, re-writing is an awareness of death. She wishes to die herself, preferring a physical death to facing reality. As she was a mighty fighter with a sword in her youth, she thinks that she can kill herself with her old familiar weapon. The sword is symbolic of humanity, materialism, authority, and masculinity. She attempts to use the power to kill herself but fails. The sword of the past is no longer useful. It is too heavy for the skinny, old woman and impossible to grip tightly. She is once again led into a more ambiguous zone between dream and waking: "Of the things that followed I cannot at all say whether they were what men call real or what men call dream."[35]

Re-writing serves Orual as a step toward her escape from the gods, but not yet of complete recognition. After she fails to commit suicide with the sword, she resolves to drown herself in the River Shennit. If the sword is a metaphor for human power, water is considered a symbol of pantheism that, in a broad sense, covers all gods. She attempts to use water as a power beyond herself to die.

At the water of the River Shennit, Orual is denied death by a god's voice. Although Psyche of *The Golden Ass* is saved by the voice at the tower, Orual is not necessarily rescued by the voice, but instead told how to die completely. She takes off her veil and puts on her girdle so as not to prolong her death, but she still cannot die. She hears a voice telling her to "die before she dies."[36] It probably means that perfect death is possible when she abandons her ego. The voice says to her, "There is no chance after."[37]

Re-writing is an experience that makes Orual re-interpret the first letter she writes (logos) in a form of vision (poiema). In this vision, she labors through a slavish mission to please the goddess of Hell: she sees herself walking in burning sands to fulfill the duty of detecting the spring from

---

35. Ibid., 277.
36. Ibid., 279.
37. Ibid.

a river in deadlands, then filling an empty bowl and giving it to Ungit: "I walked into the vision..."[38]

Orual's complaint against the gods is answered, but not in the way she expects, that the letter will be read by the Greek. Her case is accepted by a court made up of four kinds of representatives: an eagle, representing a divine messenger; ghosts who are all dead people represented by dark things; voices which include her father and her Greek tutor Fox; and a judge dressed in black. When fully clothed, she looks as if she is holding a bowl in her hand. But when naked, she finds herself holding not a bowl, but the letter or what she writes down: "only my book."[39] Re-writing reveals her hidden ugly mind—the bareness visually expressed by the removal of her veil and her garments.

READING ALOUD AND SILENTLY

Reading aloud reveals the truth of what is hidden, rejected, and suppressed in Orual. While re-writing, she reads aloud the first letter until she accepts the unexpected development of the letter in two ways: she firstly notices the difference between what she writes down and what is written on the roll, and she secondly transforms the awareness of herself from an accuser of the gods to the accused.

The letter looks, to her, noticeably different from its outward appearance—too small, too old, and wrinkled: "all a vile scribble."[40] The ragged book looks similar to the old tattered body of the Queen of Glome who introduces herself on the first page: "I am old now and I have not much to fear from the anger of gods."[41]

Orual repeatedly reads the same letter until her own voice sounds strange in her ears. The strange sound is her resistance to other characters including her father, her tutor Fox, and her Captain Bardia. She realizes the sin of devouring their lives. She even thought she loved Bardia as a man, but realizes she does not.

Reading reveals not what is written, but what is really intended to be written. The last thing she demands is her right of possession of Psyche. Her egoistic demand for possessing Psyche is repeatedly expressed with

38. Ibid., 285.
39. Ibid., 289.
40. Ibid.
41. Ibid., 3.

the word "mine": "She was *mine. Mine.* Do you not know what the word means? *Mine!*"[42]

While re-writing and reading aloud, Orual transforms her awareness of herself from an accuser of the gods to the accused. She is aware that she selfishly tries to possess everyone by playing multiple roles: a queen, a lover, a mother, a sister, a plaintiff, and a soldier, as well as the ugly and the beautiful, the male and the female. Her possessiveness is reflected in the literary rhetoric of the novel: character, narrator, writer, and reader.

Orual is prevented by the judge from reading her complaint aloud, but instead reads the letter silently among the dead congregation. Reading silently represents three aspects of her writing: reading the letter silently, the silent listening to her voice by the dead in the court, and being guided around the visual images of Psyche and Orual by her dead Greek tutor Fox.

Reading silently allows Orual to acknowledge that she is among the dead. The dead around her silently wait for her to finish the letter. In the silence, she comes to understand that her complaint is the answer; she knows that "to have heard myself making it was to be answered."[43] Through the process of interpreting and silent reading, Orual is allowed by the court to be a representative of the dead and a symbol of Hell. Orual gradually understands death and resurrection through the illusionary tour of appreciating four paintings on three walls. As Dante is both narrator and character in *The Divine Comedy*, Orual is both narrator and character through the paintings. The ghost of her dead Greek tutor Fox guides Orual around the works of art just as Dante's ideal woman, Beatrice, guides him through the nine celestial spheres of Heaven.

As discussed in chapter 2, Lewis makes an analogy of incarnation from the two roles that Dante plays in *The Divine Comedy*. First is Dante the character. Lewis sees Dante's two roles theologically as the union of the two natures of being divine and human in Christ: Dante is the author of the whole story, but he also exists and has a life of his own inside it.[44] Second, he compares Dante to Christ in the sense that just as Dante is not perceived by other people, so Christ is perceived to be God by very few people in this world, even though the author makes a whole world (poem) in which all characters exist and have a life of their own.

---

42. Ibid., 292.
43. Ibid., 294.
44. Lewis, "The Seeing Eye," 62.

Re-Writing Mythology

By appreciating the narrative stories unrolled in the wall paintings, Orual understands the meaning of the letter which she writes. The painting story tells of how she and her sister Psyche in exile are, like Demeter, the goddess of Greek mythology, to get beauty from the queen of the country of death, so that the two sisters suffer atoning pains for each other, and eventually they come to know that they suffer not for themselves, but for the sake of "the Person."

Orual's spiritual awakening is expressed by her witnessing of "two Psyches" reflected on the water. It is the reflection of the true reality of femininity in both Orual and Psyche. She comes to know the true nature of herself and Psyche: "Yes, both psyches, both beautiful. . ., yet not exactly the same."[45]

In her first letter, Orual supposes Greek philosophers to be her readers so that her accusations for their stealing Psyche will be fairly judged. In her second letter, however, she states her dissatisfaction with the lack of answer from the "gods." She imagines that both her readers and the gods are separate and plural entities.[46]

At the end of her second letter, Orual speaks to "you," referring to "you" as the singular pronoun and "Lord" with a capital "L." She expresses a profound satisfaction to know that "Lord" is the answer to her accusation. It may suggest that her idea of Greek readers and pagan gods is the reflection of a single divine being: "I know now, Lord why you utter no answer. You are yourself the answer."[47]

THE STORY THAT BEGINS WITH THE LAST WORD

TWHF seems to end with Orual's last word "might," but the story actually ends with Priest Arnom's memo of the Queen. His last statement in the last paragraph has not often been discussed in connection with Orual's last word following her two letters, but Arnom's modernist worldview is the key to comprehending *TWHF*. Her changing viewpoints are integrated in the process of her re-writing. Her recognition of the two letters reveals *TWHF* from the perspective of Christian postmodernism. Her unfinished utterances in part 1 (comprising the first letter and chapter 1 of the second letter) and part 2 (comprising the latter part of the second letter) will demonstrate

45. Lewis, *TWHF*, 309.
46. Ibid., 250.
47. Ibid., 308.

that her last sentence ending with "might" is an expression of the integration of the incompleteness of human language in word and image, as well as that which transcends human comprehension.

The reader is not informed of Orual's real motivation for writing until the end of the first letter. The Queen of Glome confesses that she originally starts to write the first letter because she is confused by hearing an old priest telling a myth. The priest in the forest of the country of Essur is one of three priests in the story. In the forest of Essur, she should have found it to be the most tranquil day of her life, but it is, in fact, the most disturbing moment.

The old priest tells Orual a story of a goddess named Istra who is destroyed by her two elder sisters because they are jealous, not only of her beauty, but also of her husband. Orual logically concludes that the priest tells the story as a myth, but she emotionally interprets his account as the genuine history of Psyche. She decides to write in order to discern the difference between fact and fiction.

The extent of Orual's confusion is reflected by her unfinished utterances. She is not capable of controlling her speech. She leaves several sentences unfinished. Her speech is disturbed when Psyche tells her about the invisible palace. She loses emotional control the most when she hears Psyche talk about her husband, who is also referred to as "Beast," especially when seeing Psyche shining with delight at her husband's name. Although Orual is proud of her motherly love toward Psyche and confident that no one understands Psyche except her, she aggressively demands her possessive right to Psyche. Her ugly mind is reflected by her staggering speech. Orual cannot end her statements properly, finishing in mid-sentences: "It's time—"[48]; "This this—"[49]; and "I think I can smell the very—."[50]

Orual's effort to express her complaints in the form of two letters is an echo of Lewis's concern over the rhetorical importance of logos and poiema, especially in the last word, "might." Joy Alexander presumes that Lewis must have applied the same technique of speech shaped for Aslan to Orual. Aslan's speech pattern of both "clarity andprofundity"[51] is combined into "the form of pure speech towards which all communication should aspire."[52] She presents Lewis as a great rhetorical stylist, especially referring

48. Ibid., 123.
49. Ibid., 124.
50. Ibid.
51. Alexander, "'The Whole Art and Joy of Words'" 47.
52. Ibid., 48.

to what the Greek tutor Fox tells Orual: "Child, to say the very thing you really mean... that's the whole art and joy of words."[53]

Unlike her disturbing attitude toward Psyche's spiritual delight, Orual speaks fluently even when she is involved in mysterious dreams and illusions. She is not linguistically affected even though she is so overpowered by a series of visions that she is unable to distinguish reality from dreams. Her speech neither falters nor finishes in mid-sentence.

It is through the process of writing that Orual assesses her own mind, rediscovers her past, and detects the memory of Psyche. Supposedly writing to the Greeks, the accuser Orual blames the gods for stealing Psyche. While writing the letter of complaint, she is reminded of Psyche as both history (her baby or sister) and as myth (Istra in Esur).

When she finishes the first letter, Orual undergoes a religious change, from a rejection of the gods to an acceptance of them; she is not atheistic but rather deistic. She does not reject belief in the existence of a Supreme Being, but believes that the divine entity does not intervene in the universe. At the end of the first letter, she concludes that the gods have no interest in her prayers: "they have no answer?"[54]

Although her shattered memory and motive are sunken, covered, and hidden, Orual's mind is "probed," as if she's a hospital patient undergoing a surgical procedure. In other words, she is closely examined with an instrument—her pen—: "to probe my wound."[55]

Orual has her selfishness exposed unexpectedly by reunions with two people whom she dislikes: one is the former guardsman of Glome, Tarin, and the other is Captain Bardia's wife, Ansit. Tarin is a eunuch ambassador of a great neighboring nation and a former lover of Redival, the second princess of Glome, whom Orual ignores as trouble-maker. He informs Orual of her sister's loneliness because of a change in her concern for Psyche from Redival. Ansit is the widow of Bardia with whom Orual is secretly in love. She uncovers Orual's selfish love toward him and charges her with a vampire-like lust for craving all people around her: "Gorged with other men's lives, women's too."[56]

Orual's selfishness is stringently denounced by Tarin and Ansit. The two challengers work to change Orual's self-recognition. She considers

53. Lewis, *TWHF*, 305.
54. Ibid., 249–50.
55. Ibid., 253–54.
56. Ibid., 265.

herself not an affectionate mother for Psyche any longer, but a selfish Ungit who steals people as victims offered to her. She has to reverse the wrong images of nuisance-sister Redival and beloved Captain Bardi. As Orual becomes newly aware of her true self, she decides not to hide herself but to take off the veil. She exposes her bare face, first to Ansit, next to her ghost-father in a dream, and then to the visionary court. She then takes off her clothes and stands completely naked in the assembly: "'Uncover her,' said the judge."[57]

With no veil and clothes, Orual reveals what is hidden and faces the truth of what she observes. She gradually becomes a character who enters into the story. Completely bare-faced, she writes down the visions in words. She tries to put her words (logos) in proper form (poiema). She writes by switching roles between a narrator and a character. In visionary images, a gradual transition takes place from the traditional Greek story of Eros and Psyche into the myths of Orual and Psyche.

Orual spends the rest of her life writing. Her creative activity in the daytime begins to overflow. In a nocturnal dream, she sees herself sorting a huge pile of seeds just like Apuleius's story of Psyche. She mentally labors from pretext.[58] The numerous visions confirm to Orual that her love toward Psyche is a reflection of her true love for "another," indicated as the pronoun "him" who shares both dread and beauty: "it was for another's sake. all that was or will be, existed for *his* sake."[59]

In the dream, two images of Orual and Psyche are integrated. In the daytime illusions, Orual sees herself as a ghost, invisible to Psyche, but walking with her. She also witnesses Psyche attempting to commit suicide in the river, just like Orual in the River Shennit. Psyche sorts the seeds, gathers gold wool on the sheep farm, and brings back the box of beauty from Queen Persephone of the Deadland. Orual also carries the suffering of Psyche, as indicated by a reflection in the water. She sees two faces, not of herself, but of two Psyches in the water: "Yes, both Psyches, both beautiful...yet not exactly the same."[60]

Orual is supposed to speak to "the Greek." She starts to write to the suppositional Greek readers and expects them to logically judge her charges, but she speaks no longer to "the Greek" in the last chapter. She speaks

---

57. Ibid., 289.
58. Ibid., 256.
59. Ibid., 307.
60. Ibid., 308.

directly to the being indicated as the singular "you" and "Lord" with a capital letter.[61] She is convinced that words, human words, exist to encounter "you" or Lord, and that "questions," or human words, did not exist before "you" because "you are yourself the answer."[62] She asserts that overestimating words deprives language of meaning, battles against words and leads to the refusal ("hate") of images.[63] She expresses her disappointment at an over-emphasis on words, but she disappears into a different dimension by writing mid-sentence with "I might-": "On *words, words*; to be led out to battle against other *words*. Long did I *hate* you, long did I fear you. I might—."[64]

TWHF seemingly ends with Orual's last word "might." In fact, her letter is not the last paragraph in the novel. The new priest, Arnom, concludes with a short report. After reading her last paragraph, many readers, overwhelmed by Orual's powerful statement, may have overlooked Arnom's last words. The concluding paragraph includes the priest's announcement of Queen Orual's death, his discovery of the undecipherable markings detected after the word "might," and his reasoning that her head might have fallen forward on the markings when she breathed her last breath.

The markings are probably meant by Orual to be the integration of both word and image, but her conclusion is beyond Priest Arnom's comprehension. Even though he is the last witness of her death, he shows no interest in her last posture, a slanting body. He simply reports what he sees. If he truly understands what she says in her two letters, he could interpret her last pose as a positive rejection of overestimating words. He might not have read her letters, except for the last sentence with "might." He probably does not understand that her final position can be interpreted as revealing her convictions: the satisfaction of her encounter with the perfect "word" as indicated by the single "you" or "Lord" with a capital L; her decision not to emulate words anymore; and her expression of spirituality so that the last sentence appears to be unfinished to the priest.

Arnom is a reformist priest who invigorates the temple system by juxtaposing two images of the goddesses: modern and traditional. The priest of pagan religion is an embodiment of the rational Greek spirit of the new age. He establishes the new image of a beautiful goddess wearing

61. Ibid.
62. Ibid.
63. Ibid.
64. Ibid.

Greek costume side by side with the old image of Goddess Ungit made of a bloody, rough stone. The priest presents a new image of the divine being, casting the old image into oblivion. He can be seen as a representative of the modern society.

Arnom's memo finishes with the word "Greece," wishing to have the Queen's letters brought to the nation by any stranger. His last word, the last word of *TWHF*, is "Greece."[65] However, if he had read all volumes of the Queen's letters, he might have understood that her letters should not be taken to Greece. Her letters of complaint had been answered in her encounter with the single "you."

By finishing her story in mid-sentence with the word "might," Orual leaves her final words to the readers. Her silence is suggestive of the death of self-assertion and the limitation of human language to describe her encounter with the Divine. Defining God can be possible only when she "dies herself" by destroying her personality as narrator, character, male, female, writer, and reader. Scholar Carla A. Arnell also regards Orual's last word "might" as a key word, although she limits the story of beauty within the two characters of Orual and Psyche. She asserts that the novel enables the reader to appreciate the beauty that transcends the human language: "written into the deep structure of the world."[66]

Orual's last scene is a depiction of accusation against the materialistic protagonist who hides behind her face the real natures of darkness, emptiness, and egoism. Lewis subverts her fixed image and reconstructs the longing for a new creation through the integration of the two letters: her logical first letter (word) and her visionary second one (image). He uses the image of non-Christian or pagan myths of gods, dead and risen, and retells the Gospel story of Jesus Christ, as the Myth of myths. As Bruce Edwards points out, Lewis's approach is effective in relaxing those "moderns" cautious about Christianity.[67] The last word, "might," is possibly the depiction of Orual's shift into a story of myth. Orual's silence with "might" is discussed by several critics. Dominic Manganiello alludes to the battle of words ended by divine intervention. He focuses on Orual's silence at the

---

65. Ibid., 309.
66. Arnell, 31.
67. Edwards, "The Lion Still Roars."

Re-Writing Mythology

end.⁶⁸ Doris T. Myers affirms that Orual's silence with "might" is an expression of rejecting the demythologizing of the Bible.⁶⁹

Joy Davidman contributes to Lewis's inspiration to rewrite the myth of Psyche from Orual's point of view. Although the extent of Davidman's impact on Orual's last word is not verifiable, Lewis owes the whole structure of this retold myth to Davidman, who contributed as editor. Don W. King affirms that she increasingly serves "as a collaborator and shadow editor for the books Lewis is writing during this time (March, 1955)."⁷⁰

RETELLING NORSE MYTHOLOGY

Norse mythology is often indicated by Lewis scholars as an essential biographical factor, but not many have made a detailed analysis of the literary impact of northern myths on his novels. Daniel Warzecha's "Nordic Mythology in C.S. Lewis's The Chronicles of Narnia" (2008) is the most recent publication on Lewis and Norse myth. He explores the eschatological impact of the Norse gods on *The Chronicles of Narnia*, but excludes *TWHF* from his research, even though the novel was written about the same time as the Narnian series. He argues that both *The Chronicles of Narnia* and Norse mythology share the teleology of eschatological destiny within the underlying confrontation of order versus disorder. He compares both sets of stories from the perspectives of nature, world, and characters, concluding that the Narnian series is not children's literature.

An analysis of *TWHF* from the perspective of the impact of Greek and Nordic mythologies, especially Loki and Yggdrasil (World Tree), will contribute to the further understanding of Lewis as a novelist of Christian postmodernism. No other research has been published in the 2000s on Lewis and Norse myth. A comparison of Norse myth, the three stories of Yggdrasil, "Loki Bound," goddess Frigg, and *TWHF*, the three women characters of Psyche, Orual, and Ansit, and one man, Bardia, will allow the reader to envision a re-creation of the female character Orual as the integration of the four tremors associated with wood. Orual is, physically and spiritually, shaken by the four kinds of wood, each of which belongs to the four characters: Psyche as the wandering Tree, Orual's writing with a wooden pen, Ansit's spinning with wooden sticks, and Bardia as a man like

68. Manganiello, "*Till We Have Faces*: From Idolatry to Revelation," 31–45.
69. Myers, *C.S. Lewis in Context*, 210.
70. Davidman, *Out of My Bone*, 242. (10n).

a big a tree. Norse mythology inspires Lewis to feel a longing for another world. He describes his first encounter with a longing or "Joy"[71] as: "a voice from far more distant regions."[72] By the capitalized term "Joy," Lewis means not the emotional expression of joy but the indescribable desire for another world. Norse myth enables him to notice the concept of "Joy" which he also calls "northernness."[73] He regards the Norse myth as one of the most important experiences that triggers the feeling of "Joy" in his mind. He ultimately finds multiple moments of Joy reflected in one single "unendurable sense of desire and loss,"[74] as if the values of Yggdrasil were integrated in Orual.

The basic concept of the desire which he calls "Joy" motivates the atheistic Lewis to seek theism. Lewis reads Norse mythology throughout his life, beginning from an early age. Lewis felt similar desires for another world through looking at his brother's toy garden and reading *The Tale of Squirrel Nutkin*.[75] In his autobiographical book *Surprised by Joy* (1955), Lewis explains the impact of Norse myth on his mind. Through Nordic mythology, he comes to know the pleasure of "Joy" (or "northernness").[76]

When reading Norse poems, in particular Longfellow's *Saga of King Olaf*, Lewis is enthralled by the cold and far world in the poem. He then is pleased by the mysterious feeling of "Joy" through reading Tegnér's "Drapa," a poem of the Nordic god, Balder. He expresses the indescribable desire of "northernness," using descriptive words such as: "I was *uplifted* into huge regions of northern sky, I desired with almost *sickening* intensity . . . *falling* out of that desire and *wishing* I were *back* in it" (emphasis added).[77]

"Drapa," which means "death song," a poem by Swedish writer Esaias Tegnér, was translated into English by American poet Henry Wadsworth Longfellow (1807–1882) and published in Longfellow's *The Seaside and the Fireside* (1849). Lewis is inspired by the death of Balder through reading the first lines that echo the sorrow of the poet.

> Balder the Beautiful
> Is dead, is dead!

71. Lewis, *Surprised by Joy*, ix.
72. Ibid., 17.
73. Ibid., 83.
74. Ibid.
75. Ibid., 16–17.
76. Ibid.
77. Ibid., 19.

> And through the misty air
> Passed like the mournful cry
> Of sunward sailing cranes.[78]

Norse mythology is of importance in understanding Lewis's concept of literature not only because he comes to know the concept of "Joy" through reading Norse myth, but also because he met two of his close friends through their shared interest in Norse mythology: Arthur Greeves and J.R.R. Tolkien. His friendship with them helped Lewis to become the writer he was.

H.A. Guerber's *Myths of the Norsemen* is a catalyst for the first meeting between Lewis and childhood friend Arthur Greeves in Ireland.[79] Lewis read many books on Norse mythology that included not only *The Ring of the Nibelung*, but also H.A. Guerber's *Myths of the Norsemen* (1908), Donald A. Mackenzie's *Myths and Legends of the Teutonic Race* (1912), and Paul Henri Mallet's *Northern Antiquitie* (1847). When Lewis finds a copy of the book in Arthur's room, the two instantly become friends.[80] This sounds somewhat like the episode in *VDT* where Lewis describes the mysterious encounter between Lucy and the Sea Girl. The two boys similarly engage in a life-long comradeship through their passion for Nordic mythology: "both knew the stab of Joy . . . shot from the North."[81]

The correspondence between Lewis and Greeves provides abundant information for Lewis's reading and writing background. His letters to Greeves are nowadays considered to be primary source material on his literary views. The two friends spend their whole lives discussing literature until Lewis's death (1914–1963).

Lewis shares with Greeves not only his attraction for the Nordic legends as a reader, but also the desire to retell the myths as a writer. "Loki Bound" is one of his earlier poems based on Nordic legends. He writes from the new angle of Loki, not as an offender but as a victim who is unfairly abused. Loki is an evil god in the old saga, bound in punishment for killing the beautiful god Balder. In his letter to Arthur Greeves (6 Oct. 1914), Lewis supposes that "Loki Bound" is patterned after Greek tragedy. This poem (written when he was an agnostic) reveals his anger against God's creation. Lewis's early work "Loki Bound" was not published, but parts of

---

78. Longfellow, *The Seaside and the Fireside*, 77.
79. Lewis, *Surprised by Joy*, 89.
80. Arthur Greeves's house was just across from Lewis's "Little Lea" in Belfast.
81. Lewis, *Surprised by Joy*, 151.

the poem were published by Don W. King in 2001: the "Loki" fragments appear as the second item in Appendix One of *C.S. Lewis, Poet: The Legacy of His Poetic Impulse*

Lewis shares an interest in the ancient sagas with scholar-friend J.R.R. Tolkien, especially Icelandic legends. They enjoy a more than forty year long friendship from the 1920s, which leads to the birth of their best known novels: *The Chronicles of Narnia* and *The Lord of the Rings*. This friendship with Tolkien is important for Lewis's Christianity. His conversations with Tolkien about the Gospel and Myth motivate him to adopt the Christian faith. He is greatly inspired by Tolkien's notion that the beauty of Christianity is that it is a mythology that happens to be true.

Spiritually, Lewis owes much to these friends, Arthur and Tolkien. He later explains the benefits to Arthur Greeves from believing God to Christ.[82] J.R.R. Tolkien and another academic friend, Hugo Dyson, joined the discussion with Lewis on the resemblance of the Gospel to myths involving a dying and rising god. He later explicates the resemblance of Christianity to mythology at an Oxford Socratic Club conference (1945).[83]

Through appreciating the visual arts, Lewis feels the same pleasure of "Joy." In particular, he likes Arthur Rackham's illustrations to a volume of *The Ring of the Nibelung*, a myth based on the Norse sagas. He finds a parallel between the impressive encounter with the legendary hero Siegfried, to that of the tragic hero Balder and sunward sailing cranes in Tegnér's "Drapa."[84]

Lewis experiences "Joy" for another world not only through reading, but also through a realistic landscape. In the visible nature of his home country, Ireland, he sees a vision of *The Ring of the Nibelung*. In the mountains, hills, and valleys of Ireland, he finds a reflection of the Wagnerian characters walking, such as Mime, Sieglinde, Siegfried, and Fafner. Sigurd, a legendary hero of Norse legend, kills the dragon Fafnir; Mime/Regin is the foster father of Sigurd; Fafner, brother of Regin, guards the gold hoard; and Sieglinde is a twin sister/lover of Siegmund and mother of Siegfried: "*Mime* might meet *Sieglinde*, . . . *Siegfried* might listen to the bird, . . . scaly body of Fafner might emerge from its cave."[85] According to Walter Hooper, Lewis first read Wagner's libretto in *The Rhinegold and The Valkyrie* in 1910

---

82. Lewis, *The Collected Letters I*, 970.
83. Lewis, "Is Theology Poetry?," 119.
84. Lewis, *Surprised by Joy*, 83.
85. Ibid., 88.

and *Siegfried and The Twilight of the Gods* in 1911: "translated by Margaret Armur, with illustrations by Arthur Rackham."[86]

In the retold story of the Greek myth, Psyche is more explicitly described as a tragic sacrifice, but in the retelling of the Norse myth, Orual's relationship with other people is the center of the story. As a modernist woman, she is focused on who is responsible not only for the death of Psyche, but also of other characters that include Bardia and Orual herself. Her guilt is emphasized in the retold version of the Nordic mythology.

In the first letter in *TWHF*, Orual raises an objection with the gods' judgment regarding Psyche. In Lewis's poem, "Loki Bound," the Norse god Loki ignores his offense of killing the beautiful god Balder, but complains that he is unfairly punished. Orual is not able to admit her wrongdoing, just as if she is Loki. "Loki Bound" is one of Lewis's early poems of Norse myth in which the evil god Loki appeals for a fair judgment. According to H.A. Guerber, there are several theories of Loki who represents two contradictory characters inside one personification: Thor and Loki, god and devil.[87] Orual similarly reveal contradictory nature through opposing the gods' judgment of unfairly stealing Psyche. Even though she is in the dock, satirically, she cannot see the reality of her guilt.

In the second letter in *TWHF*, three wooden sticks are involved in deconstructing Orual's fixed idea of herself. The wooden attributes of three female characters, Psyche, Ansit, and Orual, are related to both physical and spiritual death. Psyche is killed on the sacrifice tree and punished to be exiled for Orual. Like the Norse goddess Frigg, Ansit plies a spinning stick, spinning the fates of her husband Bardia and Orual. As Colin Duriez affirms,[88] C.S. Lewis receives the literary impact from the Northern myth, the story of Balder, Frigg, and Odin. Frigg is the goddess who is responsible for weaving the clouds (sunshine, rain, and the fertility of crops) and weaving the fates: "Frigga was goddess of the atmosphere, or rather of the clouds. . .according to her somewhat variable moods."[89] The wife of Odin

---

86. Hooper, *C.S. Lewis: A Companion & Guide*, 222.
87. Guerber, *Myths of the Norsemen*, 216–17.
88. Duriez, *The C.S. Lewis Encyclopedia*, 26.
89. Guerber, 42.

is differently spelled according to writers: "Frigga"[90]; "Frigg"[91]; and "Freya, Frea, and Frigga, Frigg."[92]

As a writer, Orual spins words with a pen, and reflects her destiny in her writings as if she is Frigg who predicts the fortune of the world. She ultimately ends her life in the destiny of self-abandonment. The three women seem to act as the collective body of one tree, as if they are Yggdrasil. Yggdrasil is a World Tree in Norse myth, symbolic of sacrifice. The Nordic great god Odin hangs himself on the tree as the sacrifice for wisdom: "sacrificial hangings from gallows trees."[93] Between Odin's voluntary death on Yggdrasil and the Crucifixion of Jesus, Cotterell finds a remarkable parallel between Mythology and Scripture: Odin was pierced with a spear, and cried out, like Christ on the cross.[94] In the Bible, the apostle John observes a soldier piercing Jesus's side with a spear, bringing "blood and water" (John 19:34 NRSV), and Christ cries out before he dies (Matt 27:46).

Psyche's voluntary sacrifice on "the Tree"[95] is the most striking reflection of the Yggdrasil sacrifice of Odin. Psyche, a woman bound on the Tree, goes into exile to bear the punishment of Orual. Orual's mind feels the shake of Psyche walking, but she tries to ignore the warning against her fake life. Her veil covers true reality, Maia, behind the outer reality, Orual. Maia, a name for Orual used by Psyche, represents multiple faces including earth, warrior, and mother. Orual, instead, signifies a binary opposition of either Maia or Orual. Orual rationally trusts the empirical world, and rejects the invisible experience inside her mind.

The modernist Queen Orual also regards the world in binary opposition: she assumes that Psyche is either insane or the wife of a god, the West Wind. She considers no third option that Psyche is simultaneously sane and the wife of a god. She finds no dead body on the Tree to which Psyche is bound.[96] From this sign, she does not interpret her sister as living a happy life in a different dimension. She resorts to unfair trickery to win Psyche back. She makes Psyche choose a binary selection: her own happiness with the West Wind or Orual's happiness.

90. Ibid.
91. Mackenzie, *Teutonic Myth and Legend*, 146.
92. Walker, *The Woman's Encyclopedia of Myths and Secrets*, 323.
93. Cotterell, *A Dictionary of World Mythology*, 250.
94. Ibid.
95. Lewis, *TWHF*, 98.
96. Ibid.

Psyche sacrifices herself for Orual, breaking her pledge with the West Wind and giving up love with her husband. The consequence of it is incurring the penalty of becoming a wandering diaspora in the world. The woman bound to the Tree looks as if she is a wandering Dryad, a female wood nymph in Greek mythology. Psyche whispers to Orual through the breeze and this voice gradually affects Orual's heart.

This empirical evidence is not enough to convince Orual, who assumes that she has no belief in the third option. As she hears the sound of the wandering tree, she goes out into the garden to ascertain its source, shouting "Psyche."[97] She immediately rejects her discovery, easing her mind by assuming that the noise may instead be that of the chain on the well swinging in the breeze: "Psyche, Psyche, my only love.[98]

Orual gradually suppresses the inner part of Maia, while Queen Orual conversely overcomes Orual, as ruler and warrior.[99] She gains trust first as ruler in place of her sick father: "I am now the King's mouth,"[100] and next when warrior Orual wins a duel over the third prince of a neighboring country.

In a similar way to Yggdrasil, Orual represents multiple faces, as her Greek name, Maia, suggests. As Maia personifies the powers of transformation, Orual reflects a multitude of sides: a goddess of war, a mother in Greek myth, and earth in Roman myth.[101] Although she manifests various aspects of self, she denies the reality of herself, instead wearing the single mask of Queen Orual. As mother, Maia of Glome nurses Psyche in place of her dead mother. For Psyche, Orual is always Maia.[102]

In Greek mythology, Maia represents the productivity and protection of life as the mother of Hermes; she is the mother of the Earth in springtime in Roman myth. The Maia in Greek mythology shares multiple faces: a mother, a grandmother, and an enchanter. The Greek goddess Maia is the mother of Hermes; a nurse for Alcas in place of his mother; "Grandmother

---

97. Lewis, *TWHF*, 190 and 224.

98. Ibid., 224.

99. Ibid.

100. Ibid., 188.

101. "In Greek mythology, the seven daughters of the Titan Atlas and the Oceanid Pleione include: Maia, Electra, Taygete, Celaeno, Alcyone, Sterope and Merope." Maia is one of the Pleiades, the seven daughters of Atlas and the sea-nymph. http://www.britannica.com /EBchecked/topic/358391/Maia.

102. Lewis, *TWHF*, 76.

of Magic"[103]; and a goddess of earth, "the Greek goddess of spring and rebirth of the dead."[104]

Maia or agrarianism is the harmony of both the visible and the invisible worlds. Wendell Berry would associate Maia with his ecological concept of agrarianism. The American environmentalist and poet defines the agrarian mind as the organic relationship of the whole creation in the world, and as the integration of both nature and culture by borrowing what John Heins states.[105]

With Maia hidden behind the veil, Queen Orual spends her whole life competing with and conquering other people. However, at the end of her life, she writes letters with a wooden pen to de-mythologize her sister Psyche, who is enshrined as a goddess in the forest of Essur. She is told by the priest in Essur that Psyche is alive within a myth, even though she spends her whole life removing the sufferer Psyche. Orual is so angry that she cannot accept the fact that Psyche is beyond her control. Listening to the beat of the wooden pen, she appeals to the reader to logically judge her complaint.

The third tremor is from Ansit, Captain Bardia's widow. Orual seems to ignore the woman engaged in spinning. Her silence conversely exposes the cruelty hidden behind her mask.

Ansit is described by Orual as a spinner twice. As the goddess Frigg of Nordic mythology predicts the future of her palace Asgard through spinning, the spinner Ansit predicts Orual's fate. Even though Orual notices Ansit spinning twice, she is intentionally silent about the significance of the spinning, making no further comment on the fact.

Ansit, however, explicitly accuses Orual of damaging other people, charging her as a killer. After she loses Psyche, Orual controls Ansit's husband Bardia as scapegoat with no feeling of guilt for her actions. Ansit blames Orual for killing others in body and mind, using the verb "eat": "as a tree that is eaten away within."[106] Orual takes her word "eating" to mean that she is a murderer: "You have made me little better than the lord

---

103. Walker, 572.
104. Ibid.
105. Berry, *The Art of the Commonplace*, 240.
106. Lewis, *TWHF*, 260.

Re-Writing Mythology

Bardia's murderer."[107] Ansit argues that Orual damages Bardia's flesh as if she is a vampire: "your queenship drank up his blood. . .and ate out his life."[108]

As narrator of the letter, Orual shows little concern for Ansit as a spinner. She is instead more impressed by the calm beauty of Ansit: "she sat at her spinning—very pale, but very calm."[109] She does notice Ansit spinning when she feels nervous about the spinner's rigid attitude: "She sat down and resumed her spinning . . . She would give me no help."[110]

Orual makes no further comments on Ansit's spinning, but the spinning woman symbolically sits down and continues spinning as if she is Frigg, the goddess of Norse myth who plies a spinning wheel. The spinner, Frigg, represents the mother of life and the prophet of everyone's fate. The famous painting of Queen Frigg by J. C. Dollman is a depiction of the goddess spinning the Clouds. A cloud, as an element of weather in the sky, is symbolic of the fates.[111]

Although Orual seemingly does not consider the effect of Ansit as a spinner, she certainly cannot avoid hearing both Ansit's accusing voice and the sound of spinning together. The wood beat is considered to affect Orual as she feels "no help" from the spinner Ansit.[112] The feeling of discomfort from Ansit works as the first step for Orual to confirm the unpleasantness inside herself.

The second step is when Orual takes off the veil. She is perplexed by the fact that Ansit is jealous of her. Although it is a small blow to her fast-closed mind, the perplexity makes her pull aside her veil and expose her hidden face to Ansit. Ansit is astonished to see "Orual" behind the veil and she "gasps."[113] She makes no further response except to weep. On the face of Orual mixed with Maia, Ansit must see an ambiguous reflection of a woman who loves and suffers for someone. Even though Ansit interprets the face as Orual's erotic love for Bardia, it is not clear what she sees on the face: "You loved him. You've suffered, too. We both . . ."[114]

---

107. Ibid., 263.
108. Ibid., 264.
109. Ibid., 259.
110. Ibid., 260.
111. Guerber, *Myths of the Norsemen*, 42.
112. Ibid., 260.
113. Ibid., 263.
114. Ibid.

Ansit works as if she is the Norse goddess Frigg. Frigg is able to see everyone's fortunes while spinning inside her home of Asgard Palace. Ansit also works as a spinner inside her home, gifted with the ability to know the fates of people in Orual's home, the Palace of Glome. She describes Orual's cruel effects upon others, not only on her and Bardia, but also the Greek tutor Fox and her two sisters.[115]

The Norse Queen Frigg, however, has one problem with her gift of prediction. As she is not able to see a vision of her beautiful son Baldor, he is killed by Loki and never returns. As Ansit's husband passes away and her son Ilerdia faithfully serves Orual, her beloved ones, both husband and son, also do not come home. For Ansit, Bardia is killed by Orual and Ilerdia is a slavish prisoner taken by Orual. Ansit expresses her displeasure to Orual: "You have taken Ilerdia now too."[116]

Lewis rewrites *TWHF* as a contemporary version of *The Songs of the Nibelungs*. *TWHF* is the drama of Ansit's revenge for Bardia against Orual. Lewis's concept of Bardia is ambiguous to the reader because his whole life is spoken from Orual's perspective as narrator of the novel. She occupies his whole viewpoint, except in her dialogue with Ansit. In *The Songs of the Nibelungs*, Kriemhild, a wife of Siegfried, seeks revenge on the murderer, Brünhild, for her dead husband. As Siegfried is avenged and killed by Brünhild for deceiving her, Orual repays Bardia because she feels "pricked" or offended by Bardia as if she is Brünhild: "blow the bubble up before you prick it."[117]

In *The Songs of the Nibelungs*, Brünhild is the Icelandic Queen who is deceived by Siegfried. Like Brünhild, Orual revenges her male partner. The warrior-lady Brünhild falls in love with Siegfried during a sword fight with him, even though Siegfried pretends to be Gunther at the time. The warrior-lady Orual similarly falls in love with Bardia through swordship with him. Lewis scholar Kazuo Takeno regards Orual's swordship with Bardia as a symbol of an unintentional action of charity.[118] As Siegfried is a warrior-hero, so Bardia is Captain of Glome, a successful soldier on the battlefield.

In contrast to Siegfried, Bardia does not intend to deceive Orual, but his statement is unexpectedly interpreted by her in a different dimension.

---

115. Ibid., 265.
116. Ibid., 264.
117. Ibid., 222.
118. Takeno, *C.S. Lewis Yorokobi No Tobira*, 229.

She takes his words as a confession of love: "the nearest thing to a love-speech. . ."[119] Her unrequited love for him can be seen on two occasions: firstly when she hears a dialogue between him and another soldier, "If a man was blind and she weren't the King's daughter, she'd make him a good wife"[120]; and secondly he raises her hand to his lips to pay respect to the victor of the duel, "Bardia's lips on my hand were like the touch of lightning."[121]

Unlike Siegfried, Bardia does not intentionally offend Orual, but she takes his words as an act of treachery. He asks her for an early end to the day: "The day's work is over."[122] His use of the term "work" is interpreted by her as an act of betrayal. She feels offended, as if she has been deceived: "I was his work; he earned his bread by being my soldier."[123]

For Brünhild and Orual, killing is a warped way of expressing concern for their lover/deceiver. Brünhild slaughters Siegfried with a spear. Orual does not kill Bardia with a weapon, but spends a long time harassing him. She indirectly kills him by repeatedly sending him onto the battlefield and keeping him away from his wife. She makes him work harder and excessively consumes his energy. Orual loves Bardia in a deformed way, as if a vampire devouring a victim.

Queen Orual hides her real face with a veil to represent a flawed model of the opposite sex. Bardia, however, discerns her spiritual defect: "The gods never made anyone—man or woman—with a better natural gift for it."[124] He expresses his grief at the fact that her advantage is limited by femininity, even though she is blessed with masculine ability. She wishes to be loved by him as a woman, but he wishes her to develop her own talents which transcend gender.

Bardia loves Queen Orual in two senses of love: he devotes himself to her out of love as *philia*, friendship or common interest, and as *charity*, agape or unconditional love. Queen Orual desires his love as *eros*, or romantic love, but he loves his wife Ansit out of love as *storge*, affection or family love. In his philosophical book *The Four Loves* (1960), Lewis divides love into four categories based on the four Greek words for love: *storge* or affection, *philia* or friendship, *eros* or romance, and *agape* or charity,

119. Lewis, *TWHF*, 92.
120. Ibid., 92.
121. Ibid., 224.
122. Ibid., 223.
123. Ibid.
124. Ibid., 197.

unfathomable love. Lewis affirms that modern literature ignores friendship, love as *philia*, between those who share a common interest or activity. Lewis states that the true friendship between David and Jonathan in the Bible (1 Samuel 20:1–42) is almost a lost art: "The modern world, in comparison, ignores it."[125]

As Lewis regards the opposite sex as a reflection of sexuality in another world, so Bardia is the mirror of Lewis's ideal sexuality. However, Orual's view of him is damaged. Lewis assumes that gender in this world, however imperfect it is, reflects an ideal human relationship in Heaven. As S.A. Barlett states, Lewis's concept of gender is not compatible with the viewpoint of feminists and psychologists such as Abraham Maslow, Bernard J. Paris, and Karen Horney: "Feminists would argue that women must resist Lewis's solution . . ."[126] Barlett judges Orual and Psyche from the perspectives of the three critics who regard a woman's self-worth as her right to define herself without depending on someone else's opinion.

Mary Steward Van Leeuwen suggests that we need to incorporate C.S. Lewis's insight into our worldview: he gradually set aside class and gender (vertical), orienting in favor of "a preference for people" (horizontal).[127] She proposes not the drastic change of Lewis's recognition of genders, but a gradual transformation from vertical to horizontal. She supports his preference for not the alternatives of two extreme opinions, but for the integration of the two.

On the surface, TWHF is a revenge drama about Ansit. In actuality, it is a story of reconciliation in human relationship. Kriemhild, wife of Siegfried, goes out to kill Brunhild for revenge. Unlike her, Bardia's wife, Ansit, never leaves home for revenge, but rather patiently waits for it. She gets her revenge on Orual not with a sword, but with her tongue. She skillfully shifts the focus of the topic from a general greeting to the one responsible for Bardia's death. In the beginning, she does not blame Orual for overworking her husband. She touches on his health with a general comment: "He was tired."[128] Next she mentions the particular reason that caused his death: "He had worked himself."[129] Lastly she emphasizes the particular person who

---

125. Lewis, *The Four Loves*, 40.
126. Bartlett, "Humanistic Psychology in C.S. Lewis's *Till We Have Faces*," 198.
127. Van Leeuwen, *A Sword Between the Sexes?*, 258.
128. Lewis, *TWHF*, 260.
129. Ibid.

was responsible: "Ten years ago he should have given over and lived as old men do."[130]

The end of Bardia is an integration of both Greek and Nordic mythology. His life finishes like Odysseus's, rather than Siegfried's. Odysseus is the hero of Homer's poem *The Odyssey*. He returns to his wife Penelope after escaping captivity by the nymph Calypso. Siegfried never returns to his wife, while Bardia returns home like Odysseus.

The vibration of Psyche's swaying tree, Orual's writing, and Ansit's spinning leads to the destruction of Orual's rational world view, her discovery of a new self-identity and the restoration of human relationship. Like Frigg, Ansit continues to spin as usual, even during the mourning period of Bardia's death. Like the musical fugue of Bach, the strokes of the three wooden sticks combined lead Orual into another world. The fugue is an expression of escaping death for postmodernists, as the structure of a fugue consists of a short phrase which is successively and endlessly repeated and developed by others.[131] The composition of fugue for Lewis is the joy of another world beyond death.[132] Lewis uses the fugue-like repetition of strokes to express his concept of the divinity and that something which lies beyond human construction.

Through experiencing invisible visions and hearing silent tremors, Orual undergoes a transformation in her recognition of beauty. Carla A. Arnell suggests that Orual's silence at the end represents the harmony of finite beauty (illusionary pictures) and recognition of the sublime, a transcendent God in the final analysis. Orual dies in the old text and lives in a new story through writing, rewriting, reading, and ending with the discovery of image, word, and beyond.

---

130. Ibid.

131. Miller, "The Late Derrida," 146.

132. Lewis, *God in the Dock*, 37.

Conclusion

A discussion of C.S. Lewis's thoughts and works from the perspective of Christian postmodernism reveals that he accepts the postmodernist approaches of both word and image, but ultimately anticipates transcendent values in another world beyond earthly media. An analysis of three of his works of fiction, *That Hideous Strength* (*THS*), *The Voyage of the Dawn Treader* (*VDT*), and *Till We Have Faces* (*TWHF*), demonstrates that he empowers story-telling through the postmodernist literary approach of creating transcendent understanding through a story within a story. Contrary to modernist literature that elevates a single interpretation of either word or image, Lewis accepts multiple interpretations of the text through the expression of both word (logical explanation) and image (imaginative description).

Ignoring modernist critics who sideline science fiction and fantasy novels from literary genres, Lewis reconstructs these genres and rehabilitates mythological story-telling from the viewpoint of Christianity. As an anti-modernist writer, he reevaluates the literary values undermined by modernist critics—mythology, science fiction and fantasy literature, recovering the meaning of a text, the reader's collaboration with the author for forming meaning, and a story within a story.

In his fiction, Lewis never uses even one theological word of Christianity, but instead re-tells a mythological story of pagan gods, dead and risen, in order to relate the story of Christ's death and resurrection. The characters of the selected novels, *THS*, *VDT*, and *TWHF*, have strong parallels with Christ's life and ordeals: Merlin and Ransom in *THS*; Aslan in *VDT*; and Psyche in *TWHF*. One problem with this is that the reader with no biblical knowledge cannot easily identify the Christian association, as the main plotline is the deconstruction of the protagonists' self-recognition

Conclusion

and the stories are set in the mythological backgrounds of Arthurian legends, the medieval voyage literature of imram, as well as Norse and Celtic mythology. It is certain, however, that Lewis's works are filled with religious elements, even if the reader should fail to connect them with the Gospel.

Lewis presents four religious elements in *The Problem of Pain* (1940): the experience of "the *Numinous*";[1] the acknowledgment some kind of morality[2]; the numinous experience as a guardian of the morality, a paradox of awe and obligation[3]; and the reader's relation to "the Something"[4] awful and righteous.

The first element, the Numinous, is a word coined by German philosopher Rudolph Otto (1869–1937) to mean paradoxical feelings of dread and enchantment. Lewis similarly creates mixed emotions of fear, awe, and bliss in the depiction of characters in his novels. In *THS* there is an eerie magician, Merlin, and mysterious angels, Eldil and Venus; in *VDT*, supernatural male and female Stars and ghostly Monopod-dwarves; and in *TWHF*, Psyche as a symbol of sacrifice and supreme beauty, as well as the enigmatic ghosts of the Father-King and the Tutor Fox. There is also Orual in a series of picturesque images.

In his *The Idea of the Holy* (1917), Ottor states that dread is associated with the numinous experience of Abraham in the Old Testament and the enchantment with the Apostle Paul's enchanting manner of speech in the New Testament. "A feeling of a creature" is a term created by him to describe Abraham's fear and awe: "It is the emotion of a creature, abased and overwhelmed by its own nothingness in contrast to that which is supreme above all creatures."[5] He asserts that Abraham is overwhelmed by "a feeling of a creature" when he courageously implores God to save the people of Sodom: "Let me take it upon myself to speak to the Lord, I who am but dust and ashes" (Gen 18:27 NRSV).

Ottor describes the second aspect of the Numinous or a feeling of "enchantment" through the way the Apostle Paul effectively uses the negative form. In his first letter to the Corinthians, Paul draws from the book of the Prophet Isaiah, a sentence with repetitive negative forms: "From ages past no one has heard,/ no ear has perceived,/ no eye has seen any God besides

---

1. Lewis, *The Problem of Pain*, 6.
2. Ibid., 8.
3. Ibid., 9.
4. Ibid., 10.
5. Otto, *The Idea of the Holy*, 10.

you,/ who works for those who wait for him." (Isaiah 64:4 NRSV). Otto proposes that Paul must have known that a positive effect of the Numinous can be generated from the repetition of negative words. He states that: "Eye hath not seen, nor ear heard, neither have entered into the heart of man, the things which God hath prepared for them that love Him."[6]

The Hebrew Apostle Paul similarly applies the negative form (the challenger's culture) to communicate with the Greek as his challenger (Acts 17:29). Lewis presents the ambiguous end of major characters who seemingly disappear into different dimensions: Merlin, Ransom, and persona "I" in *THS*, Reepicheep in *VDT*, and Orual in *TWHF*.

The second religious element is morality. As Lewis writes in *The Abolition of Man* (1943), there is a set of objective values shared by every culture, even though they may have minor differences: "the traditional moralities of East and West, the Christian, the Pagan, and the Jew."[7] With this common law, "the Tao," he criticizes modern society for abandoning the Tao or the traditional morality. In his fiction, no written statement of morality, similar to the Ten Commandments, is explicitly presented, but it is certain that St. Anne's righteous battle against the N.I.C.E. in *THS*, the transformation of Eustace in *VDT*, and Orual's face hidden within the veil (*TWHF*) is indicative of a universally inherent morality.

Morality as a religious element is, in other words, the significance of loving. Jesus summarizes this concept with two simple phrases that command us to "love one another" and "to lay down one's life for one's friends" (John 15: 12–13 NRSV). In Lewis's fiction, characters give up individual ambition to save others: in *THS*, Merlin gives up his traditional role as wizard to save the modern world; in *VDT*, King Caspian abandons his own desire for Aslan's Country to serve the nation of Narnia, and in *TWHF*, Psyche leaves her happy married life to rescue her sister Orual.

The third religious element is in confrontation with the Numinous and linked with the morality. Lewis expresses the Numinous as a necessary process to morality as a guardian: "when the Numinous Power to which they feel awe is made *the* guardian of the morality to which they feel obligation."[8] An example is observed by Ottor in the episode of the centurion at Capernaum who feels awe before Jesus[9]: "I am not worthy that

6. Ibid., 34.
7. Lewis, *The Abolition of Man*, 45.
8. Lewis, *The Problem of Pain*, 9.
9. Otto, *The Idea of the Holy*, 56.

Conclusion

thou shouldest enter under my roof" (Luke 7: 1–10 KJV). Ottor interprets the centurion's words as his feeling of nothingness when he is "confronted by the numen,"[10] and this realization leads to the desire for "atonement,"[11] or peace with God: "even holiness itself may be tainted and tarnished by his presence."[12]

Lewis's fiction similarly depicts a dreadful, but fascinating, experience in which a sleeping character is shaken, made alive, and motivated to realize that he/she has lost his/her self-recognition in the modern world. The transport depicted is between this world and another mythological world through the daily landscape as the channel: Jane's daydream in *THS*, a painting in *VDT*, and Orual's letter writing in *TWHF*. The rational thoughts of characters are unsettled by the numinous sounds of tremors—earthquakes in *THS*, waves in *VDT*, and shaking in *TWHF*. Each is motivated to desire something solid, similar to the moral standard—Ransom's light in *THS*, Aslan's wrath and compassion in *VDT*, and a contrast between Psyche's beauty and Orual's deformation in *TWHF*.

The fourth element, the most prominent postmodernist type, provides the reader with an alternative option of whether or not "the Something" is a lunatic or what the one actually says it is. The Something claims to be both "the awful haunter of nature" and "the giver of the moral law."[13] The fourth nature is what Lewis assumes as our relations to both the "awful" and the "righteous"—the personality who joins both the Numinous and morality: "the Something which is at once the awful haunter of nature and the giver of the moral law."[14] The religious element is someone associated with the Supreme deity similar to the God of Creation.

Unlike in his first two novels discussed here, *THS* and *VDT*, Lewis ambiguously suggests the presence of the divine being in the last novel, *TWHF*. In *THS*, the divine being Maleldil is mentioned as one similar to Jesus, the Second Person of the Godhead. In *VDT*, the divine presence is Aslan, the son of the Emperor-beyond-the-Sea. However, in *TWHF*, the story ends with an unclear depiction of the female protagonist, Orual, leaving the interpretation to the reader. When she is involved in an irrational experience through a confrontation with someone indescribable, the

---

10. Ibid., 57.
11. Achtemeier, ed., *Harper's Bible Dictionary*, 80.
12. Otto, *The Idea of the Holy*, 57.
13. Lewis, *The Problem of Pain*, 10.
14. Ibid.

rational Orual undergoes a numinous experience, feeling as unworthy as the centurion in the book of Luke.

Lewis finishes his last novel in a way which blurs boundaries and leaves its interpretation to the reader. The final ambiguous description of the protagonist Orual is a question for the reader—it is what she says or it is what the priest, Arnom, says. As Rudolph Ottor affirms, the ultimate part of our nature lies hidden above and beyond our rational being.[15] Lewis similarly writes to suggest the ultimate part of our existence is beyond both Orual's subjective experience (image) and Arnom's objective observation (word).

No clear identity of the mysterious person is emphatically indicated, but the story ends with two statements of her destiny: one is her own subjective account of the numinous experience with her shouts "you" and "Lord"; the other is when the modernist priest Arnom objectively reports her death and the undecipherable marks at the end of her second letter.

Lewis presents a postmodern image of humanity in the illustrations of Orual, the protagonist of his last novel. In her deconstructed perception, he fills a multi-dimensional reality as both man and woman. With her re-created personality, he reflects not the sexuality of man and woman in this world, but envisions the reality of humanity in Heaven. His communication with female writers contributes to this understanding and approach to ideal humanity: this world is a shadow-land of the true homeland, another world, in gender. Among these female contributors are Dorothy L. Sayers, Joy Davidman, and Julian of Norwich. Christian postmodernism is most reflected in Lewis's description of female characters who are involved in writing and reading.

Lewis shakes the minds of his readers as if destroying all that is not pure, until they have achieved purity. It is as if to prepare them to face God in Eternity. Such vision is echoed by what George MacDonald says in his sermons: "He [God] will shake heaven and earth that only the unshakable may remain; he is a consuming fire."[16] Lewis takes these approaches to reach the mind of the reader that is flooded with the multiple values of the contemporary world. The blurry borders between fact and fiction fundamentally indicate that this world is a very indistinct place, while suggesting that reality lies beyond the limitation of human language. Lewis ultimately wishes the reader to reconstruct the restrictions of humanity and to expect

15. Otto, *The Idea of the Holy*, 36.
16. Lewis, ed, A Preface to *George Macdonald: An Anthology*, 2.

Conclusion

what transcends the limitations of word and image from the perspective of Christian postmodernism.

Bibliography

Achtemeier, Paul J., ed. *Harper's Bible Dictionary*. San Francisco: Harper, 1985.
Alexander, Joy. "'The Whole Art and Joy of Words': Aslan's Speech in the Chronicles of Narnia." *Mythlore* 24.1 (2003) 27–48.
Alighieri, Dante. *The Divine Comedy: A New Prose Translation*. New York: Rinehart, 1954.
Anderson, John. "The Voyage of Brendan, an Irish Monastic Expedition to Discover the Wonders of God's World." *The American Benedictine Review* 43 (1992) 262–82.
Ankerberg, John, and John Weldon. *The Facts on the King James Only Debate*. Eugene: Harvest, 2003.
Aratus. *The Phenomena*. In Internet Archive. https://archive.org/details/phenomenadiosemeooarat.
Armstrong, Chris. "Dorothy Sayers: 'The Dogma is the Drama.' An Interview with Barbara Reynolds." *Christianity Today* (Dec. 16, 2005) 5pp. http://www.christianitytoday.com/ct/2005/decemberweb-only/52.0a.html?start=1.
Arnell, Carla A. "On Beauty, Justice, and the Sublime in C.S. Lewis's *Till We Have Faces*." *Christianity and Literature* 52 (2002) 23–33.
Ashe, Geoffrey. *Land to the West: St. Brendan's Voyage to America*. New York: Viking, 1962.
Augustine. *The Literal Meaning of Genesis*. Translated by John Hammond Taylor. New York: Newman, 1982.
Bacon, Francis. *Bacon's Essays*. Edited by F. G. Selby. London: Macmillan, 1889.
Bakhtin, M. M. *Problems of Dostoevsky's Poetics*. Edited and translated by Caryl Emerson. Minneapolis: University of Minnesota Press, 1984.
Barkman, Adam. "All is Righteousness and There is No Equality." *Christian Scholar's Review* 36 (2007) 415–36.
Bartlett, S.A. "Humanistic Psychology in C.S. Lewis's *Till We Have Faces*: A Feminist Critique." *Studies in the Literary Imagination* 22 (1989) 185–98.
Barratt, David. *Narnia: C.S. Lewis and His World*. Grand Rapids: Kregel, 2005.
Bell, Michael. "The Metaphysics of Modernism." In *The Cambridge Companion to Modernism*, edited by Michael Levenson, 9–32. New York: Cambridge University Press, 1999.
Benda, Julien. *The Treason of the Intellectuals*. Translated by Roger Kimball. 1928. Reprinted, Piscataway, NJ: Transaction, 2011.
Berger, Peter L. *The Heretical Imperative: Contemporary Possibilities of Religious Affirmation*. 1979. Reprinted, Garden City, NY: Anchor, 1980.
Berry, Wendell. *The Art of the Commonplace: The Agrarian Essays of Wendell Berry*. Berkeley: Counterpoint, 2002.

Bibliography

Biedermann, Hans. *Dictionary of Symbolism: Cultural Icons and the Meanings behind Them.* Translated by James Hulbert. New York: Meridian, 1994.
Bresland, Ronald W. *The Backward Glance: CS Lewis and Ireland.* Belfast: Dufour, 1999.
———. *Travel with CS Lewis.* Epsom, UK: Day One, 2006.
Browning, W. R. F. *A Dictionary of the Bible.* Oxford: Oxford University Press, 2009.
Bullinger, Ethelbert W. *Number in Scripture: Its Supernatural Design and Spiritual Significance.* Mansfield Center, CT: Martino, 2011.
Bultmann, Rudolf. *Kerygma and Myth: A Theological Debate.* New York: Harper & Row, 1961.
Cahill, Thomas C. *How the Irish Saved Civilization: The Untold Story of Ireland's Heroic Role from the Fall of Rome to the Rise of Medieval Europe.* New York: Nan, 1995.
———. *Mysteries of the Middle Ages: The Rise of Feminism, Science, and Art from the Cults of Catholic Europe.* New York: Talese, 2006.
Calinescu, Matei. *Five Faces of Modernity: Modernism, Avant-Garde, Decadence, Kitsch, Postmodernism.* Durham: Duke University Press, 1987.
Caputo, John D. *What Would Jesus Deconstruct?: The Good News of Postmodernism for the Church.* Grand Rapids: Baker, 2007.
Carlyle, Thomas. *Sartor Resartus: The Life and Opinions of Herr Teufelsdrockh.* 1896. Reprinted, New York: AMS, 1974.
Carson, D. A. "Athens Revisited." In *Telling Truth: Evangelizing Postmoderns,* edited by D. A. Carson, 384–95. Grand Rapids: Zondervan, 2000.
Cary, George. *The Medieval Alexander.* Edited by D. J. A. Ross. Cambridge: Cambridge University Press, 1956.
Chang, Curtis. *Engaging Unbelief: A Captivating Strategy from Augustine & Aquinas.* Downers Grove, IL: InterVarsity, 2000.
Chretien De Troyes. *Arthurian Romances.* Translated by W. W. Comfort. London: Everyman, 1967.
Clifford, Derek. *A History of Garden Design.* London: Faber, 1962.
Coghlan, Ronan. *The Illustrated Encyclopaedia of Arthurian Legends.* Rockport, MA: Element, 1991.
Collins, Francis. *The Language of God: A Scientist Presents Evidence for Belief.* New York: Free, 2006.
Cotterell, Arthur. *A Dictionary of World Mythology.* Rev. ed. Oxford: Oxford University Press, 1993.
Curtin, Jeremiah. *Myths and Folk Tales of Ireland.* 1890. Reprinted, New York: Dover, 1975.
Davidman, Joy. *Out of My Bone: The Letters of Joy Davidman.* Edited by Don W. King. Grand Rapids: Eerdmans, 2009.
———. *Smoke on the Mountain: An Interpretation of the Ten Commandments.* Forward by C.S. Lewis. Philadelphia: Westminster, 1953.
Ditchfield, Christin. *A Family Guide to Narnia: Biblical Truths in C.S. Lewis's The Chronicles of Narnia.* Wheaton, IL: Crossway, 2003.
Donaldson, Mara E. "Orual's Story and the Art of Retelling: A Study of *Till We Have Faces.*" In *Word and Story in C.S. Lewis: Language and Narrative in Theory and Practice,* edited by Peter J. Schakel and Charles Huttars, 157–70. Columbia: University of Missouri Press, 1991.
Donne, John. *The Poems of John Donne.* Edited by Sir Herbert Grierson. London: Oxford University Press, 1964.

Bibliography

———. *Songs and Sonnets*. Edited by Julian Lovelock. Tiptree, UK: Anchor, 1973.
Dougill, John. *Oxford: A Literary Guide*. 2002. Oxford: Oxface, 2006.
Downing, Crystal L. *Changing Signs of Truth: A Christian Introduction to the Semiotics of Communication*. Downers Grove, IL: InterVarsity, 2012.
———. *How Postmodernism Serves (My) Faith: Questioning Truth in Language, Philosophy and Art*. Downers Grove, IL: InterVarsity, 2006.
Downing, David C. "C.S. Lewis among the Postmodernists." *Books and Culture* (Nov/Dec 1998) 5pp. http://www.leaderu.com/humanities/lewis-postmodernists.html.
———. *Into the Region of Awe*. Downers Grove, IL: IVP, 2005.
———. *Into the Wardrobe: C.S. Lewis and the Narnia Chronicles*. Hoboken, NJ: Nossey, 2005.
———. "Perelandra: A Tale of Paradise Regained." In *Fantasist, Mythmaker, and Poet*, edited by Bruce L. Edwards,13–34. Westport, CT: Praeger, 2007.
———. *Planet in Peril: A Critical Study of C.S. Lewis's Ransom Trilogy*. Amherst: University of Massachusetts Press, 1992.
———. "*That Hideous Strength*: Spiritual Wickedness in HighPlaces." In *Fantasist, Mythmaker, and Poet*, edited by Bruce L. Edward, 53–70. Westport, CT: Praeger, 2007.
Duriez, Colin. *The C.S. Lewis Encyclopedia: A Complete Guide to His Life, Thought, and Writings*. Wheaton, IL: Crossway, 2000.
———. *A Field Guide to Narnia*. Downers Grove, IL: InterVarsity, 2004.
———. "Lewis and Military Service: War and Remembrance (1917–1918)." In *An Examined Life*, edited by Bruce L Edwards, 79–101. Westport, CT: Praeger, 2007.
———. *Tolkien and C.S. Lewis: The Gift of Friendship*. Mahwah, NJ: Paulist, 2003.
Duriez, Colin, and David Porter. *The Inklings Handbook: A Comprehensive Guide to the Lives, Thought and Writings of C.S. Lewis, J.R.R. Tolkien, Charles Williams, Owen Barfield and Their Friends*. Atlanta: Chalice, 2001.
Edwards, Bruce L., ed. *An Examined Life*. Westport, CT: Praeger, 2007.
———, ed. *Fantasist, Mythmaker, and Poet*. Westport, CT: Praeger, 2007.
———. "The Lion Still Roars." *World Magazine*. http://www.worldmag.com/2001/02/mailbag/page2.
———. *A Rhetoric of Reading: C.S. Lewis's Defense of Western Literacy*. Provo, UT: Center, 1986.
———, ed. *The Taste of the Pineapple: Essays on C.S. Lewis as Reader, Critic, and Imaginative Writer*. Bowling Green, OH: Bowling Green State University Press, 1988.
Eliot, T.S. *Four Quartets*. London: Faber, 1959.
———. "The Love Song of J. Alfred Prufrock." In *Prufrock and Other Observations*. http://www.gutenberg.org/files/1459/1459-h/1459-h.htm#linklovesong
Filmer, Kath. *The Fiction of C.S. Lewis: Mask and Mirror*. NewYork: St Martin's, 1993.
Flinders, Carole Lee. *Enduring Grace: Living Portraits of Seven Women Mystics*. New York: Harper, 1993.
Ford, Paul. *Companion to Narnia*. San Francisco: Harper, 1994.
Fowles, John. *The French Lieutenant's Woman*. London: Cape, 1969.
Frazer, James George. *The Golden Bough: A Study in Magic and Religion*. 1890. Repprinted, London: Macmillan, 1922.
Fredrick, Candice and Sam McBride. *Women among the Inklings: Gender, C.S. Lewis, J.R.R. Tolkien, and Charles Williams*. Westport, CT: Greenwood, 2001.
French, Rose. *Minneapolis Star Tribune*. 10 Feb. 2012. Web. 16 Sep. 2012.

Bibliography

Freud, Sigmund. *A General Introduction to Psychoanalysis*. Translated by Joan Riviere. New York: Permabooks 1953.

Gagarin, Michael, and Elaine Fantham, eds. *The Oxford Encyclopedia of Ancient Greece and Rome*. Oxford: Oxford University Press, 2010.

Galilei, Galileo. *Discoveries and Opinions of Galileo*. Translated by Stillman Drake. Garden City: Doubleday, 1957.

Giamatti, A. Bartlett. *The Earthly Paradise and the Renaissance Epic*. Princeton: Princeton University Press, 1966.

Gibson, Evan. *C.S. Lewis, Spinner of Tales: A Guide to His Fiction*. Grand Rapids: Eerdmans, 1980.

Gilbert, Douglas, and Clyde S. Kilby. *C.S. Lewis, Images of His World*. London: Hodder, 1973.

Gilbert, Sandra, and Susan Gubar, eds. *The Norton Anthology of Literature by Women: The Traditions in English*. New York: Norton, 1996.

Gill, N. S. "Who was Merlin?: Possible Men Who May Have Been Merlin." *Ancient/Classical History*. http://ancienthistory.about.com/cs/people/a/merlin_2.htm

Glyer, Diana Pavlac. "'We are All Fallen Creatures and All Very Hard to Live With': Some Thoughts on Lewis and Gender." *Christian Scholar's Review* 36 (2007) 477–83.

Godawa, Brian. *Word Pictures: Knowing God through Story & Imagination*. Downers Grove, IL: InterVarsity, 2009.

Green, Miranda J. *Dictionary of Celtic Myth and Legend*. London: Thames & Hudson, 1992.

Green, Robert Lancelyn, and Walter Hooper. *C.S. Lewis: The Authorized and Revised Biography*. 1974. Reprint, London: Harper, 2003.

Grenz, Stanley J. *A Primer on Postmodernism*. Grand Rapids: Eerdmans, 1996.

Guerber, H.A. *Myths of the Norsemen: from the Eddas and Sagas*. London: George, 1908.

Hardy, Elizabeth Baird. *Milton, Spenser and The Chronicles of Narnia: Literary Sources for the C.S. Lewis Novels*. Jefferson, NC: McFarland, 2007.

Harre, Rom, and Roger Lamb, eds. *The Dictionary of Personality and Social Psychology*. Oxford: Blackwell, 1986.

Haycraft, Howard. *The Art of the Mystery Story: A Collection of Critical Essays*. New York: Grosset, 1947.

———. *Murder for Pleasure: the Life and Times of the Detective Story*. New York: Appleton-Century, 1941.

Heaney, Marie. *Irish Myth and Legend: The Names upon the Harp*. New York: Arthur, 2000.

Heidegger, Martin. "The Age of the World Picture." In *Off the Beaten Track*, edited and translated by Julian Young and Kenneth Haynes, 115–54. Cambridge: Cambridge University Press, 2002.

Henry, Matthew. "Matthew Henry's Commentary on the Whole Bible." *Christian Classics Ethereal Library*. http://www.ccel.org/ccel/henry/mhc.i.html.

Higgins, Iain Macleod. *Writing East: The "Travels" of Sir John Mandeville*. Philadelphia: University of Pennsylvania Press, 1997.

Hooper, Walter, ed. *Christian Reflections*. Grand Rapids: Eerdmans, 1984.

———. *C.S. Lewis: A Companion & Guide*. New York: Harper, 1996.

———. *C.S. Lewis: A Complete Guide to His Life & Works*. London: HarperCollins, 1996.

———, ed. *God in the Dock: Essays on Theology & Ethics*. Grand Rapids: Eerdmans, 1970.

———, ed. *On Stories and Other Essays on Literature*. London: Harvest, 1982.

Bibliography

———, ed. *Selected Literary Essays*. Cambridge: Cambridge University Press, 1969.
Howard, Thomas. *Narnia and Beyond*. San Francisco: Ignatius, 2006.
———. "The Catholic Angler." By Patrick Henry Reardon and David Mills. http://www.touchstonemag.com/archives /article.php?id=12-05-036-i.
Huttar, Charles A. "'Deep Lies the Sea-longing': Inklings of Home (1)." *Mythlore* 26.1–2 (2007) 5–28. https://www.questia.com/library/journal/1G1171579955/deep- lies-the-sea-longing-inklings-of-home-1.
Innes, Matthew. *Introduction to Early Medieval Western Europe, 300–900: The Plough and the Book*. London: Routledge, 2007.
Jakobson, Roman. "The Dominant." In *Readings in Russian Poetics: Formalist and Structuralist Views*, edited by Ladislav Matejka and Krystyna Pomorska, 82–87. Cambridge: MIT Press, 1971.
Julian of Norwich. *Revelations of Divine Love*. 1373. Translated by Clifton Wolters. Reprinted, London: Penguin, 1966. Citations refer to the Penguin edition.
Jung, C. G. *Psychology and Alchemy*. Translated by R. F. C. Hull. 2nd ed. Princeton, NJ: Princeton University Press, 1968.
Keefer, Sarah Larratt. "C.S. Lewis's 'Edgestow' as Homophonic Polysemy." *ANQ: A Quarterly Journal of Short Articles, Notes and Reviews* 14 (2001) 40–45.
Khoddam, Salwa. "The Enclosed Garden in C.S. Lewis's *The Chronicles of Narnia*." *The Bulletin of the New York C.S. Lewis Society* 37 (2006) n.p. http://www.cslewis.org /journal/the-enclosed-garden-in-cs-lewis%E2%80%99-the-chronicles-of-narnia/.
King, Don W., ed. *Christian Scholar's Review* 36 (2007) 383–513.
———. "Introduction to the Colloquium Issue: C.S. Lewis and Gender: 'Positively Medieval?'" *Christian Scholar's Review* 36 (2007) 387–400.
———. *C.S. Lewis, Poet: The Legacy of His Poetic Impulse*. Kent, OH: Kent State University Press, 2001.
———, ed. *Out of My Bone: the Letters of Joy Davidman*. Grand Rapids: Eerdmans, 2009.
Kinsella, Thomas, ed. *The New Oxford Book of Irish Verse*. Oxford: Oxford University Press, 1986.
Kuhn, Thomas S. *The Structure of Scientific Revolutions*. Chicago: University of Chicago Press, 1996.
Kuribayashi, Teruo. "Kindai-go O Saguru Posutomodan Shingaku: Gendai Amerika No Shingaku Jijou [Postmodernism and Christianity: Trends of Contemporary American Theology]." *Kwansei Gakuin University Research for Christianity and Culture* 4 (2003) 11–55.
Lacy, Norris J., ed. *The New Arthurian Encyclopedia*. New York: Garland, 1991.
Laurence, Sterne. *Tristram Shandy*. 1759–1767. New York: Norton, 1980.
Lessing, Doris. *The Golden Notebook*. 1962. London: Penguin, 1966.
Lewis, C.S. *The Abolition of Man*. 1943. New York: Collier, 1947.
———. *The Allegory of Love: A Study in Medieval Tradition*. 1936. Reprinted, Oxford: Oxford University Press, 1958.
———. "Answers to Questions on Christianity." *God in the Dock: Essays on Theology & Ethics*, edited by Walter Hooper, 58–59. Grand Rapids: Eerdmans, 1970.
———. "Bulverism." In *God in the Dock: Essays on Theology & Ethics*, edited by Walter Hoope, 271–77. Grand Rapids: Eerdmans, 1970
———. *Christian Reflections*. Edited by Walter Hooper. Grand Rapids: Eerdmans, 1995.
———. *The Collected Letters of C.S. Lewis. Volume I: Family Letters 1905–1931*, edited by Walter Hooper. San Francisco: Harper, 2004.

Bibliography

———. *The Collected Letters of C.S. Lewis. Volume II: Books, Broadcasts, and the War 1931–1949*. Edited by Walter Hooper. San Francisco: Harper, 2004.

———. *The Collected Letters of C.S. Lewis. Volume III: Narnia, Cambridge, and Joy 1950–1963*, edited by Walter Hooper. San Francisco: Harper, 2007.

———. *The Collected Poems of C.S. Lewis*. Edited by Walter Hooper. London: Fount, 1994.

———. *The C.S. Lewis Bible*. Edited by Marlene Baer Hekkert et al. New York: Harper, 2010.

———. "De Descriptione Temporum." In *Selected Literary Essays*, edited by Walter Hooper, 9–25. Cambridge: Cambridge University Press, 1969.

———. *The Discarded Image: An Introduction to Medieval and Renaissance Literature*. Cambridge: Cambridge University Press, 1964.

———. "Donne and Love Poetry in the Seventeenth Century." In *Selected Literary Essays*, edited by Walter Hooper, 106–25. Cambridge: Cambridge University Press, 1969.

———. *English Literature in the Sixteenth Century Excluding Drama*. Oxford: Clarendon, 1954.

———. *An Experiment in Criticism*. Cambridge: Cambridge University Press, 1961.

———. Foreword to *Smoke on the Mountain: An Interpretation of the Ten Commandments*, Joy Davidman, 7–12. Philadelphia: Westminster, 1953.

———. *The Four Loves*. 1960. Reprinted, London: Harper, 2002.

———. *God in the Dock: Essays on Theology & Ethics*, edited by Walter Hooper. Grand Rapids: Eerdmans, 1970.

———, ed. A Preface to *George Macdonald: An Anthology*. New York: Harper, 1973.

———. *The Grand Miracle*. Edited by Walter Hooper. New York: Ballantine, 1986.

———. *The Great Divorce: A Dream*. London: Bles, 1945.

———. *A Grief Observed*. London: Faber, 1961.

———. "Is Theology poetry?" In *The Weight of Glory*, edited by Walter Hooper, 116–40. New York: Harper, 1949.

———. *The Last Battle*. 1956. Reprinted, New York: Harper, 1984.

———. "Introduction." *Letters to Young Churches: A Translation of The New Testament Epistles*. Translated by J. B. Phillips. London: Bles, 1947.

———. *The Lion, the Witch, and the Wardrobe*. New York: Harper, 1980.

———. "Meditation in a Toolshed." In *God in the Dock: Essays on Theology & Ethics*, edited by Walter Hoope, 212–15. Grand Rapids: Eerdmans, 1970.

———. *Mere Christianity*. London: Collins, 1952.

———. *Miracles: A Preliminary Study*. London: Geoffrey, 1947.

———. "Modern Translations of the Bible." In *God in the Dock: Essays on Theology & Ethics*, edited by Walter Hooper, 229–33. Grand Rapids: Eerdmans, 1970.

———. "Myth Became Fact." In *God in the Dock: Essays on Theology & Ethics*, edited by Walter Hoope, 63–67. Grand Rapids: Eerdmans, 1970.

———. "On Juvenile Tastes." In *On Stories and Other Essays on Literature* edited by Walter Hoope, 45–51. London: Harvest, 1982.

———. "On Science Fiction." In *On Stories and Other Essays on Literature*, edited by Walter Hoope, 55–68. London: Harvest, 1982.

———. *On Stories and Other Essays on Literature*, edited by Walter Hooper. London: Harvest, 1982.

———. *Out of the Silent Planet*. London: Bles, 1938.

———. *Perelandra*. London: Bodley, 1943.

Bibliography

———. *The Pilgrim's Regress*. London: Dent, 1933.

———. *Poems*. Edited by Walter Hooper. London: Bles, 1964.

———. "The Poison of Subjectivism." In *Christian Reflections*, edited by Walter Hooper, 72–81. Grand Rapids: Eerdmans, 1984.

———. *A Preface to Paradise Lost: Being the Ballard Matthews Lectures Delivered at University College, North Wales, 1941*. London: Oxford University Press, 1942.

———. "Priestesses in the Church?" In *God in the Dock: Essays on Theology & Ethics*, edited by Walter Hooper, 234–39. Grand Rapids: Eerdmans, 1970.

———. *Prince Caspian*. New York: Harper, 1980.

———. *The Problem of Pain*. London: Bres, 1940.

———. *Reflections on the Psalms*. London: Bles, 1958.

———. "Religion without Dogma." In *God in the Dock: Essays on Theology & Ethics*, edited by Walter Hoope, 129–46. Grand Rapids: Eerdmans, 1970.

———. *The Screwtape Letters*. London: Bles, 1942.

———. "The Seeing Eye." 1963. In *C.S. Lewis: Essays Collection and Other Short Pieces*, edited by Lesley Walmsley, 58–65. New York: Harper, 2000.

———. *Selected Literary Essays*. Edited by Walter Hooper. Cambridge: Cambridge University Press, 1969.

———. *The Silver Chair*. 1953. Reprinted, New York: Harper, 1981.

———. "Sometimes Fairy Stories May Say Best What's to Be Said." In *On Stories and Other Essays on Literature*, edited by Walter Hooper, 45–48. London: Harvest, 1982.

———. *Spenser's Image of Life*. Edited by Alastair Fowler. Cambridge: Cambridge University Press, 1967.

———. *Surprised by Joy*. London: Bles, 1955.

———. *That Hideous Strength: A Modern Fairy-Tale for Grown-Ups*. London: Bodley, 1945.

———. *They Stand Together: The Letters of C.S. Lewis to Arthur Greeves*, edited by Walter Hooper. London: Collins, 1979.

———. *Till We Have Faces: A Myth Retold*. Orlando: Harcourt, 1956.

———. "The Vision of John Bunyan." In *Selected Literary Essays*, edited by Walter Hooper, 146–53. Cambridge: Cambridge University Press, 1969.

———. *The Voyage of the Dawn Treader*. 1952. Reprinted, New York: Harper, 1980.

———. *The Weight of Glory*. New York: Harper, 1949.

———. "William Morris." In *Selected Literary Essays*, edited by Walter Hooper, 219–31. Cambridge: Cambridge University Press, 1969.

Lindskoog, Kathryn. "Links in a Golden Chain: C.S. Lewis, George MacDonald, and Sadhu Sundar Singh." *The Lewis Legacy-Issue* 69. Summer (1996). http://www.discovery.org/a/1023.

Lindval, Terry. *Surprised by Laughter: The Comic World of C.S. Lewis*. Nashville: Nelson, 2012.

Lobdell, Jared C. "C.S. Lewis's Ransom Stories and Their Eighteenth-Century Ancestry." In *Word and Story in C.S. Lewis: Language and Narrative in Theory and Practice*, edited by Peter J. Schakel and Charles Huttar, 213–31. Columbia: University of Missouri Press, 1991.

———. *The Scientification Novels of C.S. Lewis: Space and Time in the Ransom Stories*. Jefferson, NC: McFarland, 2004.

Lockett, Joseph L. "Arthurian Features in *That Hideous Strength*." https://www.prismnet.com/~jlockett/Grist/English/lewispaper.html.

Bibliography

Longfellow, Henry Wadsworth. *The Seaside and the Fireside*. Boston: Ticknor, 1949.
Loudon, J.C. *Encyclopedia of Cottage, Farm, and Villa Architecture and Furniture*. Tokyo: Athena, 2007.
Lyotard, Jan-Francois. *The Postmodern Condition: A Report on Knowledge*. Minneapolis: University of Minnesota Press, 1984.
MacDonald, George. *Phantastes: A Faerie Romance for Men and Women*. Boston: Loring, 1850. https://archive.org/details/phantastesfaerie00macd.
———. *The Princess and the Goblin*. 1872. Reprinted, London: David, 1993.
Mackenzie, Donald A. *Teutonic Myth and Legend*. New York: William, 1934. https://archive.org/details/teutonicmythandl027797mbp.
Mandeville, John, Sir. *The Travels of Sir John Mandeville*. New York: Dover, 1964.
Manganiello, Dominic. "Till We Have Faces: From Idolatry to Revelation." *Mythlore* 23 (2000) 31–46.
Markos, Louis. *From Achilles to Christ*. Downers Grove, IL: InterVarsity, 2007.
———. *Lewis Agonistes: How C.S. Lewis Can Train Us to Wrestle with the Modern and Postmodern World*. Nashville: Broadman, 2003.
Martindale, Wayne. *Beyond the Shadowlands: C.S. Lewis on Heaven and Hell*. Wheaton, IL: Crossway, 2005.
Martindale, Wayne, and Jerry Root, eds. *The Quotable Lewis*. Carol Stream, IL: Tyndale. 1990.
McGrath, Alister. *Postmodern Sekai No Kirisutokyo: 21 Seiki Niokeru Fukuin No Yakuwari* [Christianity in a Postmodern World]. Tokyo: Kyobunkan, 2004.
———. *The Journey: A Pilgrim in the Lands of the Spirit*. New York: Doubleday, 2001.
McHale, Brian. *Postmodernist Fiction*. London: Routledge, 1989.
McKillop, James. *A Dictionary of Celtic Mythology*. Oxford: Oxford University Press, 2004. http://jg8gn6xr5x.search.serialssolutions.com/?isbn=9780198609674.
Meas, Laura-Jane. "The Nineteenth Century 'Disappearance of God': Perceptions of God in Hardy and Hopkins." PhD diss., Queens University, Belfast, 2001.
Meyer, Kuno, ed., and trans. *The Voyage of Bran, Son of Febal, to the Land of the Living; an Old Irish Saga*. London: Nutt, 1917.
Meyer, Kuno, and Alfred Nutt, eds and trans. *The Voyage of Bran Son of Febal to the Land of the Living*. 2 vols. New York: AMS, 1972. https://archive.org/stream/cu31924026971030/cu31924026971030_djvu.txt.
Milbank, John, ed. *Radical Orthodoxy*. London: Routledge, 1999.
Miller, J. Hills. "The Late Derrida." In *Adieu Derrida*, edited by Costas Douzinas, 134–52. Basingstoke: Palgrave, 2007.
Morris, William. *The Well at the World's End*. London: Longmans, 1913.
Murdock, Iris. *Under the Net*. London: Chatto, 1963.
Myers, Doris T. *Bareface: a Guide to C.S. Lewis's Last Novel*. Columbia: University of Missouri Press, 2004.
———. *C.S. Lewis in Context*. Kent, OH: Kent State University Press, 1994.
———. "Lewis in Genderland." *Christian Scholar's Review* 36 (2007) 455–60.
Newbigin, Lesslie. *Foolishness to the Greeks: the Gospel and Western Culture*. Grand Rapids: Eerdmans, 1986.
Nicholi, Armand M., Jr. *The Question of God: C.S. Lewis and Sigmund Freud Debate God, Love, Sex, and the Meaning of Life*. New York: Free, 2002.
Nietzsche, Friedrich. *The Gay Science*, Edited by Bernard Williams. Translated by Josefine Nauckhoff and Adrian del Caro. Cambridge: Cambridge University Press, 2001.

Bibliography

Nott, Kathleen. *The Emperor's Clothes: An Attack on the Dogmatic Orthodoxy of T.S. Eliot, Graham Greene, Dorothy Sayers, C.S. Lewis, and Others.* 1953. Reprinted, Bloomington: Indiana University Press, 1958.

O'Meara, John, trans. *The Voyage of Saint Brendan: Journey to the Promised Land.* 1976. Reprinted, Gerrards Cross: Colin, 1991.

Otto, Rudolf. *The Idea of the Holy.* Translated by John W. Harvey. 1923. Reprinted, Harmondsworth: Penguin, 1959.

Painton, Cowen. *The Rose Window: Splendour and Symbol.* London: Thames, 2005.

Patterson, Nancy-Lou. "The Unfathomable Feminine Principle: Images of Wholeness in *That Hideous Strength*." *The Lamp-Post* 9 (July 1986) 3–39.

Pfeifer, Ludwig. "The Novel and Society: Reflections on the Interactions of Literary and Cultural Paradigms." *PTL* 3 (1978).

Poe, Harry Lee. *Christian Witness in a Postmodern World.* Nashville: Abingdon, 2001.

Polkinghorne, John. *Science and Theology: An Introduction.* Minneapolis: Fortress, 1998.

"Prester John." In *The Catholic Encyclopedia.* Vol. 12. New York: Robert, 1911. http://www.newadvent.org/cathen/12400b.htm.

Rackham, Arthur, illus. *Rackham's Color Illustrations for Wagner's "Ring."* New York: Dover, 1979.

Rascheke, Carl. *The Next Reformation: Why Evangelicals Must Embrace Postmodernity.* Grand Rapids: Baker, 2004.

Reynolds, Barbara. "Dorothy Sayers: The Dogma is the Drama." *Christianity History* 88 (2005). http://www.christianitytoday.com/ct/2005/decemberweb-only/52.0a.html.

———. *Dorothy L. Sayers: Her Life and Soul.* New York: St. Martin's, 1993.

Rossi, Lee D. *The Politics of Fantasy, C.S. Lewis and J.R.R. Tolkien.* Ann Arbor: UMI, 1984.

Rowe, Karen. "Till We Have Faces: A Study of the Soul and the Self." In *An Examined Life*, edited by Bruce L. Edwards, 135–56. Westport, CT: Praeger, 2007.

"Saint Patrick's Breastplate." *The Prayer Foundation.* http://www.prayerfoundation.org/st_patricks_breastplate_prayer.htm.

Sammons, Martha C. *"A Far-Off Country": A Guide to C.S. Lewis's Fantasy Fiction.* Lanham, MD: University Press of America, 2000.

———. *A Guide through C.S. Lewis' Space Trilogy.* Westchester: Cornerstone, 1980.

Sayer, George. *Jack: A Life of C.S. Lewis.* Wheaton, IL: Crossway, 1994.

Sayers, Dorothy L. *Are Women Human?* Grand Rapids: Eerdmans, 2005.

———. *Creed or Chaos?: Why Christians Must Choose Either Dogma or Disaster (or, Why It Really Does Matter What You Choose).* 1949. New York: Harcourt. Reprinted, Manchester, NH: Sophia, 1999. Citations refer to the Sophia edition.

———. *Gaudy Night.* London: Gollancz. Reprinted, London: Harper, 1986. Citations refer to the Harper edition.

———. "Gaudy Night." In *The Art of the Mystery Story: A Collection of Critical Essays*, edited by Howard Haycraft, 208–21. New York: Grosset, 1946.

———. *The Mind of the Maker.* 1941. Reprinted, London: Continuum, 2004. Citations refer to the Continuum edition.

———. "Why Work?" In *Creed or Chaos*, 89–116. Manchester, NH: Sophia, 1999.

Schakel, Peter J. "The 'Correct' Order for Reading the Chronicles of Narnia?" *Revisiting Narnia: Fantasy, Myth and Religion in C.S. Lewis' Chronicles*, edited by Shanna Caughey, 91–111. Dallas: BenBella, 2005.

———. *Imagination and the Arts in C.S. Lewis: Journeying to Narnia and Other Worlds.* Columbia: Missouri University Press, 2002.

Bibliography

Schakel, Peter J, and Charles Huttar, eds. *Word and Story in C.S. Lewis: Language and Narrative in Theory and Practice.* Columbia: University of Missouri Press, 1991.

Schideler, Mary Mcdermott. "Introduction." In *Are Women Human?*, by Dorothy L. Sayers. Grand Rapids: Eerdmans, 2005.

Schultz, Jeffrey D., and John G. West Jr., eds. *The C.S. Lewis Readers' Encyclopedia.* Grand Rapids: Zondervan, 1998.

Severin, Tim. *The Brendan Voyage—Sailing a Leather Currach from Ireland to Newfoundland.* New York: Modern, 2000.

Sheldrake, Philip. *Living Between Worlds.* London: Darton, 1995.

Sibley, Brian. *The Land of Narnia: Brian Sibley Explores the World of C.S. Lewis.* London: Collins, 1989.

Shippery, T.A. "The Ransom Trilogy." In *The Cambridge Companion to C.S. Lewis*, edited by Robert MacSwain and Michael Ward, 237–50. Cambridge: Cambridge University Press, 2010.

Smith, James K.A. *Who's Afraid of Postmodernism?: Taking Derrida, Lyotard, and Foucault to Church.* Grand Rapids: Baker, 2006.

Spark, Muriel. *The Prime of Miss Jean Brodie.* 1961. Reprinted, London: Penguin, 1965.

Spenser, Edmund. *The Faerie Queene*, edited by A.C. Hamilton. 1590. Reprinted, London: Longman, 1977. Citations refer to the Longman edition.

Stephens, James. *The Crock of Gold.* London: Macmillan. 1912. http://sacred-texts.com/neu/celt/cog/index.htm.

Takeno, Kazuo. *C.S. Lewis Yorokobi No Tobira* (*C.S. Lewis: Door of Joy*). Tokyo: Iwanami, 2012.

Travers, Michael. "The Letters of C.S. Lewis: C.S. Lewis as Correspondent." In *An Examined Life*, edited by Bruce L. Edwards, 19–47. Westport, CT: Praeger, 2007.

Van Leeuwen, Mary Stewart. "A Sword between the Sexes: C.S. Lewis's Long Journey to Gender Equality." *Christian Scholar's Review* 36 (2007) 391–414.

———. *C.S. Lewis, Poet: The Legacy of His Poetic Impulse.* Kent, OH: Kent State University Press, 2001.

———. *A Sword Between the Sexes?: C.S. Lewis and the Gender Debate.* Grand Rapids: Bazos, 2010.

Vaus, Will. "Lewis in Cambridge: Professional Years (1954–1963)." In *An Examined Life*, edited by Bruce L. Edwards, 197–218. Westport, CT: Praeger, 2007.

Walker, G. Barbara *The Woman's Encyclopedia of Myths and Secrets.* New York: Harper, 1983.

Walmsley, Lesley, ed. *C.S. Lewis: Essays Collection and Other Short Pieces.* New York: Harper, 2000.

Walton, Izaak. *The Compleat Angler.* 1653. Reprinted, Oxford: Oxford University Press, 1983.

Warzecha, Daniel. "Nordic Mythology in C.S. Lewis's the Chronicles of Narnia." In *Re-Embroidering the Robe: Faith, Myth and Literary Creation since 1850*, edited by Suzanne Bray et al., 17–31. Newcastle, UK: Cambridge Scholars, 2008.

Waugh, Patricia. *Metafiction: The Theory and Practice of Self-Conscious Fiction.* New York: Routledge, 1996.

White, James. *The King James Only Controversy: Can You Trust Modern Translations?* Ada, MI: Baker, 2009.

Wittgenstein, Ludwig. *Philosophical Investigations.* Translated by G. E. M. Anscombe. Oxford: Blackwell, 1968.

Bibliography

Wolfe, Ransom Gregory. "Essential Speech: Language and Myth in the Ransom Trilogy." In *Word and Story in C.S. Lewis: Language and Narrative in Theory and Practice*, edited by Peter J. Schakel, and Charles Hutta, 58–75. Columbia: University of Missouri Press, 1991.

Yuasa, Kyoko. "Awoken and Integrated: *That Hideous Strength* and *The Abolition of Man*." *Sapporo University Women's Junior College Bulletin* 45 (March 2005) 61–84.

———. "Christian Postmodernism: *The Dawn Treader* as C.S. Lewis's Mappa Mundi." In *Proceedings of the Annual International Conference on Language, Literature and Linguistics* (June 2012) 294–98.

———. "C.S. Lewis and Christian Postmodernism: Merlin and His Enclosed Garden Recreated." *Christianity Literature Study* 29 (May 2012) 144–55.

———. "C.S. Lewis's *The Great Divorce*: Christian Postmodernism and 'The Inverted Telescope.'" In *Persona and Paradox: Issues of Identity for C.S. Lewis, His Friends and Associates*, edited by Suzanne Bray, and William Gray, 93–105. Newcastle, UK: Cambridge Scholar, 2012.

———. "Dorothy Sayers and C.S. Lewis: Christian Postmodernism beyond the Boundaries." *US-China Education Review A & B* 2 (July 2012) 533–43.

Zambreno, Mary Frances. "A Reconstructed Image: Medieval Time and Space in the Chronicles of Narnia." In *Revisiting Narnia Fantasy, Myth and Religion in C.S. Lewis' Chronicles*, edited by Shanna Caughey, 253–66. Dallas: Benbella, 2005.

Index

Achtemeier, Paul J., 177
Alexander, Joy, 140, 156–57
Anderson, John, 133
Ankerberg, John, and John Weldon, 23
Anti-modernist (anti-modernism), 2, 4, 19, 21–26, 38, 41
Apuleius, 142, 143, 144, 145, 152, 154, 158
Aquinas, Thomas, 49
Aratus, 48
Arnell, Carla A., 140, 160, 173
Ashe, Geoffrey, 127–28
Atheism (atheist), 42, 62, 162
St. Augustine, 49

Bach, Johann Sebastian, 107, 173
Bakhtin, Mikhail, 8, 37–38
Barfield, Owen, 24, 25
Barkman, Adam, 59
Bartlett, S. A., 172
Bendan, Julian, 90
Bell, Michael, 5, 11, 12, 14
Berry, Wendell, 168
Bible (scripture), 3, 7, 13, 23–25, 29, 33, 47–49, 55, 72, 73, 76, 77, 98, 101, 108–9, 112–13, 121, 131, 133, 134, 136, 166, 172, 175–76
Boron, Robert de, 52, 70, 71
Bresland, Ronald, 52
Browning, W. R. F., 103
Bullinger, Ethelbert W., 129
Bultmann, Rudolf, 25
Bunyan, John, 80
Burger, Peter, 29–30

Cahill, Thomas C., 107
Calinescu, Matei, 5, 11, 12, 14
Caputo, John, 15, 17, 18
Carlyle, Thomas, 113
Carroll, Lewis, 75
Carson, D.A., 49
Cartesianism (Cartesian), 86–87
Cary, George, 123–24
Chang, Curtis, 49, 143
Chaucer, Geoffrey, 77, 123
Christ (Jesus), 2, 29, 40, 50, 77, 98, 108, 121, 128, 134–35, 138, 140–41, 160, 164, 166, 174, 176
Christianity (Christian), 3, 12–15, 17, 19–20, 25, 27, 29, 33–34, 36–40, 42, 47, 49–50, 58, 71, 73, 88, 105, 143, 147, 164, 174
Christian Postmodernism, 1, 2, 4, 6, 9–11, 15, 17, 18–19, 21, 26, 28, 30, 31, 35, 47, 49, 57, 59, 63, 102, 135, 139, 142, 155, 178, 179
Christopher, Joe R., 59
Clarke, Arthur C., 19
Clifford, Derek, 76–77, 79, 81
Coghlan, Ronan, 71
Coleridge, Samuel Taylor, 134
Collins, Francis S., 26, 31–35
Collins, William, 75
Community, 5, 15–16, 17, 57, 69, 94, 101, 125, 135
Cotterell, Arthur, 76, 110, 166
Creation, 16, 31–33, 133, 136
Creator, 34, 42, 78, 92
Cross of Christ (Crucified, Crucifixion), 32, 98, 108–9, 166

193

Index

Curtin, Jeremiah, 76

Dante, 52, 54, 60, 151, 154
Darwin, Charles, 13, 25
Davidman, Joy, 5, 8, 37, 57–58, 62–63, 161, 178
Death (dead), 45–46, 50, 56, 152, 154, 159, 173–74
Defoe, Daniel, 46
Derrida, Jacques, 19, 20, 45–46
Digby, Sir Kenelm, 75
Dillard, Annie, 35
Donaldson, Mara E., 148
Donne, John, 46, 83, 95–96
Downing, Crystal L., 2, 4–6, 11, 13–15, 18–20, 38, 43
Downing, David C., 4, 6, 19, 20, 56, 64, 68, 70, 85–86, 93, 105, 109, 122
Dualism (dual/duality), 26, 30, 31, 62, 90, 92
Durietz, Colin, 5, 78–79, 134, 165
Duriez, Colin, 50
Dyson, Hugo, 164

Eden, Richard, 124
Edwards, L. Bruce, 3, 4, 6–8, 10, 16, 19–22, 47, 148, 160
Flinders, Carole Lee, 64–65
Eliot, T. S., 21, 26, 39, 87, 95, 122
Endicott, Lizzie, 50

Fact and fiction (history and myth, non-fiction and value), 2, 4, 7, 29–30, 37, 43, 46, 50, 54–55, 63, 82, 111, 178
Filmer, Kath, 140
Ford, Paul F., 111, 129, 134
Foucault, Michel, 4
Fowles, John, 8, 37, 44–45
Frazer, James George, 38, 39–40
Fredric, Candice, and Sam McBride, 58
Freud, Sigmund, 12, 25, 32, 94
Fugue, 45–46, 173

Gender, 58–60, 65, 172
Geoffrey of Monmouth, 52, 70, 71
Giamatti, A. Bartlett, 76, 77, 79
Glyer, Diana Pavlac, 59

God, 14–16, 18, 31–33, 35, 45, 60, 65, 72, 77–78, 80, 92, 95, 98, 101, 122, 131, 133–34, 141, 164, 173, 175
Godawa, Brian, 49
gods, 2, 154, 164
Gospel, 2–4, 7, 15, 16, 25, 29, 31, 36, 41, 47–48, 50, 111, 141, 143, 160, 164, 175
Green, Graham, 26
Green, Miranda J., 76
Green, Robert Lancelyn, 40
Greeves, Arthur, 5, 38, 51–56, 147, 163
Grenz, Stanley J., 1, 2, 11–18, 43
Gresham, William, 62
Griffiths, Dom Bede, 63
Grosz, George, 88
Guerber, H. A., 51, 163, 165–66, 169

Hardy, Elizabeth Baird, 53
Harington, Lucy, Countess of Bedford, 79
Haycraft, Howard, 60
Heaven, 13–14, 98, 109, 152, 178
Heaney, Marie, 76
Henrietta Maria, 83
Heidegger, Martin, 12
Heins, John, 168
Herbert, Mary, 79
The Holy Spirit, 16, 98, 134
Hooper, Walter, 8, 40, 70, 78, 105, 164–65
Howard, Thomas, 68, 83, 84, 95, 140, 143
Humanity (human nature), 1, 57, 59, 61–62, 86, 109, 113, 135, 152, 178
Huttar, Charles, 102, 105–6, 108
Hyper-realism, 18, 23

Imagination (imaginative), 17–18, 28, 33, 50, 53, 55, 61
Imram, 9, 104, 107, 131, 133
Incarnation, 31, 34, 50
Innes, Matthew, 102
Ireland (Irish), 53 110, 119–20, 127, 132, 136, 163, 164

Jacobson, Roman, 12
Jean d'Arras, 119

Index

Johnson, Ben, 83
Jones, Inigo, 78, 81
"Joy," 32, 33, 51, 63, 163–64, 173
Joyce, James, 40, 41
Julian of Norwich, 8, 57, 63–65, 178
Jung, C. G., 119

Keefer, Sarah Larratt, 68
Khoddam, Salwa, 76, 105
Kilby, Clyde, 141
King, Don W., 59, 62, 164
The Kingdom of God, 103, 106, 111, 112, 122, 126, 133
Kinsella, Thomas, 55
Kuhn, Thomas S., 20, 28–29
Kuribayashi, Teruo, 5–6

Lacy, Norris J., 71
Layamon, 70
Lessing, Doris, 8, 37, 43–44
Lewis, C. S.
 The Abolition of Man, 21, 22, 66, 85, 176–77
 The Allegory of Love, 53, 77, 81, 84
 "Bulverism," 21
 Christian Reflections, 16
 The Chronicles of Narnia, 5, 19, 26, 105, 107, 109, 161
 The Collected Letters of C.S. Lewis I, 2, 3, 40, 50, 52–54, 56, 141
 The Collected Letters of C.S. Lewis II, 8, 64, 147
 The Collected Letters of C.S. Lewis III, 18, 64, 141
 The Collected Poems of C.S. Lewis, 40
 The C.S. Lewis Bible, 30
 "De Descriptione Temporum," 21, 25, 36, 38–41
 The Discarded Image, 2, 20, 123–25, 128
 "Donne and Love Poetry in the Seventeenth Century," 96
 "Dymer," 78
 English Literature in the Sixteenth Century, 47, 79, 87
 An Experiment in Criticism, 3, 16, 141, 148
 Foreword to Smoke on the Mountain, 36
 The Four Love, 84, 172
 God in the Dock, 3 10, 22–23, 25, 50, 64, 173
 The Great Divorce, 48, 54, 57, 64, 109
 A Greif Observed, 63
 The Horse and His Boy, 9
 The Last Battle, 110, 132
 Letters to an American Lady, 8
 Letters to Young Churches, 21
 The Lion, the Witch and Wardrobe, 114, 116, 121
 The Magician's Nephew, 76
 "Meditation in a Toolshed," 21, 22, 28
 Mere Christianity, 21, 25, 31, 33, 82–83
 Miracles: A Preliminary Study, 18, 21, 23, 26, 34–35, 45, 64
 "Modern Translation of the Bible," 23
 "Myth Became Fact," 111
 On Stories, 1, 7–8, 18, 54, 56, 103
 "On Science Fiction," 18
 Out of the Silent Planet, 57
 "The Pains of Animals," 64
 Perelandra, 47, 57, 92
 The Pilgrim's Regress, 6, 38, 41–43, 57
 Poems, 39
 "The Poison of Subjectivism," 21, 22
 A Preface to George MacDonald: The Anthology, 55
 "A Preface to Paradise Lost," 27, 61, 148
 "Priestesses in the Church?," 57
 Prince Caspian, 109, 121
 The Problem of Pain, 33, 175, 177
 Reflections on the Psalms, 33, 136
 The Screwtape Letters, 27, 57
 "The Seeing Eye," 52
 Selected Literary Essays, 25, 80
 The Silver Chair, 112, 121
 "Sometimes Fairy stories May Say Best What's to be Said," 52
 Space Trilogy, 60, 75, 92
 Spenser's Image of Life, 53

Index

Lewis, C. S. *(continued)*
  Surprised by Joy, 7, 21, 24–25, 37, 38, 47, 50–55, 119, 162, 163
  That Hideous Strength, 4, 9, 22, 28, 31, 46, 52, 57, 66–101, 174–77
  They Stand Together, 40
  Till We Have Faces, 4, 9, 46, 57, 62, 139–177
  The Voyage of the Dawn Treader, 4, 9, 46, 102–38, 174–77
  "William Morris," 56
Lewis, Warren, 38, 54, 63, 86, 147
Limited (Limitation), 1, 21, 28, 32, 36, 43–44, 47, 61, 64–65, 84, 103
Lindskoog, Kathryn, 85–86
Lindval, Terry, 89
Lobdell, Jared C., 90, 93
Logos and Poiema, 3, 5, 61, 141, 148, 152, 158
Longfellow, Henry Wadsworth, 163
Lorris, Guillaume de, 99
Lyotard, Jean-Francois, 5, 14–15

MacCann, Patsy, 51
MacDonald, George, 5, 7, 52, 54–55, 178
Mackenzie, Donald A., 163, 166
Magritte, Rene, 88
Mallet, Henri, 163
Malory, Thomas, 52, 69, 70–71, 92–93
Mandeville, John, 104, 125–26
Manganiello, Dominic, 160–61
Markos, Louis, 5, 11, 13–14, 19, 41, 49
Martindale, Wayne, 47, 148
Materialism (materialist), 34, 42, 58, 73, 135
McGrath, A. E., 5, 15–18
McHale, Brian, 5, 11–12, 14
McKillop, James, 104
Meas, Laura-Jane, 113
Meta-fiction (metafictional), 37, 43, 45, 48
Meyer, Kuno, 110
Middleton, J. Richard, 13
Miller, J. Hills, 45–46, 173
Milton, John, 27–28, 77–78
Miracle, 21, 23, 26–27, 31, 34

Modernism (modernist, modern, modernity, modernistic), 3–5, 10, 11–14, 19–25, 27–28, 34, 36, 38–43, 52, 62, 66–67, 69, 74, 87–90, 94, 96–98, 101, 113–14, 147, 174, 177
Modernized Christianity (Modernist Christian), 3, 14, 19, 25–26, 33, 35, 160
Morris, William, 7, 52, 55, 56, 147
Multiple, 16, 34, 37, 43, 50, 52, 62–63, 70–71, 103, 121, 178
Murdoch, Iris, 8, 37, 43, 44
Muriel, Spark, 8
Myers, Doris T., 59, 68, 75, 96, 140, 161
Mystic (mysticism), 9, 57, 63, 64, 65
Mythology, 3, 7, 25, 33, 36–38, 40, 47, 49, 50–51, 66, 71, 76, 81, 84–85, 93–94, 98–99, 109, 111, 118, 121, 130, 135–36, 138–39, 141–43, 147, 155, 157, 160–75; Irish myth (Celtic), 50, 51, 173; Greco-Roman, 9, 141–43, 165–67, 173; Norse, 50, 51, 141, 161–73, 175

Narrator, 82, 93, 109, 111, 149, 154
Naturalism (natural), 2, 23, 26, 29, 31, 35, 46, 70, 98, 135
Nietzsche, Friedrich, 12
Nennius, 71
Newbigin, Lesslie, 26, 28–31
Nicholi, Armand M., 32
Niebuhr, Reinhold, 13
Nott, Kathleen, 26–28

O'Meara, John, 105, 112, 128–34
Onis, Federico de, 13
Ottor, Rudolf, 106–8, 175–78

Paracelsus, 119
Pascal, Blaise, 31
Pater, Walter, 147
St. Patrick, 55
Paul (The Apostle), 7, 31, 47–49, 108, 175–76
Penelope (Sister), 8
Persona "I," 46, 54, 73–75, 82, 92, 111
Phillips, J. B., 24

Index

Pluralism (plural), 13, 16, 18
Poe, Harry Lee, 6, 59
Polkinghorne, John Charlton, 34
Porter, David, 50
Postmodernism (postmodernist), 2, 4–6, 9, 11, 14–15, 18–20, 24, 37, 43, 45–46, 54, 74, 102–3, 143, 173–74, 177–78

Rackham, Arthur, 164–65
Rascheke, Carl, 2
Rationalism (rational), 25–26, 28, 87–88, 95, 113–14, 130
Raynolds, Barbara, 60–61
Reader, 1, 3–4, 7–9, 23–24, 30–31, 34, 37, 41, 43–44, 47–48, 56–57, 59–60, 62, 64–65, 69, 71, 75, 78, 88, 138, 144, 147, 149, 163, 174–75, 178
Reading, 3, 4, 6–7, 15, 17, 19–20, 32, 41, 47, 60, 117, 135
Reed, J. O., 80
Resurrection, 50, 108, 121, 174
Re-writing, 147, 149–53
Richards, I. A., 16
Root, Jerry, 47
Rowe, Karen, 140, 143

Sammons, Martha C., 68, 94
Satan, 27, 77, 79
Saussure, Ferdinand de, 41
Sayers, Dorothy L., 8, 26, 37, 57, 59, 60–62, 97, 178
Schakel, Peter J., 129, 139
Schultz, Jeffrey D., 68
Science and religion, 26, 28, 31, 35
Severin, Tim, 128
Sexuality, 47, 57–58, 60, 94, 95–99, 101, 172
Shelburne, Mary Willis, 8
Sheldrake, Philip, 107, 133, 135
Shideler, Mary McDermott, 62
Shippery, T. A., 68
Sibley, Brian, 125–27
Sidney, Sir Philip, 83
Singh, Sundar, 85

Smith, James K. A., 4, 13, 15, 16
Spark, Muriel, 37, 43–44
Spenser, Edmund, 52–53, 83
Stephen, James, 51
Sterne, Laurence, 52
Story within a story, 44, 46, 174
Supernaturalism (supernatural), 2, 4, 9–10, 23, 25–26, 28–29, 31–32, 34–35, 46, 72–73, 97, 102, 114, 129

Takeno, Kazuo, 170
Tegnér, Esaias, 162, 164
Theist, 38, 62
Tolkien, J. R. R., 5, 37, 58, 106, 163
Toynbee, Arnold, 13
Transcend (transcendence), 1–3, 18, 26, 32, 62, 103, 160, 179
Trinity, 16, 60, 77, 98
Troyer, Chretian de, 52, 70–72, 99

Van Leeuwen, Mary Stewart, 58–59, 172
Vau, Louis le, 86
Vaus, Will, 39

Wace, Robert, 70–71
Walker, G. Barbara, 166–68
Walsh, Brian J., 13
Walton, Izaak, 80
Warzecha, Daniel, 141, 161
Waugh, Patricia, 8, 37, 41, 44–45
West, John G., Jr., 68
Williams, Charles, 37, 58, 70
Wittgenstein, Ludwig, 15
Wolfe, Gregory, 68, 95
Wollstonecraft, May, 95
Woolf, Virginia, 40–42
Word and Image, 1, 2, 4, 6, 9, 18, 36, 57, 63, 65–66, 135, 159, 160, 173–74, 178–79

Yeats, W. B., 51

Zambreno, Mary, 102

www.ingramcontent.com/pod-product-compliance
Lightning Source LLC
Chambersburg PA
CBHW070327230426
43663CB00011B/2245